# ALL THE PRESIDENT'S MONEY

# ALL THE PRESIDENT'S MONEY

## Investigating the Secret Foreign Schemes That Made the Biden Family Rich

JAMES COMER

BROADSIDE BOOKS
*An Imprint of* HarperCollins*Publishers*

FIRST EDITION

Library of Congress Cataloging-in-Publication Data

Names: Comer, James, 1972– author.
Title: All the president's money : investigating the secret foreign schemes that made the Bidens rich / James Comer.
Description: First edition. | New York : HarperCollins Publishers, [2024] | Includes index
Identifiers: LCCN 2024022628 (print) | LCCN 2024022629 (ebook) | ISBN 9780063420014 (hardcover) | ISBN 9780063420021 (ebook)
Subjects: LCSH: Biden, Joseph R., Jr.—Family. | Biden, James. | Biden, Robert Hunter, 1970– | Biden family. | Wealth—Political aspects—United States—History—21st century. | United States—Politics and government—2021– | Political corruption—United States—History—21st century. | Governmental investigations—United States—History—21st century. | Presidents—United States—History—21st century.
Classification: LCC E918 .C66 2024 (print) | LCC E918 (ebook) | DDC 973.934—dc23/eng/20240605
LC record available at https://lccn.loc.gov/2024022628
LC ebook record available at https://lccn.loc.gov/2024022629

ISBN 978-0-06-342001-4

24 25 26 27 28 LBC 5 4 3 2 1

Sandra Lucile Witcher Comer
January 26, 1948–April 24, 2010

*Photo credit: Tompkinsville First Baptist Church Directory*

Words can never describe my thanks, appreciation, and love to you. You were the leader of our family, a constant presence at First Baptist Church of Tompkinsville (where you always required your two sons to attend each Sunday with you) and the source for both my strength and knowledge of the fundamentals of politics.

You can't get rich in politics unless you're a crook.

*—Harry S. Truman*

# CONTENTS

# INTRODUCTION

When Joe Biden was sworn in as vice president of the United States in 2017, he got a raise from his Senate salary of $174,000 to his new salary of $230,700. He had worked for the government most of his life, but when he moved into the Naval Observatory, he moved out of a mansion worth millions. Immediately after leaving office, he bought a second multimillion-dollar mansion.

Most people with salaries in that range don't live in a mansion, and they also usually don't pay their bills through a bookkeeper and a law firm they share with their son. But Joe Biden did.

Over the past twenty years, that son, Hunter Biden, has not had a traditional job like his father. In his congressional testimony, he said he taught some courses, wrote a book, served on boards, and "founded and built the successful small business in advising global infrastructure and alternative investment clients."

If Hunter and James Biden had turned their last name into $100,000, it would be a scandal. If they had turned it into $1 million, it would be a scandal. Somehow, as they've raked in as much as $30 million, it has failed to register as a scandal for the mainstream media.

While all of this went on, family man Joe Biden famously stayed close to his brother and son, talking to Hunter nearly every day. Somehow, we are to believe Joe Biden never thought to ask his son what he did for a living.

Presumably when a major Democratic donor started spending millions to quell various Hunter Biden scandals in the run-up to the 2020 election, Joe Biden didn't ask that donor what he expected in return.

If you only have the network news to go by, none of this makes sense. Surely poor recovering addict Hunter Biden hasn't admitted to most of this? But he has. Wouldn't law enforcement have done something about it? Many of Hunter Biden's domestic and foreign business associates are currently in prison. Of course, in his testimony he categorially denied his father was involved in any of this.

All of us conservatives knew from birth that the media was overwhelmingly liberal and had been since the days of the ridiculous Adlai Stevenson, and the professionalization of journalism after World War II. The coming of the J-schools ironically marked the end of balanced journalism.

But about a decade ago this began to change. A new kind of reporter came onto the scene, one totally uninterested in even *seeming* to be balanced. These were not just liberals, they were activists. They'd gone to college and taken out massive student loans to obtain journalism degrees with the express purpose of overthrowing what they viewed as an unjust society—America!

Their extreme left-wing opinionated journalism pulled the American left with it. In fact, it would be more accurate to say that the Democratic Party is an arm of the Mainstream Media Establishment than vice versa. These days, the tail seems to wag the dog. Although I think of mainstream media journalists as little better that public relations flacks and admen for the Democratic Party, it is probably more accurate to view the Democrats as terrified hostages to a media run amok, and suffering a massive case of Stockholm syndrome.

One thing is for certain: I went into my chairmanship of the House Oversight Committee thinking that there must be some good and true journalists out there willing to engage with objective ideas and clear evidence. I have now arrived at the point where I know the mainstream media to be beyond reform and the enemy of most everything I hold dear, especially the truth.

Of course, there is still a subgroup of decent journalists, and I'm thankful for them every day as we try to get the message out. Those are generally on the right-leaning and conservative side of news and opinion. I hate to say it, but these good people are thin on the ground, and they do not control the dissemination of information in anything like the totalitarian manner of their left-wing contemporaries.

The mainstream media rule the narrative as of today. And you can be sure that always, every time, and everywhere, their goal is to further the interest of the left and of the Democratic Party.

They are the fleas who have eaten up the dog.

So don't wonder how the Bidens got away with it. Wonder that the truth is making any inroads in the narrative at all. But let me assure you, we'll keep fighting.

For a long time, the mainstream media thought they had everything sewn up nice and neatly for Joe Biden. Let's take a look at the story line they had carefully crafted with a cloud of misdirection and magical Democrat gaslighting dust, with fake media narratives.

## ONE: HUNTER BIDEN'S LAPTOP WAS RUSSIAN DISINFORMATION.

FIFTY-ONE FORMER INTELLIGENCE officials signed a letter saying so. The creation of that letter, we learned, had been secretly led by Antony Blinken. But never mind that: these august intelligence has-beens (who were, curiously, mostly left-wing Democrats and Trump haters) stated in orotund prose that the laptop had all the makings of a Russian disinformation campaign to propel Donald Trump's reelection. The mainstream media took the letter, mixed it with a dollop of Rudy Giuliani drama, and ran with it for all it was worth. Social media companies joined in and suppressed the *New York Post* story that accurately described the laptop and its damaging contents. All of this was enough to discredit the laptop long enough for Biden to take the election.

Hunter Biden's laptop was determined to be legitimate after CBS conducted a forensic audit in early 2023 (I'll discuss this at length later), and in the lawsuit that Hunter filed against John Paul Mac Isaac—his computer laptop repair store owner—whom he accused of improperly sharing the contents of his laptop.[1] And finally, when the Garland Department of Justice announced it had used it as evidence in Hunter Biden's June 2024 conviction of lying on a gun application. Ironically, Hunter Biden committed perjury during his deposition when he was asked by Representative Matt Gaetz if he dropped his laptop off at Mac Isaac's store. He said no.[2] Of course, at that time he was well into a lawsuit with Mac Isaac in which he accused Mac Isaac of mishandling the laptop contents. That is, the contents of the laptop *that he dropped off there for repair and never picked up*. Here's proof that when you lie so many times in so many ways, it is often difficult to keep track of which false trail of deceit you've gone down at any particular time.

## TWO: THE BIDEN FAMILY WERE LEGITIMATE INTERNATIONAL ENTREPRENEURS JUST LIKE THE TRUMPS AND KUSHNERS.

IN THE MEDIA'S never-ending defense of the Biden menagerie during the 2020 election, decades of reporting on the Biden family's countless conflicts of interest had to be rewritten. The secret, they discovered, was the strategic pivot to Donald Trump's family. The *Trumps* also had overseas business dealings. The Bidens were just like *them*!

It didn't matter that the Trump family's international business interests were right out in the open. You could touch them, visit them, wear them, and eat them. These endeavors included golf courses, hotels, apartments, office buildings, real estate development, steaks and wines, and, yes, a line of clothing that was made in China.

My only goal is the truth. In March 2024, I did an interview where, when asked about the difference between Jared Kushner's deal with Saudi Arabia and Hunter Biden's foreign deals, I stated that in my opinion Kushner did cross the line of ethics. I rejected the desirability of a congressional hearing on that specifically. But, as I've stated repeatedly, I very much want to change the law to restrict such ethically dubious dealings. I do intend for Oversight to look into the general problem. That is why Rep. Katie Porter (D-CA) and I introduced the bipartisan Presidential Ethics Reform Act to define exactly what influence peddling is and ban it from happening in the future. American citizens can currently be charged for bribing a foreign official, but the laws are much more relaxed for those taking advantage of foreign deals and investment back at home.[3] The next day a GOP consultant close to both Kushner and Representative Kevin McCarthy called telling me that I needed to change my statement.

I explained to him that my statement was correct, and that my only regret was that I unintentionally defended Kushner when I accurately stated the difference between his and Hunter Biden's activities. Kushner *does* have legitimate businesses with assets and a transparent purpose. Kushner negotiated the Abraham Accords with the Saudis and then started a business to make money from the new trade rules. At least there's a noncorrupt explanation for the business, something Hunter Biden has rarely offered. Nevertheless, I felt that Kushner tested ethics by going to Saudi Arabia so soon after leaving office to secure a legitimate $2 billion investment into those businesses. I explained to the GOP consultant (who was obviously a mouthpiece for Kushner) that under my planned legislation to ban influence peddling, Kushner's dealing would not be legally allowed.

I figured I had a direct line to Jared Kushner at that moment, so I finished up the call by instructing the consultant to tell Kushner to f— off. I hoped Kushner was listening on speaker phone.

In his book about political families cashing in, consummate corruption scourge Peter Schweizer says of Jared Kushner and his wife, Ivanka Trump, "These relationships hardly equate with the large private equity deals and real estate partnerships that Biden and Kerry family and allies struck with the Chinese."[4]

No reason for the Biden "deals" has been offered besides vague references to payments for advice. Look as you will, you could not find a single substantial legitimate business that the Biden family had . . . anywhere! The Bidens did not appear to have any assets other than cash. But, boy, did they have a lot of that. They did not produce, manufacture, or sell anything while Joe Biden was in office.

Whether you and I like it or not, it is currently legal in the U.S. to work for certain foreign concerns so long as you abide by the requirements of the Foreign Agents Registration Act, or FARA. Also, the penalty for violating FARA is severe—a maximum of five years in prison and a $250,000 fine.

Hunter Biden doesn't appear to have registered to lobby for any of the foreign actors with whom he was involved when his deals went down.*

Decades earlier, Hunter Biden had briefly been a lobbyist, but he'd long ago realized that was no way to get rich. Too many limitations. Hunter set out to be *filthy* rich. Rolling in cash.

---

* When, in his March 2024 Oversight Committee appearance, Tony Bobulinski told Representative Alexandria Ocasio-Cortez that he witnessed Joe Biden committing a crime, a FARA violation is one of the crimes he was referring to. More on that confrontation in chapter 16.

But if he were to get there by selling his father's influence (and what other skills did Hunter have to offer? a useless law degree?), FARA restrictions would have to be thrown out the window. So he would become a dealmaker, an investment something-or-other. That was the ticket.

## THREE: THE BIDENS NEVER TOOK ANY MONEY FROM CHINA.

JOE BIDEN SAID that during the 2020 presidential debate against Donald Trump, so it must be true. In fact, Biden went even further. The only person on the debate stage whose family took money from China was President Trump. In fact, Hunter Biden's companies took in over $6 million *that we know about* from CCP-controlled companies and individuals.

CEFC was allegedly a private Chinese financial investment company based on energy holdings. America's pitiful mainstream media accepted the notion that CEFC was a private company simply because Hunter said it was, but I was skeptical from the moment I heard about how it operated. The name itself should have given the "private company" label away as a lie. The letters stand for "China Energy Fund Committee," and the company was run very much like a Chinese Communist Party department, a state-owned enterprise (SOE), rather than an independent company.

"It has a Communist Party Committee and a Youth Committee, which are staples of SOEs," *Fortune* reported in 2016. The company awards staff prizes such as "Model Worker," "Excellent Party Member," and "ping-pong champion."[5]

CEFC might have been a separate political canton, but it was no independent entity.[6]

CEFC was ruled over by its chairman, Ye Jianming, who had been, among many other shady occupations, a former Chinese secret police official. The CEFC money allegedly came from government-controlled oil and gas. It helps if we understand that China is energy-poor and a fossil fuel importer. It doesn't have vast oil riches like the U.S. does in Texas and Alaska. Lack of energy resources is, in fact, the primary strategic weakness of the People's Republic of China (PRC).[7] So where did the money actually come from for this gigantic conglomerate that suddenly sprang onto the field of the world's economy? We don't know specifically, but assuredly from the coffers of the communist government of the PRC.

CEFC was, at base, a state-controlled enterprise (which, in China, means Chinese Communist Party–controlled) used by the PRC to spread its influence around the world while maintaining deniability. Its billionaire chairman was a particularly adept bureaucrat, possibly one of the PRC "redbloods,"[8] a son of one of the incredibly powerful and wealthy political families who run things in Beijing (although Ye claimed to come from a family of "modest fishermen").[9,10] Whoever he was (and *was* is the operative word; he's probably dead or, at best, rotting in a Chinese prison camp presently[11]) he had by 2017 carved out for himself a little dukedom within the CCP establishment.

Sound like anybody we know here in America?[12]

During this period, China was fully engaged in its Belt and Road Initiative, an international scheme to build infrastructure out for semideveloped and third-world countries by issuing loans the Chinese knew those countries could never repay. When a nation inevitably defaulted, China would then set the terms of the bankruptcy. What this usually meant was that China took over, say, an entire port, staffed it with Chinese nationals, and began operating it as a military base (all shipping in China is ultimately controlled by the People's Liberation Army Navy, or PLAN).

CEFC was right there in the Belt and Road Initiative money

mix, "investing" in dubious enterprises, making loans, and paying off local officials right and left through "goodwill" nonprofit offshoots that it wholly controlled.

It was an outfit tailor-made to channel money to Joe Biden's brother and son.

The largest investments from within CEFC during 2017 were within the Czech Republic.[13] So much CCP money flowed in that the Czech president named Ye an "economic advisor."[14] But the big deal that Chairman Ye was working toward was a $9 billion agreement to become part owner in the Russian state-owned enterprise Rosneft, which controls 40 percent of Russia's energy output. China, remember, badly needs imported oil and gas to keep its economy functioning, and Russia was right next door to provide it. But bad blood between PRC president Xi Jinping and Russian president Vladimir Putin doomed the deal.[15]

When the Rosneft deal fell apart, the PRC president cut down Ye like a dead cornstalk in winter—and Hunter Biden and Jim Biden lost arguably the greatest "sugar brother" of their lifetimes, and certainly the richest. In typical Biden fashion, part of Ye's downfall can be attributed to Hunter and Jim's ineptitude as fixers[16]—but more on this later.

America's pitiful mainstream media never had a clue about the Biden spin factory's "private company" lie about CEFC because they never looked for clues, which were abundantly obvious all along.

## FOUR: JOE BIDEN NEVER MET ANY OF THE PEOPLE WHO DID BUSINESS WITH HIS FAMILY.

CANDIDATE JOE BIDEN promised that there was an absolute wall between him, the government, and his family's business dealings, and that he hadn't met any of Hunter's associates.

"It's a bunch of lies. I did not. And it's a bunch of lies," said Joe Biden in a press conference, adding, "They're lies."[17]

In almost every case, he now says he doesn't recall meeting with them, and when he does, he knows he didn't discuss business with them.

The Oversight Committee investigation revealed that the Biden family influence-peddling schemes operated at full speed from mid-2014 until late 2018. Once Joe Biden made the decision in 2014 that he would not run for president in 2016, thus marking the seeming end to his political career, Hunter went to work identifying potential sources of income leveraging the power of the vice presidency. In 2018, Hunter's business model self-destructed with a series of bombs that included the arrest and conviction of CEFC's Patrick Ho, the out-of-control drug addiction of Hunter Biden (not that any of his oligarch "bros" cared, but this signaled to all of the shady foreign actors who had hoped to gain access that the family middleman was out of commission), the IRS investigators closing in on the tax evasion that Hunter Biden is being prosecuted for, and the imminent announcement that Joe Biden would seek the 2020 Democrat nomination for president.

The years 2019 and 2020 were lean ones for Hunter Biden. As evidenced by subpoenaed bank records, the massive influx of foreign wires came to a screeching halt. The surplus of cash in his many bank accounts dwindled to the point that many of the accounts became overdrawn. The advisors to the Biden presidential campaign wisely ordered Joe to spend his time in his basement, and for Hunter to spend his time out of the picture and away from his controversial foreign benefactors.

When Hunter made the near-fatal mistake of leaving his laptop with all of its incriminating evidence behind at a Wilmington, Delaware, computer repair store, Biden allies in the Deep State, led by future secretary of state Antony Blinken and director of national intelligence James Clapper, stepped up to order their friends in the mainstream media to follow a false narrative that the laptop was not real, but rather another attempt by Donald Trump and his buddy Vladimir Putin to spread Russian disinformation through their chief propagandist, Rudy Giuliani, in a coordinated effort to take down Joe Biden's campaign.

# ALL THE PRESIDENT'S MONEY

# Chapter 1

## SHOW ME THE MONEY

During the 2020 presidential campaign, Joe Biden repeatedly assured voters that he was not involved in his family's shady business schemes. He also claimed that he kept a strict wall between his family's business activities and the government to prevent any conflicts of interest from ever arising.

As Biden famously told President Donald Trump in an October 2020 debate, "I have not taken a penny from any foreign source, ever in my life."[1]

Information from research publications, conversations with former business associates serving as whistleblowers to the committee, and a review of Hunter Biden's abandoned laptop all point to Joe Biden being central in his family's international money-making scheme. Evidence suggested that Hunter Biden made millions from shady characters in adversarial countries spread across the globe by simply selling access to Joe.

"Joe Biden was the brand being sold by the Biden family," Tony Bobulinski said to Oversight Committee interviewers in 2024, referring to deals before and after he left office.[2]

The Grassley-Johnson Report cited 150 Suspicious Activity Reports involving Hunter and Jim Biden filed by their bankers. The SARs suggested many serious possible crimes, ranging from money laundering to potential bribery, but are not in themselves evidence of any wrongdoing.

Hunter Biden had been under a U.S. Department of Justice (DOJ) investigation for a range of infractions, including failure to pay federal income taxes for years at a time. From May 2014 to April 2019, the president's son was paid in excess of $5 million by Burisma Energy in Ukraine for occupying a fanciful board position. In addition to Hunter's legal woes, President Biden's two brothers, Jim and Frank Biden, plied their trade of influence peddling. Before it became verboten for American mainstream media to criticize the Biden family for fear this would aid the dreaded Trump, members of the Biden family were often in the news with political and financial scandals as they peddled access to Joe Biden or forgot to pay their taxes, all while residing in a state where Joe exercised almost total political control.

During the first two years of Joe Biden's benighted presidency, I was the top Republican (the ranking member) on the U.S. House of Representatives Committee on Oversight and Accountability. Though I was in the minority, I aggressively pursued information and sought to do what I was elected to do: provide oversight and hold bad government actors accountable. This task was made nearly impossible because Republicans were not in the majority and were not granted subpoena power by the Democrats. My Oversight Committee requested over two hundred documents from the Biden administration during those two years and did not receive a single response. Their excuse? That I was not the actual chairman.

It takes a lot of hubris and pomposity for these unelected administration timeservers to turn up their noses to a U.S. congressman duly elected by citizens of the United States of America and empowered by law to oversee their activities and hold them accountable for corruption, irresponsibility in carrying out the law, and other ethical breaches, but our requests were ignored repeatedly.

Meanwhile, I bided my time and made plans for being in the

majority in Congress. As it happened, I had two years to consider this, two years to plan how to investigate the Biden family once Republicans flipped the House. When that happened, I would become chairman of Oversight and possess subpoena power. Believe me, I thought long and hard about what to do with that instrument.

I knew from my banking experience that there would be more to the story regarding those 150 SARs, not only due to the sheer number of violations—far greater than any that I or anyone I consulted with in the banking sector ever heard of—but also because I was aware that no bank would file a SAR on a family member of the sitting vice president of the United States without a great deal of confidence that a serious financial crime had been committed.

The Grassley-Johnson Report mentioned all those SARs existed. I wanted to get into the gritty details, and I knew I and my staff had the expertise to do so. I had to get Treasury to give up the details so that I could closely examine the SARs. Such reports are rightly protected by federal bank privacy laws because they contain a great deal of very sensitive information. For example, if the banks suggested the Bidens were money laundering, then the SARs would not just list other bank accounts involved; they would also list all the account owners. This would lead to opportunities to subpoena more bank accounts and potentially discover new sources of illegal transfers and new coconspirators in the influence-peddling schemes.

With the power of the subpoena, I could follow the money trail from source to end.

Those SARs would be the key to opening up the sordid tale of Biden corruption.

## THE HEART OF BIDEN DARKNESS

WHO DID THEY *think they were dealing with?*

On Sunday, July 30, 2017, Hunter Biden believed he had had enough nonsense from his annoying Chinese associates. He was visiting his father's house in Delaware and decided this would be the perfect time to text his frustration and let them know in no uncertain terms that the time had come to pay up for services rendered. He took out his phone and typed in a text to someone he knew would understand the plain English he was about to deploy in making his displeasure known—CEFC chairman Ye's personal secretary and translator, Raymond Zhao.

"Z- Please have the director call me- not James [Gilliar] or Tony [Bobulinski] or Jim [Biden]- have him call me tonight. I am sitting here with my father and we would like to understand why the commitment made has not been fulfilled." Hunter continued, "All too often people mistake kindness for weakness --- and all too often I am standing over top of them saying I warned you. From this moment until whenever he reaches me."

"Copy, I will call you on WhatsApp," Zhao replied.

"Ok my friend - I am sitting here waiting for the call with my father," Hunter texted. "I sure hope whatever it is you are doing is very very very important."[3]

This was Hunter Biden informing Zhao that Joe Biden was sitting next to him and together they would seek revenge if their prior commitment was not fulfilled.

Ten days later, CEFC had wired a total of $5.1 million to Hunter Biden–linked accounts.[4]

The Biden family and their associates took in over $8 million from China. Starting with a $3 million wire into the Robinson Walker LLC[5] a few weeks after Joe Biden left the vice presidency (as Rob Walker testified, a "thank you" from CEFC[6]), to the

$5 million wire that Hunter's Hudson West III received days after he sent the WhatsApp message demanding money from CEFC's Raymond Zhao, Chairman Ye's right-hand man, and beyond.

## THE BUSINESS THAT ISN'T

AFTER SUBPOENAING AND reviewing thousands of pages of bank documents from multiple financial institutions, reviewing hundreds of pages of banking red flags at the Treasury Department, reading hundreds of emails and messages pertaining to various money transactions, and listening to dozens of hours of sworn testimony from the Bidens, as well as their former associates, I can honestly say that I do not know of one single *legitimate* business that the Bidens owned or operated.

It's astounding.

Take Jim Biden's Americore adventure. Americore had always been a benighted business, billing itself as an attempt to take over America's network of rural hospitals, which are much needed but have often become financial drain holes for small counties trying to support them. The idea was that Americore would centralize and economize these, using a multi-hospital network.

"I was sold that Americore was going to be the salvation of rural hospitals," a former executive told *Politico*. "The whole thing was a scam, and it didn't take that long to figure it out."[7]

Americore was in the process of imploding in 2018 when Jim Biden, who seemingly could smell a swindle a hundred miles away,* offered to come in and save the struggling company with a

---

* The actual connection was through Jim Biden's friend and colleague convicted felon Joey Langston, the judge-bribing upper-story man of infamous trial lawyer (and also a convicted felon) Dickie Scruggs. See Curtis Wilkie's well-written account of the tawdry tale, "The Fall of the House of Zeus: The Rise and Ruin of America's

bridge loan from a hedge fund, followed by investment from "the Middle East."

Jim Biden made sure everyone at Americore knew whose brother he was and what he could do for the company. He arranged the hedge fund cash infusion, then promptly gave himself a $600,000 "loan" issued by Americore from the proceeds. Americore wired the funds to Jim Biden's accounts in separate payments. The terms of this loan were not revealed, and it's not clear when or how they planned to pay it back.

Jim Biden kept up his Joe Biden Banter. He told company executives that he wanted to give Joe Biden equity, and that they should install Joe onto their board of directors. His brother could promote the company's "rural business model" in a future presidential campaign.

Jim Biden moved like a Hoover vacuum through the company's funds. At least three Bidens got jobs at Americore, including Jim Biden's wife and daughter. Hunter Biden met with the CEO, and head-of-the-family Joe Biden had several encounters with Americore executives and associates.[8]

Jim Biden's imaginary oil sheik investment never materialized. Of course even if it had, the investment could not have saved what amounted to an imploding alleged kickback scheme managed by nincompoops. Americore went through the bridge loan and was soon struggling again. Jim Biden did not repay his "loan" from the company, and in 2020 Americore declared bankruptcy. The hedge fund clients were screwed. And, as I'll expand upon later, the rural people in need of a nearby hospital were screwed.[9] After the bankrupt company sued him, Jim Biden eventually paid back $335,000, coming out $250,000 on top on the deal.[10]

---

Most Powerful Trial Lawyer," AbeBooks, January 1, 1970, https://www.abebooks.com/9780307460707/Fall-House-Zeus-Rise-Ruin-0307460703/plp.

Did Jim Biden pocket that money? Only $50,000 of it personally.

As the Oversight staff discovered through our careful search of bank records, on March 1, 2018, $200,000 of the Americore "loan" flowed into Jim Biden's bank account. That same day, Jim Biden wrote a check to Joseph R. Biden for $200,000. The subject line read, "loan repayment."[11]

You read that right. Two hundred thousand dollars of Americore money went to Joe Biden.

There's no doubt about this. We have a copy of the check.

"Loan."

There's that Jim Biden word again.

I'm reminded of the scene in *The Princess Bride* where Inigo Montoya says to Vizzini, "You keep using that word. I do not think it means what you think it means."

## THE BRAND IS EVERYTHING

THE LEGAL DEFINITION of a "business" is a person or entity performing an activity carried on for the production of income from selling goods or performing services. The Bidens did not own hotels, casinos, office buildings, apartment complexes, apparel companies, wineries, or a social media company. Hunter Biden did not even have a website or real office location that I could ever find on any of his thirty LLCs. The only business activity that we discovered in the investigation was sales. And what was for sale?

The "Biden Brand."

The customers? A rogues' gallery of shady operatives from corrupt countries around the world.

What were they buying?

Hope for political action and influence. A truth-seeking prosecutor fired here, tacit acknowledgment of an illegal extension of a totalitarian country's boundaries there, a corrupt oligarch taken off a U.S. no-entry list somewhere else, and "a wealth of introductions and business opportunities at the highest levels."[12] What else could the Biden Brand possibly be trafficking in? In a presentation to Qatari officials asking for $30 million, Jim Biden listed his qualification as the "Brother and Campaign Finance Chair of former Vice President Joe Biden."[13] They have nothing else. When it walks like a duck and quacks like a duck—it's a duck. Even if that duck is swimming in a lake of "plausible deniability," as Jim Biden put it to Tony Bobulinski.

When asked what exactly they did to receive millions of dollars in payments from CEFC, Jim Biden testified that they were paid to find American investments for the Chinese Communist Party–linked company. When asked if he or Hunter ever actually found CEFC anything to invest in, Jim testified, "No."[14]

I do not believe that the Bidens received $8 million from China to seek investment opportunities. I believe it was a Chinese intelligence operation. Its purpose: after the Bidens' failure to deliver a single realistic investment to the entity that for all practical purposes was the Chinese government, Joe Biden would be compromised. Furthermore, he would be easy to threaten. In other words, blackmail. Do a service for us or your family goes down. Espionage agencies have been using the trick for centuries.

Or maybe it's not that. Maybe the answer is much less convoluted. Maybe it was payment for being soft on China back when Joe was in office or if he ran for president. It makes more sense to me than Hunter's story, that being on the board of Amtrak made him an invaluable connection for one of the richest men in China.

## THE CLIENT LIST

SUBPOENAED BANK RECORDS proved that most of the money Hunter Biden took in through his shady dealings arrived while Joe Biden served as vice president of the U.S. The investigation also revealed that Hunter Biden started receiving $1 million from corrupt Romanian oligarch Gabriel Popoviciu weeks after Joe Biden flew home in Air Force Two from delivering his now-infamous "anti-corruption" speech to Romanian citizens.[15]

In addition, the investigation revealed that Hunter received two extravagant gifts: a diamond from the CCP-linked CEFC, and a sports car from a Kazakhstani oligarch. Money for this Porsche was paid through an account where Hunter Biden was listed as the corporate secretary.[16] Hunter would contradict himself during his deposition by saying he was not affiliated with that account.

There is no evidence to suggest that CEFC was anything other than a wholly owned investment arm of the Chinese Communist Party. Many of the banks where Hunter Biden had accounts also assumed CEFC to be a state-owned entity. Because China does not have the same securities laws that the U.S. has that require public filings of ownership, it was impossible to determine the true ownership of the corrupt and now-defunct Chinese entity. Following the multiple changes in ownership of the entity, it appears that today all of its assets are in possession of the Chinese government.

The Oversight Committee's transcribed interviews revealed that Joe Biden—after pledging to the American people countless times that he had never met any of the shady characters involved in wiring his family money through a series of transactions flagged by major banks for potential corruption through shell companies—actually met nearly every single person. In fact, on April 16, 2015, he had dinner at Georgetown's Cafe Milano with Yelena Baturina, who days later sent Hunter Biden $3.5 million, as well as Kazakhstani oligarch Kenes Rakishev and Burisma corporate secretary Vadym Pozharsky.[17] Hunter Biden stressed in his congressional testimony that his father did not have substantive conversations with any of these people.

During Eric Schwerin's interview, we discovered that he was both Joe Biden's bookkeeper and Hunter Biden's bookkeeper, and worse, that Schwerin never received one penny for doing Joe Biden's bookkeeping while Joe was vice president.[18] Not only was there no wall between Joe and Hunter, as evidenced by the fact that they used the same private bookkeeper, but Joe Biden never paid Schwerin for those bookkeeping services.[19]

This in itself is an ethics violation. An elected official can't accept free services from a company. In addition to bookkeeping services, Joe and Hunter also shared the same Delaware law firm, Monzack Mersky and Browder.[20] This became relevant to the investigation with the discovery of two payments to Joe Biden from Jim Biden where Jim testified that the payments came from a law firm trust account. That same firm also represented at least five of Hunter's LLCs as well as Joe Biden's CelticCapri LLC.

There certainly was no wall—financial, legal, or otherwise—between Joe and Hunter Biden.

## RUSSIAN DOLL OF CORRUPTION

BY ALL ACCOUNTS, Joe Biden gave only two speeches overseas solely focused on corruption during the eight years of his vice presidency. One was in Romania to civil society groups and students on May 21, 2014,[21] and one to the Ukrainian Rada on December 9, 2015. In both speeches, Vice President Biden touted American democracy and strongly condemned corruption.

"Corruption is just another form of tyranny," said the vice president in Romania. "And corruption can represent a clear and present danger not only to a nation's economy, but to its very national security. There are nations, and we've seen it recently, that exploit corruption to exercise malign influence and undermine the very sovereignty and independence of their neighbors. In this way, corruption has become an instrument of foreign policy for some nations."[22]

I highly doubt that there was ever a more "pot calling the kettle black" moment in the history of our country than during and after these two diplomatic speeches delivered by then Vice President Biden.

A little over a year after Biden's speech in Romania, he welcomed Romanian president Klaus Iohannis to the White House. Within five weeks of this meeting, a Romanian businessman involved with a high-profile corruption prosecution in Romania, Gabriel Popoviciu, began depositing large sums of money into a Hunter Biden associate's bank account—money that inevitably made its way into Biden family accounts though incremental payments. Popoviciu made sixteen of the seventeen payments to the Biden associate account, ultimately totaling over $3 million, while Joe Biden was vice president of the United States. Biden family accounts ultimately received approximately $1.038 million.

Joe Biden's much-debated speech to the Ukrainian Rada was similar. The difference was that Hunter Biden was receiving significant payments from the allegedly corrupt Ukrainian energy firm Burisma *before* the speech. These payments were under threat because of international investigations of allegations of widespread corruption by Burisma executives. Britain had seized some of the oligarchs' assets the same month the owner of Burisma got the U.S. vice president's son to join his board.

According to a panel discussion that Joe Biden participated in at the Council on Foreign Relations on January 23, 2018, the vice president admitted that he told then–Ukrainian president Petro Poroshenko that he would withhold $1 billion in U.S. loan guarantees to Ukraine unless the Ukraine government fired prosecutor Viktor Shokin, the man charged with investigating Burisma. Biden gave them a timeline of six hours before he boarded Air Force Two to fly home. Later, Biden added his famous line, ". . . son of a bitch, they fired him!" After the termination of Shokin by parliamentary vote in March 2016, Hunter Biden continued to receive hundreds of thousands of more dollars in additional payments from Burisma. In 2018, the replacement Ukrainian prosecutor ended the investigation of Mykola Zlochevsky, owner of Burisma, without filing any charges.

By 2014, Vice President Joe Biden had already gotten the horrible news that his political prodigy son Beau had been diagnosed with glioblastoma multiforme, an aggressive form of brain cancer. Also, by this time it was apparent to Biden that most of the pundits in the Democratic National Committee as well as many in the Obama administration had decided that Hillary Clinton was their best shot to carry on Barack Obama's legacy of expensive left-wing policies. It was apparent to everyone, including Joe Biden, that his long and accomplished political career as U.S. senator from Delaware and as vice president was nearing an end. And at Joe's age, coupled with the fact that Hillary appeared destined to be the first female president—and surely a two-term president at that—the chances of Joe ever returning to political service were essentially zero. So, Joe Biden started planning for his future outside politics.

Former vice presidents who never became president often had similar careers outside the vice presidency. Younger vice presidents like Walter Mondale briefly practiced law or served as an ambassador, or both. Dan Quayle worked with the Hudson Institute and became an investment banker. Al Gore founded a television channel, Current TV, which he later sold to Qatari-owned Al Jazeera for a huge sum. The much older Dick Cheney—who had made his fortune prior to becoming vice president by serving as CEO of Halliburton—lived more or less like a normal retiree. All four of these former VPs wrote books. Joe Biden was much closer in age to Dick Cheney, but, unlike Cheney, who became rich after successfully working for years in the private sector, Biden had no visible personal income apart from his government pension when he left office.

Our investigation suggested that Joe Biden's most marketable skill after leaving office would be consulting with wealthy foreign entities. He had experience both as a senator who chaired the Senate Foreign Relations Committee, and as a vice president whose primary role had been presiding over a Senate rapidly becoming obsessed with giving out massive sums of foreign aid. Plus, as VP, he'd made a specialty of traveling to corrupt foreign countries and handing out massive aid checks. Unfortunately for the rest of us, the practice of consulting/lobbying on behalf of foreign entities became legal once Joe Biden left office, so long as he registered as a foreign agent.

More than likely, Hunter learned his impressive skill in financial deception while he worked as a young man at MBNA bank as a fraud investigator. Had Hunter Biden not gotten addicted to drugs and left his laptop behind at a Delaware computer repair shop, likely while under the influence, the lucrative deals would have gone undetected by anyone other than the handful of IRS and DOJ employees who spent years investigating the Bidens, only to be made to stand down prior to interviewing both Hunter and Joe Biden.

## EARLY STRATEGY FOR SUCCESS

AS THE 2022 fall election drew closer and the possibility grew that we Republicans would flip the House, I realized that if we did, I would become chairman of the Oversight Committee. I began even then to strategize how I would approach the investigation. I knew that it would be extremely difficult to obtain evidence from a sitting president of the United States and hostile Department of Justice. I was also extremely cognizant of the fact that in the final analysis every major congressional investigation over the past twenty years had underperformed, and all had failed to achieve their purposes.

We had several tasks, as I saw it.

First, we needed to prove that the Hunter Biden laptop was real and not Russian disinformation. The media and the Deep State had practically stamped this untruth into the minds of most Americans through sheer repetition of the falsehood.

My strategy was to secretly work with a credible mainstream media reporter, ideally one not ideologically in cahoots with the capital's political class. I heard through sources that CBS News' Catherine Herridge had a copy of the Hunter Biden laptop hard drive and was secretly conducting a credible forensic audit to determine its authenticity. My Oversight communications staff stayed in close contact with Herridge and knew this forensic audit would be completed soon after the midterm election.

Herridge verified the drive's authenticity.[23] She lived up to her reputation for objectivity and proved to be one of the few reliable and honest mainstream reporters throughout our investigation.

Second, we needed financial records that would show *that* the Bidens were hiding money, and *where* they were hiding it. After all, when the details became known of Hunter Biden's dissipated, foolish lifestyle and blinkered decision-making, an observer might legitimately imagine he'd spent every dollar that the Chicom party apparatchiks, Eastern European oligarchs, and Middle Eastern cut-out men might have paid him on crack cocaine and meth.[24] Of course, there were other Bidens besides Hunter. There was, for example, Joe Biden's brother James, whom the president describes as "my best friend, my buddy."[25] Jim Biden has always been considered Joe Biden's right-hand man in the family, sticking close to his brother at "nearly every critical juncture in Joe's personal and political life."[26]

Third, if I were incoming Oversight Committee chair, I knew that I needed access to the Suspicious Activity Reports (SARs) that the Grassley-Johnson Senate investigation of Biden corruption had previously turned up. Fifth, I had to depose a bunch of hostile former Biden associates. Finally, I needed to pin some hope that new evidence would emerge, perhaps coming from whistleblowers, that would force the shady Biden associates to tell the truth.

Sixth, I had to ignore a lot of well-intentioned but misguided advice. Several right-wing political commentators were pushing me to use my subpoena power to acquire Joe Biden's tax records. This could not have worked. First, Joe Biden had already voluntarily disclosed his tax returns while he was vice president and while he was president. Second, the House Ways and Means Committee is the only committee with the authority to access presidential tax returns. So I could not have subpoenaed President Biden's tax returns even if I'd wanted to.

I'd spent years on a bank board of directors. I'd seen enough tax returns to know that most dishonest people cheat or fudge their returns. There would be no smoking gun there.

Bank records, however, do not lie. People can hide or manipulate income in both legal and illegal ways when paying their income taxes. Bank statements represent the *actual* money. They show every penny of income as well as the source of that income. Possessing bank records would allow us to trace where the funds came from and where they went. Criminals try to obscure these sources. They hide money through various money-laundering activities. It can be a labyrinth. But, in a sense, the records *are* the money. An assiduous investigator can trace that currency back like an explorer seeking the origin of a river.

As expected, the Bidens have the best legal team in America. I knew going in that they would try to obstruct my investigation at every turn. I figured they would expect me to finagle the rules and attempt to subpoena the tax returns for Hunter Biden and possibly Jim Biden as my first act. This was what any lawyer might do.

Seventh, I'd have to catch his team napping. I came out of the gate with subpoenas for bank records of all the shady associates of Hunter Biden (an amazing assortment of hedge fund con men, political bloodsuckers, social charlatans, financial knaves, and playboy trust fund scions). These records I hoped would lead to sources of cash and the real bad guys—hostile foreign governments and other political entities attempting to suborn American democratic institutions. I also wanted to show how the money flowed to the Bidens themselves. Experience told me this was likely how they operated. An associate would receive the foreign wire and then pass it along to the Bidens, who then claimed it as a consulting fee or some other innocent-sounding payment made from a legitimate American company.

Senators Chuck Grassley and Ron Johnson had already done groundbreaking work that brought to light many aspects of Hunter Biden's influence-peddling operation. In the course of the investigation, Grassley and Johnson had turned up 150 SARs filed on transactions related to entities connected to the Bidens. This stood out to me like a sore thumb. As a kid who'd grown up around banking, I suspected that nobody else in the history of America had that many SARs. It was a given. Just one SAR was a mark to draw the suspicion of any bank or creditor, and—more ominously for the bank itself—the attention of investigators and regulators. One hundred and fifty was an incredible number!

I also knew that no bank would issue a SAR on the son of a sitting vice president of the United States unless they were *certain* that son had committed a very serious crime. Banks do not like to issue SARs, not only because it's added paperwork, but because it's an instant invitation for bank examiners to arrive at their doors. One violation can draw an examiner and cost the bank thousands of employee hours assisting and complying with the investigative process. Imagine what one hundred SARs would mean in terms of disruption and possible reputational damage. A bank that made such a report would want to be on very sound footing when filing.

There had to be more to the story of the SARs than had been previously revealed. I needed access. The Biden SARs were protected by bank privacy laws that would prevent me from ever obtaining them simply by asking. Secretary of the Treasury Janet Yellen would not have allowed me to visit the Treasury Department premises to read them. The only way that would happen would be if I used congressional legal pressure to coerce Treasury to show them to me.

The last part of my initial strategy was always going to be the most difficult. Getting all of the shady characters involved in the Hunter Biden influence-peddling scheme to willingly come in, turn over crucial documents, and tell the truth about the malfeasances they committed seemed highly unlikely. What I needed most was the power to grant immunity. If I could provide legal immunity, then they could tell the truth about possible crimes they may have been involved in without being held accountable for those misdeeds.

But there was a catch. The only possible way I could grant immunity was with the permission of Attorney General Merrick Garland, who was a fanatical defender of Biden and the pack of quislings who made up the Biden administration. That wasn't going to happen. So immunity would be out of the question. How to flank Garland's obstinacy and get that essential information?

We needed government whistleblowers to come forward with knowledge of both the crimes committed and the investigative cover-ups performed by government agencies involved in investigating the Bidens. Joe Biden and his brood had been political fixtures since 1972. There were decades of investigations and possible crimes to consider.

Before that could happen, I knew I must build trust with the American people that this investigation was credible, and that I, as lead investigator, could be counted on to tell the truth. Fortunately, along came two of the most forthright and believable public servants a lead investigator could ever wish for.

# Chapter 2

## UNLOCKING THE SARS

The first week of February 2023 saw the Oversight Committee come out of the gate hard. We held our first official hearing and it was titled "Federal Pandemic Spending: A Prescription for Waste, Fraud, and Abuse." I wanted to demonstrate that my committee was serious about its core mission: wasteful spending. Over the previous two years while the Democrats were in control of Oversight, I never remember them having one single hearing on wasteful spending.

During my hearing, we got a glimpse of how Representative Jamie Raskin's warped, partisan mind works. Every other word out of his mouth was "Donald Trump." Raskin and his members also interrupted my members several times while they were speaking. In general, the Democrats on the House Oversight Committee displayed their simplistic business model: attack Trump and defend the Bidens.*

On any given day that I was in Washington, my communica-

---

* We also saved Washington, DC, from itself that February. Oversight has jurisdiction over the District of Columbia, and we rescinded Washington, DC's ridiculous criminal justice reform legislation that, among other things, allowed every criminal in the crime-ravaged city to go free without serving one day in prison. Jamie Raskin called Republicans racists and micromanagers but the crime in DC was so out of control that even the Democratic Senate surprisingly passed H.J. 26 and President Biden signed it into law. Raskin and his Democrat House colleagues should have been humiliated and roasted by the media for being slapped down by their own president. Right. That didn't happen.

tions director, Austin Hacker, would be contacted by some media outlet wanting to do an interview. In the beginning, I granted just about every request. One day Jonathan Swan and Luke Broadwater of the liberal *New York Times* stopped by my office to interview me for a profile. I knew their article would end up being a hit piece, but being the competitor I am, I decided to try to convince them otherwise. I invited Swan to travel with me around my Kentucky district over the upcoming recess to watch me and have full access to both me and my constituents.

Bad idea. Two thousand twenty-three marked the year I went from being skeptical-but-hopeful about the mainstream media to knowing them for what they are: paid Democratic Party hacks and closet left-wing conspiracy fanatics masquerading about in the skin suit of their trade's former greatness. I'd rather listen to my dog bark at a crow than hear one more reporter whine to me that he's only trying to get the truth out there—while reaching around to stick a shiv in my back.

## WOODWARD'S WARNING

SPEAKING OF OLD-TIME real reporters, in early February 2023 I managed to have dinner with Bob Woodward. I'd read many of his books over the years, including my favorites, *The Agenda* and *The Choice*, which were about Bill Clinton. While I never voted for any Clinton, I enjoyed reading books about Bill Clinton's climb from a small southern town to the top of the political ladder. Woodward had credibility in a town full of journalists with absolutely zero credibility.

He and Carl Bernstein were instigators of the most famous congressional investigation of all time, Watergate. Also present at the dinner was Bob Costas of CBS News. The three of us enjoyed a quiet homemade dinner prepared by Woodward's wife. After the dinner, where he mainly talked about old Watergate era stories, we turned to the business of why I was there. Woodward and Costas were doing a book on Joe Biden's presidency and wanted to interview me because they thought my investigation might have an impact.

I gave them their interview, then asked Woodward what he thought about my investigation. He replied that he thought Joe Biden had obviously worked the system his entire political career, and that his son and both brothers had a troubled financial history. He predicted that my investigation "would either be bigger than Watergate or it would end up being a big nothingburger." The receipts had to show the money flowed all the way to the top.

Woodward explained that everyone in DC knew that Joe allowed his family to sell access to him, but as far as he was aware, that was not illegal. He added that it should be, but it wasn't. "You will have to prove all of Joe Biden's wrongdoing," he said, "and you will likely not be able to do that."

I told Woodward that I was going to subpoena all of the Biden characters' bank accounts, then trace the money from all the countries back to the Bidens, and then I would subpoena all of the associates and the Biden family and make them answer questions that would incriminate them, because I had their bank records. Bank records do not lie.

Woodward and Costas looked at each other incredulously and winked at each other, both probably thinking what we say back home when someone nice says something unrealistic. "Well bless your little heart!"

Woodward commented that he did not think that Biden's high-priced legal team would ever allow me to have access to their bank accounts, and the banks would never let me have them.

Costas piped in and said that everyone knew Joe Biden had always been cash-strapped and always tried to live beyond his means. But he added that it was his understanding that the family was very good at covering its tracks. I took that as an admission that all of the mainstream media knew that the Biden family was corrupt, but for whatever reason they were bent on covering it up.

Toward the end of the evening, Bob Woodward told me that the difference in my Oversight Committee today versus the Watergate hearings from 1975 was the press corps. He said the Watergate congressmen had aggressive reporters in the wings who were hungry to find information and worked hard to develop their own reliable sources. He proudly declared that *he* solved the Watergate crime, not the senators. They just copied and pasted his work. Today's reporters are the least curious of all time, Woodward continued. They do not have any sources outside of politicians and political operatives.

Woodward's remarks turned out to be an accurate prediction. Thinking about how the most famous DC reporter of all time actually felt about the DC press corps confirmed my own misgivings. Every time I read another dishonest or dismissive article about the investigation, I take great pride in knowing that Bob Woodward has no respect for that reporter either.

## TWITTER CENSORSHIP OF THE HUNTER BIDEN LAPTOP STORY

AFTER HOLDING TWO substantive hearings on major bipartisan issues, our third hearing got down to Biden investigation brass tacks. It was titled "Protecting Speech from Government Interference and Social Media Bias, Part I: Twitter's Role in Suppressing the Biden Laptop Story." This was our first hearing on the Biden influence-peddling schemes. The hearing came about due to my meeting with Elon Musk and the release of his "Twitter Files."

My objective: to prove to the skeptics that the Hunter Biden laptop was real.

By this point in February 2023, most mainstream media outlets were still misreporting that the laptop had been altered by Russia or Rudy Giuliani.

We were at a precarious point in early 2023. The mainstream media's false narrative had become dominant, and the flacks and liars had nearly succeeded in drowning out the truth. This was due in part to a previous series of unfortunate and avoidable mistakes on the Republican side.

## GIULIANI VEERS OFF MESSAGE

BRINGING IN RUDY Giuliani as an advisor to President Trump was one of them. Rudy Giuliani was a great New York mayor. There is no doubt he saved the place from ruin and returned its self-respect during his tenure there. But after an abortive presidential run, cancer, and simply growing old, Giuliani has become a shadow of that aggressive U.S. attorney who was once the terror of Empire State organized crime.

Unfortunately, this would not become apparent until too much responsibility was placed on the old guy's shoulders and, well, he flubbed it badly and did near-irreparable harm to the Biden family influence investigation in the process.

Giuliani's role did bear one important fruit.

Hunter Biden's laptop from hell.

After the DOJ deep-sixed computer repairman John Paul Mac Isaac's FBI interview along with the Hunter Biden laptop, Mac Isaac heard about the former mayor's efforts and gave a copy of the laptop hard drive to Giuliani. From there it ended up in the capable hands of Miranda Devine and a team of resourceful and competent reporters at the *New York Post*.

Yet Giuliani's reputation allowed the FBI to falsely label what was obviously Hunter Biden's actual laptop a Russian disinformation operation, perhaps with Giuliani serving as an accomplice to hurt Joe Biden's election chances. Giuliani's unfortunate reputation also caused President Trump's DOJ, led by the too-often-gullible William Barr, to dismiss the factual information he had accumulated on the Bidens and Burisma.

This lack of attention by the DOJ, whether Deep State conspiracy or mere bureaucratic incompetence, led Trump to call Ukrainian president Volodymyr Zelenskyy and simply ask about the true corruption and quid pro quo between VP Biden and Viktor Shokin. The idea that Trump was demanding his own tit-for-tat, or anything other than the truth from the Ukrainians, was ridiculous.

## REPAIRING THE FIELD

I NEEDED TO correct that disinformation, because the laptop contained hundreds of emails that served as key parts of incriminating evidence, as well as bank records that were my basis to obtain subpoenas.

During the opening statements from the former Twitter employees, they all admitted the Hunter Biden laptop was real and unaltered (since this was obviously true), and they apologized for their mistake of censuring the *New York Post* after the *Post* accurately broke the story. It was a revelation that most political experts think could have swung the 2020 election to Trump—and that very fact was the explanation for the entire operation to paint it as a Russian info operation.

It is important to remember that at the time of the censuring of content on Facebook and Twitter, Donald Trump was the president. It was Trump's own treacherous FBI director and his Department of Justice making the censorship requests. Of course, such government bullying has only gotten worse under Biden. Neither I nor Jim Jordan was satisfied with many of their answers, so we moved the investigation over to Jordan's Judiciary Committee.

The admission of Twitter employees to government collusion with censorship should have been a humiliating experience for the mainstream media who slandered the *New York Post*, conservative media outlets, and the Wilmington, Delaware, computer repairman John Paul Mac Isaac, who initially discovered the Biden computer contents and turned it in to the FBI. Recall that Hunter Biden abandoned his laptop in Mac Isaac's store. After waiting the contracted time, it and its contents became Mac Isaac's property.

As Miranda Devine acerbically comments, "The laptop is real. Nobody else could have created such an abomination. It is Hunter's greatest work of art."[1]

Not only were the mainstream media not humbled, but they also barely noted the hearing other than to falsely disparage it.

## INTO THE VAULT OF SARS

MY CONSTANT PRESENCE on conservative TV led to being asked to speak at high-profile events, major fundraising, and requests to attend campaign events for my congressional colleagues seeking reelection. I spoke at my very first Conservative Political Action Conference (CPAC). I was on a panel with Mollie Hemingway that discussed holding the Biden family accountable. The energetic crowd loved the topic. There was a sea of Trump flags being waved and MAKE AMERICA GREAT AGAIN hats being worn. I felt like I was back in Kentucky—and let me assure you, I have never once felt that way about being in Washington, DC, before.

In addition to invitations from conservative events, I started attending GOP major donor meetings. These, combined with my new small-dollar donor online fundraising efforts, turned me into one of most prolific fundraisers in Congress. I needed those reserves in my campaign account.

I was certain to be the target of a major offensive by Democrat dark money come the next election cycle.*

The Democrats have an enormous fundraising apparatus that in most ways dwarfs the Republican efforts.[2] They outspent us by hundreds of millions. It is based on tech money from San Francisco, specifically the usual suspects such as Jeff Bezos (and his ex-wife), Bill Gates (and his ex-wife), Mark Zuckerberg (of the infamous 2020 election "Zuck Bucks" scam[3]), eBay founder and George Soros fanboy Pierre Omidyar, as well as European billionaire donors who think their money ought to have a say in America's elections, such as Switzerland biotech magnate Hansjörg Wyss, whose name sounds like that of a perfect Bond villain.[4]

After spending the first two months of my chairmanship fighting with Treasury secretary Janet Yellen to access the 150 Suspicious Activity Reports accumulated by Hunter or James Biden, Yellen finally caved.

It was a victory that nobody in the mainstream media ever dreamed we would have. It all came from knowing just where to look. From my years of experience in banking, I suspected that nobody on the planet had ever had anywhere near that many serious banking violations. I also suspected that the banks would not issue

---

* Throughout my first six years in Congress, I had a grand total of zero members ask me to travel to their House districts to campaign for them. Now that I was the chairman of Oversight, I had sixty-eight such requests to speak at a plethora of GOP Lincoln-Reagan Dinners or other fundraising events. I also had many candidates for either open House seats or races against Democrat incumbents reach out and request my presence in their districts. I took this as a sure sign that a majority of the Republican base as well as badly needed independent voters appreciated our oversight efforts. I traveled to twenty states from Connecticut to Arizona to campaign for Republican candidates in an effort to keep the House Republican majority in 2024.

SARs on a prominent family unless they were very confident that the family was breaking the law.

My A-team on the Oversight staff traveled to Treasury to start the long process of combing through the Biden SARs. I assumed that one week would be ample time because most SARs were only one or two pages. However, after many new discoveries and three full weeks of staff work, we left the Treasury Building with a trove of new and concerning evidence on a multitude of potential Joe Biden and Biden-family crimes.

We also found many new and previously unknown accounts and shell companies that Hunter Biden had owned at various times. Most surprising of all, we found that Hunter Biden had *170* Suspicious Activity Reports—twenty more than previously known—from six different U.S. banks. The Bidens were also subjects of an additional fifty SARs filed against other people.

I traveled to the Treasury Building with four of my Oversight colleagues—Byron Donalds, Nancy Mace, Tim Burchett, and Marjorie Taylor Greene—to review the SARs. Upon entering we were informed that the elevators were out of order and we had to take the steps. When we got to the top of the building, I told my gasping colleagues, "It's a good thing we didn't have any senators with us, or they would have passed out halfway up!"

The SARs were worse than what I could have possibly imagined. It was obvious to the informed reader that the banks believed the Bidens were taking large amounts of money from rogue countries like Russia, Romania, Kazakhstan, and China and then running it through a bunch of LLCs to several Biden family members. As a "politically exposed person," the banks would have viewed this not only as suspicious, but as a possible threat to our national security.

Though the Biden attorneys and their coconspirators in the media were disappointed that I was granted entry into Treasury (and

I still think they had something to do with those elevators being out), they were comforted because the Right to Financial Privacy Act of 1978 prevented us from leaving the Treasury Building with the 170 SARs. We would have to initiate the subpoena process to obtain and publish them, and that process would inevitably take time and be subject to litigation.

If anyone thinks that it's perfectly common to rack up 170 SARs from six different banks, then I invite them to ask their local banker—or anyone who simply works in a bank—what they think about the Biden family's 170.

Byron Donalds understood as well as anyone the severity of what he was seeing. He did an outstanding job throughout his many interviews of explaining the complex series of potentially illegal transactions the banks suspected Biden-associated entities engaged in. Nancy Mace was also shocked by the sheer number of possible crimes the banks were noting.

# Chapter 3

## A BIDEN HALL OF MIRRORS

I issued my first subpoena for bank records on February 27, 2023, for the accounts of John Robinson Walker and issued a report on the results two weeks later.[1] Rob Walker was a Biden family associate and particular crony of Hunter Biden. He was from Arkansas and had gotten into politics via the Clinton machine.[2] Additionally, Walker's wife, Betsy, served as assistant to Jill Biden during Joe Biden's vice presidency. He was a frequent visitor to the White House during the Obama administration.[3]

My committee had information that led me to believe Walker's company, Robinson Walker LLC, was being used to receive and transfer money to Biden family members. Walker established his company in 2008 as an LLC (limited liability company) in Delaware. Previous reports from research indicated that Walker had received a large wire from a Chinese Communist Party–related entity that was sending money to up to ten Biden family members.

We got the bank records days after the subpoena was issued, and sure enough, my information was correct. From 2015 to 2017, Biden family members and their companies received over $1.3 million in payments from the Walker-related accounts. The Biden family members who got the money included the usual suspects of Hunter and Jim Biden, but also two new members, Hallie Biden (Beau's widow and Hunter's former lover) and an unknown Biden. The unknown Biden transfer was the most unusual financial wire

I had seen in my banking career. Most wires are filled out like a personal check. You list who the payment is going to as well as the dollar amount, date, and the purpose of the payment. In this instance, the wire was sent to "Biden." That's right, no first name or business name, just Biden. And consistent with all of the wires that we would go on to discover that went to the Bidens, nothing was ever listed for the purpose or subject of the wire. I will always believe that the Biden whom the wire went to was none other than Joe.

In addition to the payments that streamed into the back pockets of the Biden family members, no wire to Hunter Biden would be complete without going through a series of his shell companies first. The portion that went to Hunter was funneled through three of these companies, including Owasco PC, JBBSR Inc., and RSTP II LLC. Of course, as was almost always the case when Hunter funneled money through these shady LLCs, the banks participating would issue SARs, the official notification to bank regulators of possible money laundering, tax evasion, or bribery from foreign sources.

The most troubling revelation from the bank records of Robinson Walker LLC was the source and time frame of the major foreign wire that was used to funnel money into the Biden family bank accounts. On March 1, 2017, less than two months after Joe Biden left the vice presidency, State Energy HK Limited, a suspicious Chinese company, wired $3 million to Robinson Walker LLC. At the time of the wire, the Walker account had a balance of less than $160,000, so a $3 million inflow represented a sum greater than the typical balance for the account over several years. That wire also resulted in a SAR from the bank due to the fact that the account had never received anything close to that amount before, and the source was an unknown Chinese company. Furthermore, the transfer came into an account that never had any prior Chinese activity.

The following day, Robinson Walker LLC wired $1.065 million to European Energy and Infrastructure Group in Abu Dhabi, a company associated with James Gilliar. Gilliar, a bullet-headed former British special forces operative who has since gone to seed, was another business associate of Hunter Biden and involved in several opaque foreign transactions with the Biden family.

Approximately six days after receiving the $3 million wire from China, Robinson Walker LLC started sending incremental payments to the Biden family. These payments stretched over ten weeks until the Bidens received their cut of exactly $1,065,692.

Rob Walker's personal bank records revealed that on November 9, 2015, Rob Walker sent a wire to Hunter Biden in the amount of $59,900. Near the same time, he also sent James Gilliar the exact same amount. That would suggest that Walker, Hunter Biden, and Gilliar had a three-way split agreement of some sort. They performed a similar split with the Chinese money two years later. All of this happened *while* Joe Biden was vice president.

## DEMOCRAT SIDESHOW

THE INVESTIGATION BEGAN as promised. We started to follow the money, careful to be transparent with the media and the American people about any evidence we would accumulate. My investigation was designed to be the complete opposite of Adam Schiff's Russia hoax, a carnival show that had relied on the Steele dossier to press a narrative that Donald Trump was involved in some ill-defined but ominous Russian misdeed.

But even as we started to advance, Jamie Raskin began what would be a consistent rearguard misinformation campaign about the bank records we produced. Raskin and his minions would either issue a completely false or grossly mischaracterized statement that twisted the facts, or speak directly to the Washington press corps as if he were the ultimate authority on any matter. Raskin proclaimed that Joe Biden's bank records contained little more than receipts for Papa John's and Starbucks. He left out the small fact that the other accounts received $3 million from an unknown Chinese entity, and that three or four Biden family members got a cut that topped $1 million. This would be an embarrassing omission for the average person, but Jamie Raskin is not average. He is a special kind of liar who rushes to the aid of the Bidens and never fails to defend the indefensible.

## BIDEN INFLUENCE PEDDLING COMES INTO FOCUS

IN THE SECOND bank memorandum, issued May 10, 2023, we focused on evidence that clearly showed a complex web of LLCs associated with Hunter Biden doing business with two adversarial countries (China and Romania). The trail led right up to Joe Biden's door.

This type of investigation is exactly what the House Oversight Committee was created for. Influence peddling, violations of federal ethics laws, improper financial disclosures, risks to national security, and overall public corruption needed to be properly and thoroughly investigated. We were the only entity in America doing that with the Biden family. It was obvious that the FBI, Department of Justice, and Internal Revenue Service sure as hell were not interested in investigating the Bidens. Instead, they were actively obstructing *our* investigation.

In a nationally televised presidential debate on October 22, 2020, soon-to-be-president Biden was asked directly whether there was anything unethical about Hunter's business dealings in China or Ukraine.

"My son has not made money in terms of this thing about, what are you talking about, China," he replied. "I have not had—the only guy who made money from China is this guy [referring to Donald Trump, who was standing next to him in debate format]. He's the only one. Nobody else made money from China."[4]

Thanks to the thorough and substantive work from our investigation, that statement from President Biden will go down in history as the biggest lie ever told by a major presidential candidate. It was one of many lies that Joe Biden has made over his lengthy political career. But this one was truly impressive (and tragic for the country). China is our biggest enemy and arguably the most serious threat to the national security in our nation's great history.

What else could the money be for but for China to win over one Joseph Robinette Biden Jr.?

Despite previous reports from many sources that the Bidens took large sums of money from China, the Second Bank Records Memorandum uncovered information that had not been previously known. Evidence pointed to the fact that Hunter Biden was actively and successfully involved in a Romanian influence scheme while Joe Biden was vice president.

The Romanian scheme involved a corrupt foreign national by the name of Gabriel Popoviciu, mentioned earlier. Popoviciu was the subject of a widely publicized criminal probe and later prosecution in Romania.[5] True to form, then–vice president Biden gave speeches in Romania in 2014 and 2015 decrying corruption in the country while his family participated in it (similar to what he would later do in Ukraine prior to withholding $1 billion in foreign aid to Ukraine unless they fired the prosecutor investigating Burisma for fraud). This scheme of Biden traveling on Air Force Two to corrupt foreign countries that received substantial American tax dollars in the form of foreign aid to deliver generic speeches about corruption while Hunter served as cleanup man behind him displayed a pattern of behavior that would be consistent throughout the investigation. It had the character of a stage play. Or a con job.[6]

And so, on May 21, 2014, we find then–vice president Biden delivering this speech to Romania's political leaders.

> Corruption is a cancer, a cancer that eats away at a citizen's faith in democracy, diminishes the instinct for innovation and creativity; already tight national budgets, crowding out important national investments. It wastes the talent of entire generations. It scares away investments, and jobs. And most importantly, it denies the people their dignity. It saps the collective strength and resolve of a nation. Corruption is just another form of tyranny. And corruption can represent a clear and present danger not only to a nation's economy, but to its very national security.

Meanwhile, at the time of Biden's speech, the high-profile corruption prosecution case involving Gabriel Popoviciu was underway. Popoviciu would be convicted of a bribery-related offense. (Popoviciu would be the first of many characters sending money to an LLC associated with Hunter Biden who would later be convicted of "unrelated" bribery.)

Romanian president Klaus Iohannis visited Vice President Biden at the White House on September 28, 2015. The reported purpose of the meeting was to "focus on anti-corruption efforts and rule of law as a means to strengthen national security and promote greater investment and economic growth." Iohannis stated after the meeting that Biden "voiced satisfaction over Romania's progress against corruption."

Less than five weeks later, Robinson Walker LLC's accounts received deposits from Bladon Enterprises, which is reportedly the Cypriot company that Gabriel Popoviciu used for business in Romania. Bladon Enterprises wired Robinson Walker LLC over $3 million between November 2015 and May 2017.[7]

From the millions wired to Rob Walker's account, the Romanian money was then distributed to at least Hunter and Hallie Biden, in much the same manner that Chinese money was later parsed out. The Bidens got slightly more than one-third of the cut; in this case they received exactly $1.038 million through seventeen incremental payments. Sixteen of the seventeen payments occurred while Joe was vice president. Not only did we discover a new country from which the Bidens received over a million dollars, but we also proved that it happened *during* his term as vice president of the United States. The pre-investigation mainstream media narrative that Joe Biden's family never took any mysterious or unethical money while he was vice president had been forever dispelled.

Previous press accounts by NBC News mentioned Vice President Biden's great work on pushing to crack down on corruption in Romania, but failed to mention anything about the veep's son working for a central figure involved in corrupting Romania to begin with. Joe Biden went to a country and made vague statements of praise about anticorruption efforts, but without mentioning any matters the government might find inconvenient, and generally going easy on the foreign government. He was in turn lauded by the fawning media as a model of ethics.

An October 25, 2019, story by the *New York Times*[8] (a story meant to diminish the effects of Rudy Giuliani's mentions of potential corruption by the Bidens in Ukraine and Romania) managed to accidentally acknowledge that George Mesires, Hunter Biden's attorney at the time, had stated "that Hunter Biden referred Mr. Popoviciu to both Boris Schiller Flexner, the law firm where Hunter worked at the time and Mr. [Louis] Freeh's firm Freeh Group International Solutions."

But as is always the case with the *New York Times*, they casually discredited Mesires in the same piece, as they do anyone who suggests liberal showboat Joe Biden (who presided over the now-infamous attempted "high-tech lynching" in 1991 of Supreme Court nominee Clarence Thomas,[9] among many other sacred moments for the left) would do anything wrong. The media was united in the fall of 2019 just as they were throughout the 2024 Biden investigation, and they continued to parrot the Democratic National Committee and the Biden legal team's attacks on anyone who would suggest any wrongdoing. They would go even further and indoctrinate their readers and viewers in the fairy-tale story that there really was no evidence, even though they continually redefined what counted as evidence. And after this song-and-dance there would be the inevitable pivot to how Donald Trump and his ultra-MAGA followers were somehow the guilty party for "pouncing" on the poor Bidens.

Throughout President Biden's time in office, he has continued to lie to the American people about the fact that he and his family have received money from China, despite the evidence of subpoenaed bank records and the testimony from Hunter during the Lunden Roberts child support hearing. In 2017 alone, our investigation revealed that the Bidens received millions of dollars from companies controlled by Chinese foreign nationals.

# Chapter 4

## THE DEEP STATE STRIKES BACK

In May 2023, House Oversight Committee staff director Mark Marin got a message from a former Charles Grassley staffer that the FBI had evidence that Joe Biden took a bribe while he was vice president. I had seen enough to convince me that President Biden was the type to take a bribe, so I met Senators Grassley in a downtown Washington law firm that represented Grassley's mysterious FBI sources. Two FBI agents sat in another room, and I did not meet them in an effort to protect them. We followed strict whistleblower protocols in observing FBI form FD-1023—a record of an interview with a confidential informant—containing the allegation that Hunter, and possibly Joe Biden, took bribes from a Ukrainian oligarch in the winter of 2015.

FBI director Christopher Wray later called the 1023 interviewee one of the FBI's most trusted informants. The timeline of the bribes alleged by the informant coincide with Joe Biden's trip to Ukraine and leveraging that $1 billion foreign aid package for the termination of Ukrainian special prosecutor Viktor Shokin.

The FBI agents leaked this to Grassley because their colleagues never once investigated any of this. Bidens were off-limits. I felt that the 1023 form was a longshot—it didn't point us to new accounts or witnesses to subpeona. However, as Bob Woodward told me, investigate every lead you get, regardless of how unlikely it may seem. The informant turned out to be an American,

Alexander Smirnov. In the end, as I'll relate, the informant was subsequently indicted for lying, and the whole exercise proved a distraction.

I don't know Alexander Smirnov, but I would be surprised if I didn't determine his fate by visiting the law office that day. Like many who have information on the Bidens, if you tell the wrong people (that is, stalwart investigators) and even if you are just doing your job, you may end up in prison.

## WRAY DODGES AND WEAVES FOR THE BIDENS

THE 1023 DOCUMENT also claimed it would take investigators ten years to unravel the maze of complex bank accounts that the money was allegedly laundered into.

Senator Grassley's sole focus of the 1023 form was the fact that, according to the FBI leakers whom Grassley had a close relationship with for many years, the FBI never once investigated it. However, the intelligence community spent years investigating bogus claims of Russian collusion against Trump and even offered $1 million to Christopher Steele if he could validate the details of his "dossier." My focus was much different. I was investigating the Bidens for influence peddling and already had plenty of evidence in hand.

On May 31, 2023, Grassley, Jim Jordan, and myself, along with some staffers, had a conference call with FBI director Christopher Wray. It was held in a small "hideaway" office on the Senate side of the Capitol. Grassley knew Director Wray very well, but the call was the first time I had any interaction with him. Grassley started the call off with some introductory pleasantries and then handed it over to me. I told the director that it had been brought to my attention by sources that a 1023 existed on Joe Biden that alleged he and his son took $5 million in bribes from a corrupt Ukrainian oligarch. I added that my investigation revealed that the potential bribe was consistent with the way the money had flowed in, based on what I had already found in Romania and China.

After a few seconds Director Wray chimed in. He talked to me on the phone like he would always testify in Congress: by carefully choosing his words with the ultimate goal of saying absolutely nothing relevant to the issue at hand. I then asked Wray again for the release of the document and a briefing for all of my Oversight Committee members. Once again Wray beat around the bush. Even though he was speaking to the three most powerful investigators in Congress, Wray never would even admit that the document existed. Wray knew two days in advance that this call was about to take place and he knew exactly that the subject was the 1023, but he was acting as if the document didn't even exist. I looked at Grassley and made a "what do I do" gesture with my hands.

At that point the ninety-year-old senator from Iowa sprang to life. He pounded the table by where the phone was centered for the call and said, "Damn it, Chris, the chairman has the 1023! He has read it. We know it exists. So quit wasting our time and answer his damn questions!"

Everyone in the room was shocked, in a pleasant sort of way. I looked at Jordan and he was grinning ear to ear. I did not realize Grassley had it in him. But he did. We all saw it. It just took the Deep State's number one defender in chief to patronize the chairs of Oversight and Judiciary as well as the former chair of the Senate Judiciary Committee to bring it out.

Director Wray then started talking about the 1023 as if the first five minutes of the call never happened. I asked several questions about the 1023, including whether the FBI investigated it (which Grassley's FBI sources claimed the FBI never did) and who the informant was. The informant was not named in the original version of the 1023. I obviously wanted to interview the informant to determine the accuracy of the claim.

Wray would not answer whether the FBI had investigated the claim, but he did partially answer a question about the informant. He told the three congressmen and a handful of staffers that he could not and would not reveal the name of the informant because it could jeopardize the informant's life, and the FBI went to great lengths to protect the identity of their informants. Wray added that the informant was "one of the highest-paid, most trusted informants in the entire Bureau."

Wray then offered to bring the 1023 to the sensitive compartmented information facility (SCIF) and allow me and Ranking Member Raskin—along with necessary staff that had a security clearance—to view the document. He would bring FBI staff to give us a classified briefing and answer questions. Even though the 1023 was not a classified document, I felt like the Wray offer was a step in the right direction. In less than fifteen minutes I went from the FBI director acting like the 1023 did not exist to him admitting its existence, confirming the credibility of the source, and offering me a briefing.

In May 2023, the FBI brought the 1023 to the congressional SCIF for only me and Jamie Raskin to view, along with our committee staffers with a security clearance. I had my two main Oversight staff attorneys, Jessica Donlon and James Mandolfo, accompany me.

Fox News host Steve Doocy's daughter, Mary Doocy, is the assistant general counsel for the FBI.[1] She was in the SCIF as part of a four-member FBI briefing team when Jamie Raskin and I viewed the FD-1023 form.

The FBI knew that I had already viewed the 1023 in unredacted form in a law office with Senator Grassley weeks before the SCIF meeting. Now, in the SCIF, Mary Doocy handed me the official copy from the FBI. It was about one-quarter redacted. It looked like someone had taken a random Sharpie to it with the aim of making it incomprehensible. It was a ridiculous act of bureaucratic petulance.

Upon receipt of this 1023 and seeing its heavy redactions, I slid the four full-page document right back at Doocy with a look on my face, I'm sure, of indignation. I certainly felt offended. As an FBI lawyer, I knew she'd likely been part of creating this charade of a document.

My hasty return of the 1023 to her seemed to piss Mary Doocy off. Maybe it's just a coincidence, but her father, *Fox & Friends* host Steve Doocy, and her brother, Fox White House correspondent Peter Doocy, would soon become my biggest critics on Fox News for the remainder of the investigation. And they didn't let up off camera either. Many of the White House videos criticizing me, and many of the legacy media outlets' false narratives citing disparaging comments about me and the investigation, were from the Doocys.

In any case, I had already read the original, unredacted 1023, so I knew what had been blacked out. I asked the FBI who the informer was, and they said that they could not tell me other than to once again assure me that he was one of the Bureau's "highest-paid and most trusted informants."

They added that the FBI had used this source to successfully prosecute other cases.

As soon as everyone was done with his questions, Raskin left the SCIF and rushed out to his friends in the mainstream media. I remained in the room outside the press gaggle and watched an impromptu TV press conference by Raskin before I walked out to answer a few questions.

Jamie Raskin loved the DC press corps, and they loved him

back. Raskin and the DC reporters had a lot in common: They were arrogant, usually dishonest, card-carrying liberals in good standing with the Democratic Party. Raskin—with his trademark chest bowed out and head cocked back (much like what we of the Appalachian foothills call a banty rooster)—said that the FBI declared that there was no ongoing investigation of the Biden family, not by U.S. Attorney David Weiss or anyone else.

That was a bald-faced lie. The FBI said at least three times to direct questions I asked them that there *was* an ongoing investigation of the Bidens.

That Raskin moment dashed any hope that the Biden influence-peddling investigation might be bipartisan, as Watergate had been, with members of Congress in both parties participating in meaningful questions and research.

Unfortunately, in Oversight I had been shackled with a vainglorious fool as my ranking minority member.

Of course, the corrupt mainstream media immediately wrote exactly what Raskin and his coconspirators in the White House told them to. After seeing the press, I called Speaker McCarthy to tell him that I wanted the FD-1023 form released to the public or else I was going to hold Christopher Wray in contempt of Congress.

## THE CONTEMPT THREAT WORKS

MCCARTHY WAS CAUGHT off guard by my sudden outburst. I like to think I am usually a no-drama, low-maintenance member. But desperate times called for desperate measures. I knew that the FBI, the DOJ, and the White House were in cahoots with the mainstream media and House Democrats in spreading disinformation about a lack of evidence, and I wanted to get the truth out to discredit both the mainstream media and Jamie Raskin.

## THE MIKES ARE OF NO HELP

TWO IMPORTANT HOUSE committees I requested assistance from during the investigation refused to help. To charge President Biden with a violation of the Foreign Corrupt Practices Act, we needed to show proof of policy decisions he made in exchange for all the gifts his immediate family received before and after he was vice president and president.

These policy changes were not relegated to the distant days of the Obama administration either. One obvious policy change was President Biden's decision in his first days in office to cancel the FBI's China Initiative. He followed through with many policy decisions that essentially put China first and America last.[2] It seemed to be almost a programmatic march.

The House Intelligence Committee, led by Representative Mike Turner, and the China Task Force, led by Representative Mike Gallagher, had access to all classified information from the FBI, which in turn had possessed a full staff devoted to investigating Biden's soft-on-China policies as they influenced America's security. But both Turner and Gallagher (who was one of three Republicans who voted against impeaching homeland security secretary Alejandro Mayorkas) had no interest in assisting my Oversight investigation. This attitude persisted throughout. It seemed clear they were cowed by the FBI when it should have been the other way around, with the FBI and the intel community working for *them.*

It isn't impossible to wrangle bureaucrats. It's just hard work, like moving cows out of brush tangles. But it's one of the jobs the American people elected us to do.

After a few days of political maneuvering* and public threats

---

* The next day after my call with McCarthy about my drastic proposal to get the 1023 released, I got a call requesting a meeting with Mike Turner and Brian Fitzpatrick. I agreed to their request but brought with me my staff director Mark Marin. Turner was

from me that the Oversight Committee would hold Wray in contempt of Congress, I got a call from Oversight staff saying that Wray's attorneys had reached out to offer me a deal. Their proposal was to let everyone on the Oversight Committee* view the 1023 in the SCIF.

---

the chairman of the House Intelligence Committee and Fitzpatrick was a former FBI officer who also served on the Intelligence Committee. Both men were very close with McCarthy and very close with Wray. Both men had heard that I wanted to hold Wray in contempt, and both strongly encouraged me to abort my idea.

Their arguments as to why it was a bad idea to hold Wray in contempt mainly revolved around their fear that Wray would halt giving the Intelligence Committee their regular classified briefings. I made matters worse by questioning both men as to whether they actually believed anything the intelligence community representatives were telling them when they were holed up in the SCIF. I had certainly not seen anything that would demonstrate any level of trust in the intelligence community.

After some stern, irreconcilable differences of opinion, we politely agreed to disagree. But I got the subliminal message from them that most of the Intelligence Committee members would not vote in favor of holding Christopher Wray in contempt. That meant that I could never get to the 218 votes needed for approval. I learned at that moment just how difficult it was going to be to pass anything needed to hold all the bad actors accountable in this investigation.

My opposition this time was not the usual suspects in the Freedom Caucus or the moderates; it was the Intelligence Committee, whom I considered to be some of the more rock-solid members in our slim majority. I had started out with a lot of respect for Turner, and he is a significant improvement from his Democrat predecessor, Adam Schiff, but we view the world from a different perspective when it comes to foreign policy and confidence in the intelligence community.

Despite the obvious lack of votes to pass contempt on the House floor, I decided to proceed. I knew I had the votes in Oversight to pass it through committee, despite Mike Turner also being a member. I could lose two Republican votes for the bill to still pass out of committee with a partisan vote, and that was the only one I would possibly lose.

My plan was to pass it out of committee if I did not get what I wanted from Wray, then make the Republican leadership deal with it. Just because a bill passes out of committee does not mean it will ever go to the Rules Committee, which would then schedule a floor vote by the entire body.

I knew the pressure from the right to hold Wray in contempt would make McCarthy have to get the Intelligence guys in line, and they were some of the very few who would do what McCarthy asked of them.

* My Oversight Republicans are fighters, but they want to be in the loop. Most seldom got the chance to go to the SCIF. And not only would viewing this document be a rare experience, it would allow them to be able to go on TV and talk about it. There

June 20, 2023, was the big day that resulted from my stare-down with FBI Director Wray. Every member of the House Oversight Committee got to go down to the SCIF and view the FBI form FD-1023 that I had first encountered from Grassley's FBI whistleblower, and then in the SCIF with Raskin.

The document that the FBI brought that day for the rest of the committee was heavily redacted. In fact, I was insulted by just how much. According to committee members who viewed the 1023, they estimated that at least 25 percent of the unclassified document was redacted, including the part about the recordings that the informant had alleged existed. The FBI briefers also repeated to Oversight members their claim that the informant in the 1023 was one of the FBI's highest-paid and most trusted.

At the end of this 1023, there was a tiny footnote that referenced *other* 1023s. I would later point this out to my fellow Republicans on Oversight. Together we demanded the release of any other 1023s pertaining to Joe Biden. Round two with Wray had begun and is ongoing.

## ANOTHER FBI WEASEL MOVE

BY DECEMBER 2023, the DOJ would arrest Alexander Smirnov. I'll discuss this more fully in chapter 17. Was it an attempt by the FBI to discredit him and his part in the Oversight investigation? I think we know the answer to that.

I did not know the validity of the allegation or if *tapes backing up*

---

are twenty-one Republican men on my committee including me, and they agreed that accepting the deal was the best decision. I have five Republican females on the committee. Not only did they all disagree with my decision to punt on the contempt vote, but they let me have it. Everyone knows that MTG, Lauren Boebert, and Nancy Mace are tough, but never underestimate Lisa McClain and Virginia Foxx. I am blessed to have the toughest and meanest women to ever serve in Congress on Oversight.

*the allegation* really existed. Director Wray told me the informant was one of their best, but then worked with the corrupt mainstream media to imply that *I* had made the statement about the informant's credibility. The FBI, which generally takes the lead on counterintelligence within the U.S., is a frightening weapon in the hands of the Deep State because it still holds credibility with so many. But I believe that brand has become tarnished, maybe forever.

"The Federal Bureau of Investigation, as its name states, is only a bureaucracy. It is not a sacred institution," J. Michael Waller writes in *Big Intel*, his great history and critique of the FBI and CIA. "Its brand and mythology are not to be protected at all costs. It is a bureaucratic structure mandated to perform necessary functions to investigate federal crimes, combat foreign spies, and not much more."[3]

I will never believe anything the intelligence community says about Joe Biden, his family, or Ukraine. The lack of transparency is bad enough, but the downright lying, hiding of facts, coordination with the corrupt mainstream media to create false narratives, and cover-ups are enough to make me commit whatever time I have left in Congress to fighting and dismantling the Deep State intelligence community, beginning with Christopher Wray at the FBI.

# Chapter 5

## A GAME OF CHINESE CHECKERS

The Second Bank Memorandum details payments from China to the Bidens, using the bank records as solid evidence.[1] Ye Jianming is a central figure in our investigation. Ye, a slim, well-dressed man who resembled a Chinese version of Hunter Biden, was not only chairman of the Chinese Communist Party–linked company CEFC, which funded the Bidens, but was for years a Chinese communist espionage chief! CEFC wired millions of dollars to various shell companies that would eventually be passed through Biden family members' bank accounts, large sums of which ended up in Joe Biden's pocket. CEFC had a huge interest in doing business with Joe. They enlisted his assistance in helping China navigate the various federal bureaucracies and to remove the growing numbers of barriers to entry for Chinese investment in the United States. Biden, who was the spearhead of U.S. policy in the region, sat back and watched China build military bases that shut down navigation rights to the South China Sea, which is shared by Vietnam, Indonesia, and the Philippines and provides sea passage from the Far East to India.

In December 2015, a former president of the United Nations General Assembly and Serbian politician named Vuk Jeremic tried to introduce Ye Jianming and the CEFC to Hunter and his crew. Whether or not that particular meeting between Jeremic, Biden, and CEFC actually took place is not known. Soon afterward,

Hunter Biden and Ye would develop a lucrative business relationship. By 2017, the two had forged a partnership in which Joe Biden was slated to share office space with them at the House of Sweden office complex just outside Washington, DC.

When I say Ye was a spy chief, I'm not kidding. He was the real deal. From 2003 to 2005, Ye was the deputy secretary-general of the China Association for International Friendly Contact (CAIFC), which was an international outreach arm for the People's Liberation Army. It was also a platform for undercover intelligence gatherers.[2] According to Oversight Committee research, CAIFC was a front organization for the former General Political Department and performed dual roles of intelligence collection and conducting propaganda and perception management campaigns.

In other words, Ye Jianming was once the leader of the Chinese version of the CIA. Pause a moment to take that in.

He was the spy chief for China tasked with not only leading the legendary spy ring, which has stolen many of the private sector intellectual property and patents that American industry invests billions of dollars annually in research to develop, but also directing the propaganda network that has become widely known through their ownership in social media outlets like TikTok. Ye Jianming is the man whom the Bidens chose not only to work for in the private sector but also to share office space with.

They might as well have booked a cubicle with Joseph Stalin's KGB director, Lavrentiy Beria.

By the mid-2010s, Chinese president Xi Jinping had placed Ye atop a Chinese business empire worth an estimated $44 billion (a sovereign wealth fund, created not with private capital, but with money from the Chinese government treasury). His purpose was to use CEFC to implement China's Belt and Road Initiative.

## BELT AND ROAD BRIBERY AND EXTORTION

THE BELT AND Road Initiative is the hallmark of Chinese president Xi's foreign policy platform, a global infrastructure development strategy that was incorporated into the Constitution of the Chinese Communist Party in 2017. Belt and Road invests in more than 150 countries and international organizations—at what has turned out to be usurious rates that often bankrupt the countries and municipalities that take them up on their "deals." In short, the Belt and Road Initiative is China's sadly effective plan to dominate the world economy.

A major practice the Chinese use to implement their strategy is called "debt trap diplomacy," where they prey on poor third-world countries and compromised political leaders and their families to loan money for projects that China wishes to own itself. Local politicians get the short-term boost that always comes with construction jobs. China lends them the funds knowing they will be difficult or impossible for the borrowers to pay back. Once the debtor defaults, China takes possession of the asset. In banking, that is called a foreclosure, and China has done it time and again around the world.

The Belt and Road Initiative is one of the biggest threats not only to our American economy but to our national security and that of our international allies. The business model of loaning money to compromised political leaders and their families seems to be made to order to capture the Biden family enterprise, especially the future president's drug-addicted and morally bankrupt son. China played the Bidens like a fiddle.

For cover purposes, Ye acted as China's unofficial global energy envoy (a role much like John Kerry performs in the Biden administration). CNN would even report that Ye traveled the world to promote a company that "aligned itself so closely with the Chinese government that it was often hard to distinguish between the two."[3] According to the *Washington Post*, Vuk Jeremic described Ye as "young and dynamic, with top level connections in his country."[4] In a speech delivered to CEFC in 2017, Ye said, "CEFC China's vision is very simple, which is to obtain overseas resources to serve the national security." CEFC China employed the Bidens so that Joe Biden would help remove barriers to entry for China into American markets. For a few paltry hundred millions, they could reap billions in profits—and, far more importantly, undermine, subvert, and outright steal from their chief international rival. China wanted to buy American energy companies, American manufacturers, and American farmland, but Congress and most state legislatures were in the midst of passing legislation to ban China from being able to invest their massive piles of cash in America because of national security risks. China needed the Bidens to implement their Belt and Road Initiative in the United States and, true to form, Hunter Biden and his colleagues lusted for all that money.

Ye Jianming was closely aligned with President Xi's inner circle and was present for high-level meetings with Xi and foreign leaders. According to the *Financial Times*, "When Chinese President Xi Jinping welcomed Czech President Milos Zemen to the Great Hall of the People in Beijing in mid-September 2015, he was flanked by a slim, clean-cut businessman named Ye Jianming."[5]

## THE CEFC COLLAPSE

YE OFTEN USED CEFC funds allegedly to bribe and corruptly influence foreign officials. This was all part of the successful business model China was using to rapidly grow their international economic footprint. One of Ye's agents in both the United States and abroad was Patrick Ho. On March 25, 2019, the U.S. Department of Justice in the Southern District of New York got Ho sentenced to three years on international bribery and money-laundering offenses because of his work in Africa for CEFC. Ye's role in the bribery schemes for which Ho was convicted was mapped out in the DOJ conviction:

> Ho also advised his boss, Ye Jianming, then the chairman of CEFC China, to provide $500,000 cash to [Ugandan president Yoweri] Museveni, ostensibly as a campaign donation, even though Museveni had already been reelected. Ho intended these payments to influence [Ugandan minister of foreign affairs Sam] Kutesa and Museveni to use their official power to steer business advantages to CEFC China.[6]

Because Ye had the unfortunate luck of operating while Donald Trump was president, his schemes became partially exposed. In 2018, Ye was called back to China from his swank new apartment in New York City. He was then detained by Chinese authorities. It was initially reported by the *South China Morning Post* that his "detention in China was ordered directly by the Chinese president Xi Jinping." Ye's current whereabouts are unknown. Most assume he is rotting in a Chinese prison.

The fact that Ye is missing has interesting implications, as does the disappearance of other players in the international Biden influence-peddling scheme. Did President Xi apprehend Ye because he was sloppy? Or did Xi apprehend Ye to use him as collateral in a scheme to blackmail President Joe Biden? After all, Ye has direct knowledge of the millions of dollars the Bidens have made off China. Unfortunately for our investigation, only President Xi knows the answer at present. For some reason, I was unable to get him to come in for a deposition!

## OTHER PLAYERS AT THE TABLE

ANOTHER KEY CHINESE figure in the investigation is Gongwen "Kevin" Dong. According to an email verified by both Hunter

Biden and his sympathizers at the *Washington Post*, Gongwen Dong served as Chairman Ye's CEFC emissary in the United States. Dong was closely associated with CEFC's U.S. business activities.[7] In fact, many of the entities the Oversight Committee is investigating were registered by Dong but contain transactions to the benefit of Ye. Kevin Dong was obviously Ye Jianming's factotum and bagman.

Many of the entities that Dong used in the United States were named with a variation of the phrase "Hudson West," but other names included FRLV Investments LLC and CEFC Infrastructure Investment. Dong formed a number of LLCs in Delaware, a state noted for its legal and liability protection of established corporate laws. This made investigating all the dozens of Delaware LLCs affiliated with the Bidens an absolute nightmare for the committee. Basic corporate filing information you can easily get from LLCs in the other forty-nine states are nearly impossible to acquire in murky Delaware.

The sheer number of shell companies (see Appendix A for the staggering list) raised another point of concern about how Hunter and James Biden operated, a concern that most of the banks the Bidens did business with pointed out in their Suspicious Activity Reports (SARs) filed with Treasury. The layering of these companies and how they transferred money is a pattern that was mentioned often in the 170 SARs the Bidens had filed against them as well as the additional fifty SARs of which they were subjects. Add in the fact that each of the Bidens is what is referred to in banking as a politically exposed person (PEP) and that many of these LLCs' bank accounts were essentially dormant prior to massive foreign cash infusions by wire, huge amounts of money that immediately were pumped out to journey through other Biden-affiliated LLC accounts as the Biden family received incremental payments. It is very easy to understand why the IRS spent years investigating the

Bidens for potential financial crimes. The big question the Select Subcommittee on the Weaponization of the Federal Government, chaired by Jim Jordan, may be able to answer is just who exactly told these investigators to stand down and why, as two brave IRS investigators later testified.

Dong became known in 2017 throughout New York City when he made two massive real estate purchases. The first was a $50 million home at 15 Central Park West. The second was an apartment at 432 Park Avenue, which cost approximately $33 million.

Subpoenaed bank records obtained by Oversight and cited in the Second Bank Memorandum indicate that, from June to August 2017, Ye Jianming transferred over $130 million to entities that Dong controlled. At that same time, Hunter and Dong set up a company called Hudson West III LLC. Dong did it through Hudson West V, and Hunter through Owasco PC. Each man owned 50 percent of Hudson West III.

According to the bank records, James Biden–related companies received over $75,000 from Hudson West III between August 2017 and October 2018. Hunter Biden was sent more than $4 million in the same period.

When Chinese authorities apprehended Ye Jianming in 2018, word started to spread about Hunter Biden's potential involvement. In an email that was verified by the *Washington Post*, Hunter revealed that he realized his financial relationship with CEFC was a problem. He tried to disassociate from the scandal: "I am not in a [joint venture] with CEFC. I am not partners with CEFC. I am not employed nor funded by CEFC." That is completely untrue, in each particular. Hunter Biden did what Hunter Biden always does when he gets in trouble—lie and wait for Daddy to make it all go away. And the *Washington Post* did what the *WaPo* always does when it has evidence of wrongdoing by the Bidens: they turned a blind eye!

## A COMPLICATED SHELL GAME

ONE OF THE often cited and unfortunately fair criticisms of my investigation was that I and the other members on Oversight did not do a good job of explaining in a manner the average American could understand the alleged crimes the Bidens committed. I do not dispute this. I spent countless sleepless nights and sought advice from people whom I considered outstanding communicators on ways to better explain how those dozens and dozens of oddly named companies piped those millions and millions of dollars through a series of complex financial transactions to several Biden family members. Add to that the fact that most of those payments originated from shady characters with foreign names that I could not begin to correctly pronounce! It was a nightmare to explain.

I'm afraid I haven't yet succeeded in communicating just what was going on to a significant percentage of Americans. Some, particularly in the media, did not have the patience to follow the massive number of complex transactions. Some (this would also include the media and most Democrats) hated Donald Trump so badly that they did not want to hear anything negative about Joe Biden. They were going to vote for Biden against Trump regardless, even if he had gold bars from Egypt in his closet (as Senator Robert Menendez from New Jersey actually *did*), or payoff cash wrapped in a pie crust box in his freezer (like former representative William Jefferson from Louisiana). Democrats have a habit of holding their noses over sullied candidates and pulling the voting machine lever regardless.

In my defense, I am going to detail one payment of $100,000 that traveled to Hunter Biden's account from Gongwen "Kevin" Dong through a series of transactions over a two-month period:

- On May 11, 2017, Dong formed CEFC Infrastructure in Delaware as an LLC. Hudson West V—the company previously mentioned that received a $24 million wire from Ye and formed a partnership with Hunter Biden—was the sole equity member of CEFC, with Dong listed as a director and the company's address as Shanghai, China.

- One week later, on May 18, 2017, Hudson West V assigned 100 percent of its interest to Shanghai Huaxin Group Ltd, a company registered in China.
- On June 30, 2017, Shanghai Huaxin funded the CEFC Infrastructure bank account with a significant injection of $10 million from China.
- Approximately one month later, on August 4, 2017, CEFC Infrastructure wired $100,000 to Owasco PC, which was one of Hunter Biden's companies.

Can you imagine my explaining that in a thirty-second sound bite on Fox News? Or how about in a press conference to a bunch of short-attention-span reporters looking to advance their publication's existing narrative? Or even worse, to a bunch of members of Congress whose sole priority was self-preservation?

I lost them at "Dong."

If anyone can come up with a better way to explain that transaction, please message me and I'll buy you a barbecue sandwich in Monroe County, Kentucky. And please understand, that was just *one* of *hundreds* of transactions that the outstanding and hardworking staff on the Oversight Committee had to trace. Hunter and James Biden made these transactions as complex as possible to confuse investigators at the DOJ and deceive auditors at the IRS.

Yet that one transaction, $100,000 from Dong to Hunter, disproved Joe Biden's long-standing claim that his family never received any money from China. If Joe were a Republican, the mainstream media would shout from every rooftop that he was a liar. The corporate records we subpoenaed showed that Dong attempted to hide the foreign source of the money by layering LLCs formed in Delaware.

## THE ART OF THE PAYOFF

AT THE TIME of the First Bank Memorandum, a $3 million wire was discovered from an unknown Chinese entity associated with the Chinese Communist Party to Robinson Walker LLC, which was then split with members of the Biden family. The name of that Chinese entity was State Energy HK. Our investigation revealed that State Energy was another vehicle Ye used, in this case to funnel money and purchase lucrative "gifts." Despite the company's name, and consistent with most of the company names included in the Biden web of shell companies, few if any of the financial transactions have anything to do with a company that's in the energy business. The significant purchases of very expensive jewelry, for example, are more consistent with a Chinese company laundering money and facilitating payments through luxury items, which are difficult to trace. Our investigation also revealed that in addition to jewelry, the Chinese used artwork as vehicles to launder money to American criminals.

High-end modern art. Does that ring a bell?

Could it explain why, after the Chinese deals blew up as a result of Hunter's reckless lifestyle and Joe's election to the presidency and its spotlight, Hunter Biden became one of America's highest-paid artists overnight?

## THE THREE-CARAT BRIBE

FROM 2016 TO 2017, State Energy HK made over $23 million in purchases from a retail diamond/jewelry business. The timing of the diamond purchases is significant to our investigation. In late

2016 and early 2017, State Energy HK bought over $2 million worth of diamonds from one specific retailer. These transactions align with the large diamond Ye sent to Hunter Biden after a Miami dinner. The *New Yorker* confirmed in a July 1, 2019, story that Hunter Biden met Ye in Miami and that Biden received a 2.8-carat diamond.[8] A valuation of $80,000 was put on the diamond by Hunter Biden's first wife in their divorce proceedings following Biden's flagrant affair with his dead brother's widow, but Hunter claimed it was worth just $10,000. Clearly Kathleen Buhle Biden was aware of such a diamond's existence.

Hunter now claims that he gave the diamond to an unnamed associate and forgot about it. In other words, Hunter's Chinese diamond is missing, like so many of the foreign bad actors in the Biden influence-peddling scheme.

In addition to purchasing large amounts of valuable items unrelated to an energy firm, State Energy HK made several million-dollar donations to a think tank associated with Vuk Jeremic, the Serbian associate of Hunter Biden whom we met earlier. The Center for International Relations and Sustainable Development had locations listed in both Belgrade and New York.

Where so-called dark money (*dark* means the donors are not disclosed) comes from in American political funding remains a big mystery. It definitely flows from many foreign sources. Certainly it would be no surprise if China were one of those sources or if China had even created some American entities to spread its propaganda and undermining lies. On the other hand, Chinese propaganda is so similar to Democrat talking points that it would be hard to tell the difference.

But I do wonder how many of the left-wing dark money groups come from China. We know China is a huge anonymous donor to many of America's most liberal universities, whose very purpose seems to be to subvert American mainstream values. I suspect that a large percentage of the dark money funding the unachievable Green New Deal campaigns does as well. Nobody stands to gain more from America losing our energy independence than China. The fact that America has a great deal of energy resources while China has relatively few hydrocarbons and is an importer of oil and gas is one of the key imbalances that keeps China from displaying even more aggression.

If anyone needed more reason to be suspicious of the United Nations, consider that Vuk Jeremic finished a close second in the race to be UN secretary-general. Hunter Biden helped Jeremic in his effort by leveraging the support of none other than his vice presidential father, Joe. In an email dated June 16, 2016, Jeremic wrote to Hunter and his associate Eric Schwerin asking if he could meet with Vice President Biden's national security advisor, Colin Kahl. On July 2, Jeremic confirmed to Hunter that his meeting with Kahl went well.[9]

The meeting Hunter set up with his father's top-level staffer and Jeremic is evidence that Hunter utilized the office of the vice president. And like almost every other time this happened, the use of a cutout such as Kahl allowed Joe Biden to conveniently claim plausible deniability.

Chinese-linked State Energy HK made suspicious donations to Jeremic's think tank while he was running for UN secretary-general in what could credibly be argued was an attempt to buy influence with the prospective leader of the world body. This is consistent with the business model China uses to manipulate vulnerable politicians. And less than two months after Joe Biden left office as vice president, State Energy HK wired $3 million to Robinson Walker LLC, which in turn paid the Bidens over $1 million.

The Bidens make the Grant administration grifters look like amateurs. They even put to shame those masters of the game of influence peddling, Bill and Hillary Clinton.

# Chapter 6

## OLIGARCHS FOR BIDEN

To fully appreciate all the previously unknown information that the Oversight Committee discovered in our fifteen-month investigation about potential crimes by members of the Biden family, one must go back to the pre-investigation false media narratives, particular these four whoppers.

- Hunter Biden's abandoned laptop was a Russian disinformation operation.
- No Biden ever took money from China.
- The Bidens were real businesspeople who had legitimate businesses.
- No money ever changed hands between shady foreign nationals and the Bidens while Joe Biden was vice president.

Thanks to the investigation, we now know that all four of those false narratives concocted and disseminated from the 2020 presidential through the 2022 midterms were 100 percent false. Fake news!

Oversight published a Third Bank Memorandum on August 9, 2023,[1] that explored in depth the last two false media narratives as the nature of the Biden businesses and how much money changed hands while Joe Biden was serving in the second-highest office in the land. Much like the Second Bank Memorandum focused on money received from China and Romania, the Third Bank Memorandum focused on money the Bidens received from foreign entities in Russia, Ukraine, and Kazakhstan. Six different banks were subpoenaed and thousands of pages of bank records were turned over to the committee.

The committee found that nearly $30 million in payments from foreign sources was paid to the Biden family and their associates with no known products or services being provided in exchange for those payments aside from vague claims of networking and advising, all while Joe Biden served as vice president. Hunter Biden and his former best friend and associate Devon Archer used many of their vast Rosemont Seneca entity accounts to receive the foreign payments before they would then be dispersed in incremental payments to various Biden family members after being passed through a series of shell companies.

Nearly all the foreign money that was transferred from shady foreign entities to the LLCs associated with Hunter Biden while Joe was VP was first sent through a shell or receiving company owned by associates such as Devon Archer, Eric Schwerin, or Rob Walker. It then tumbled through a complex maze of companies that consisted of a name and a bank account before some of it reached its final destination—the back pockets of various Biden family members. Hunter vehemently denies that payments went to his father: "All I know is this: My father was never involved in any of my business, ever. Never received a cent from anybody or never benefited in any way. Never took any actions on behalf in any way. And I can absolutely, 100 percent state, that is not just in my case but in every family member's case."

Why go to this trouble?

Because it is both illegal and highly unethical (not to mention very damaging politically for both Vice President Biden and President Barack Obama) for the immediate family of a sitting vice president to get significant gifts or payments from foreign nationals. These gifts (including multicarat diamonds) or payments would have to be disclosed and explained. What exactly did the Bidens do to earn such lucre? It certainly wasn't savvy management acumen those shady foreign entities were paying for. What *were* they paying for? The brand. And the brand being sold, as Devon Archer stated, was Joe Biden.[2]

The brand is Joe Biden. Political influence is the product. It's as simple as that.[3]

Or, as Hunter Biden puts it in a laptop email, "The Bidens are the best I know at doing exactly what the Chairman wants from this partnership. Please let's not quibble over peanuts."[4]

Devon Archer. Rob Walker. James Gilliar. The primary role of all the Hunter Biden associates appears to have been to accept the initial unethical payment from the foreign entity and then make payments through a series of wire transfers betwixt and between Hunter Biden's massive portfolio of strange LLCs. The first three bank memos established this pattern of financial deception.

As the memo details, midway into the second term of the Obama administration in February 2014, a Russian oligarch sent $3.5 million to a shell company associated with Hunter Biden and Devon Archer. Yelena Baturina, Russia's second-wealthiest woman,[5] transferred $3.5 million to Rosemont Seneca Thornton (one of the many shell companies with the word *Rosemont* in its name). From that payment approximately $1 million was transferred to Archer and the remainder was used to initially fund a new account, Rosemont Seneca, which Archer and Hunter Biden would later use to receive additional foreign wires.

## THE BURISMA BOARD GAME

IN THE SPRING of 2014, a Ukrainian oligarch placed both Devon Archer and Hunter Biden on the board of the infamous Burisma energy company and agreed to pay them each $83,333 a *month*, or $999,996 per year.[6] Hunter admitted on ABC News' *Good Morning America* in 2019 that he had no experience in the energy sector and that the only reason he was put on the board of Burisma was his last name.[7] But what needs to be understood and appreciated about Hunter's placement on the board is the sheer excessiveness of the salary he received.

As RealClearInvestigations journalist Mark Hemingway puts it, "A 2017 Harvard study looked at the compensation of board members at private companies with annual revenue of less than $500 million. Board members were typically paid between $55,230 and $82,986 annually. In 2018, Burisma reportedly had revenue of $400 million. Burisma paid Biden more every month than board members at similar-sized companies could expect to receive in a year."[8]

Hunter made $4 million overall from his stint on the Burisma board.[9] If that alone were not bad enough, he was being paid the excessive salary while his father was not only serving as the vice president but also was in charge of administering foreign aid to the country where Burisma was domiciled *and* was currently being investigated for fraud by the country's top government prosecutor.

Burisma Holdings' corporate secretary was a man named Vadym Pozharsky. He worked directly for Mykola Zlochevsky, the owner of Burisma. Hunter was initially hired by Burisma to work as a legal counsel for the company despite Biden's having no previous legal experience in the energy sector. But that wasn't enough. After Pozharsky and Zlochevsky met with Hunter at a conference at Lake Como, in Italy, they decided to put Hunter on the full board of directors of Burisma instead, perhaps to justify Hunter's ridiculous "salary" and assuage his inflated ego. Or perhaps Zlochevsky and Pozharsky realized that Hunter could not do a single thing that an ordinary energy lawyer would be required to do.

Or was the quid pro quo already in? Was it possible Hunter Biden then and there guaranteed that his father could help get the Ukrainian prosecutors off these Burisma executives' backs? Either way, the meeting in Italy was a huge short-term success for Hunter, as he later wrote in his memoir, "The board fee had morphed into a wicked sort of funny money. It hounded me to spend recklessly, dangerously, destructively. Humiliatingly. So I did."[10]

Soon after the meeting in Italy where Hunter completed his meteoric—damn near miraculous—rise through the organizational charts of the corrupt Ukrainian energy company, Vice President Joe Biden would visit Ukraine. In fact, Hunter and Devon Archer had just begun receiving payments when the official visit occurred.

These directors' payments to Hunter and Archer were not made directly to them individually (unlike nearly every other director's compensation in the history of the free world) but rather were wired to the Rosemont Seneca Bohai shell company. From there they were transmitted to Hunter Biden's many different business accounts in increments. The only logical explanation? Deception.

We would later learn from IRS whistleblowers that the agency's investigation of Hunter Biden centered on these payments from Burisma and his failure to pay one penny of federal income tax on the millions he received from Burisma. One imagines that in Hunter's world, only the little people pay taxes! If so, Biden's sense of entitlement would seem to be justified. His friend and lawyer Kevin Morris later laid out $2 million to cover years of Hunter's missing taxes.[11]

## THE YEAR OF THE BIG HAUL

TWO THOUSAND FOURTEEN was certainly a banner year for the Biden family influence-peddling ring. Around the time that Hunter Biden received millions from the Russian oligarch, and millions more from the corrupt Ukrainian oligarchs heading up Burisma, he received one of the nicest gifts—and certainly one of the fastest—in the history of American political scions receiving supremely expensive gifts from mysterious foreigners. A brand-new Porsche. And the "luck" continued. Vice President Biden, who was in the middle of his second term in office, did not get hit with a major ethics violation for failing to list gifts to immediate family members over $250 in federal disclosures as required. He also managed to avoid a federal indictment under the Foreign Corrupt Practices Act. It was Hunter Biden's car, after all, not Joe's! Of course, as Devon Archer would tell the committee, Hunter would never be caught dead in a Kentucky-made Toyota Camry or an old Ford farm truck like the one I drive. No, he received a car more becoming of his brilliant mind and fabulous lifestyle. Hunter Biden got a white Porsche Panamera GTS.[12] It was a gift from Kazakhstan. Well, actually he was wired the cost of the sports car he had his eye on, and the next day Hunter went Porsche shopping.[13]

In February 2014, Hunter met with Kenes Rakishev at a Washington, DC, hotel. Rakishev worked closely with the prime minister of Kazakhstan, Karim Massimov. In April, Rakishev, who was a Kazakhstani oligarch and served as a director at Kazakhstan's state-owned oil company KazMunayGas, wired $142,300 to Rosemont Seneca Bohai. The very next day a payment was made from the Rosemont account to a car dealership for the exact same amount of $142,300 to purchase his fancy new sports car. A few months later, in June, Devon Archer and Hunter arranged for Burisma executives to visit Kazakhstan to evaluate a three-way deal among Burisma, a Chinese state-owned company, and the government of Kazakhstan.

The Kazakh oligarch who bestowed this fabulous new Porsche on Hunter Biden and called Hunter his "brother from another mother"[14] was Kenes Rakishev. Rakishev maintained close ties to Prime Minister Massimov, with whom he and Hunter worked closely to try to get an energy deal set up between the Chinese and Kazakhstani governments involving Burisma. Massimov was later sentenced to eighteen years in prison for treason, abuse of power, and attempting a coup.[15]

## BAD PEOPLE IN BAD COUNTRIES

A COMMON THEME I stated during countless interviews throughout the investigation was the manner in which the "Bidens took millions and millions of dollars from bad people in bad countries around the world, and we have no idea what they did to receive the money."[16] Thus, the important purpose of our vitally important investigation of public corruption from our current commander in chief was to determine exactly what the Bidens did for all that dirty money and if, in fact, President Joe Biden was compromised. Any credible media outlets should have praised the Herculean effort of the Oversight Committee to honestly and credibly investigate the biggest public corruption scandal in America's proud history. In the past, they would have. Not today's mainstream media, composed as it mostly is of lazy, liberal-elite trust funders and partisan lackeys.

Soon after the Third Bank Memorandum, we learned from our transcribed interview with Devon Archer[17] of another Joe Biden lie. Despite Joe saying multiple times that he never met any of the shady foreign nationals who mysteriously wired money to his son's multiple bank accounts, Vice President Biden had dinner with Russian oligarch Yelena Baturina, the leadership of Burisma, and Kenes Rakishev on various occasions in 2014 and 2015 in Washington, DC. Oddly—or perhaps not so much—there are no Secret Service records to verify these meetings. After the committee publicly released information of Archer's testimony that the meetings had, in fact, occurred, nobody from the White House disputed it. The meetings obviously took place.

## THE VERY DEFINITION OF BRIBERY IN JOE BIDEN

I'VE MAINTAINED IN every interview from September 2023 until the end of the investigation that I would vote to impeach Joe Biden without hesitation if given the chance. Winning that vote in the House depends on how many of my colleagues feel we've proven Vice President Biden's family was the vehicle to receive bribes intended for him.

As the evidence mounted over the first eight months of the investigation, the White House's constant refrain was that Joe Biden had no knowledge of his son's business activities. But the release of the Third Bank Memorandum provided validation that the laptop was real, and photos of Joe Biden meeting with international shady actors implicated in sending funds to Biden family accounts were in fact real and not AI-generated.

After the Devon Archer testimony, the White House did an about-face and drastically changed the goalposts and their narrative. White House press secretary Karine Jean-Pierre nonchalantly stated during a routine press conference that the "president was not in business with his son!"

Well now. That was a huge deviation from their previous mantra: "The president had no knowledge of his son's business dealings."

That statement in itself should have been marked as a victory for the Oversight Committee, but the only media mention the White House's sudden shift in explanation received was from conservative and independent news sources. Obviously, the call had gone out for the mainstream media to behave as if this sudden and massive deviation had been the explanation all along. Nothing to see here! Throughout our investigation, the mainstream media has never strayed from its obedience—you might as well call it slavish submission—to the White House narrative.

# Chapter 7

## GUILT AND CORROBORATION

Gary Shapley and Joseph Ziegler were the two best government-employed witnesses ever to testify in front of the Oversight Committee in my eight years in Congress. They were genuine people who were true public stewards of our tax dollars and made the brave decision to come forward and blow the whistle on the most powerful family in American politics, despite knowing the probable consequences of their appropriate action.

Shapley and Ziegler told Congress that they were not allowed to do their normal investigation. Even as they discovered evidence showing President Biden might be involved, the two were prevented from looking into it. This took guts to come forward with because even though Shapley is a registered Republican, he says he has voted for Democrats before, including President Bill Clinton. This is even more true for Ziegler, who is openly gay and a Democrat, and not likely making many of his friends happy by coming to the Capitol.

Shapley supervised the IRS team on the Hunter Biden case for more than three years. Ziegler worked on the case since its very beginning in 2018. Both men gave previous testimony behind closed doors to the House Ways and Means Committee, which quickly voted to make it public, so I knew in advance of my hearing the incriminating evidence both men possessed on the Biden family.

Despite Oversight Democrats' best efforts to disrupt, dispute, and even publicly shame Shapley and Ziegler, both men delivered performances for the ages. The nationally televised hearing displayed the IRS whistleblowers' sincerity, knowledge, and facts that proved our federal government was involved in a massive and historic cover-up of the biggest political corruption story of our lifetime. The hearing also allowed the American people to see what great lengths congressional Democrats would go to to discourage and intimidate honest, legally protected whistleblowers from coming forward to shine a light on massive corruption.

The IRS whistleblowers testified to five very damaging points that proved that, in addition to the many financial crimes that President Biden's family had committed, there was a massive cover-up at the hands of our very own federal government, which served to protect the corrupt first family. This explained why, despite numerous media stories over the years about Biden influence peddling and tax evasion, no charges were ever filed against any Biden family member. This was the ultimate evidence of both a two-tiered system of justice and the fact that the rules do not apply to ruling-class families like the Bidens.

First off, Joe Biden's role in his son's financial schemes was never investigated by the federal government. Shapley testified that despite many instances in his investigation where there were multiple references to Joe Biden, investigators were not allowed to question Joe. Shapley said he could not remember a single time in his fourteen years of service with the IRS that he was not allowed to question a key witness in a serious financial crimes investigation.

Second, Attorney General Merrick Garland lied when he stated that then–U.S. attorney David Weiss had the independence to prosecute Hunter Biden. Both Ziegler and Shapley testified that Weiss was blocked from bringing tax fraud charges against Hunter by his father's appointed U.S. attorneys in California and Washington, DC. And both IRS whistleblowers confirmed their professional beliefs that Hunter did in fact commit multiple financial crimes.

Third, Hunter Biden was tipped off by Justice Department authorities on a planned search and visit by IRS investigators. Years of research by the IRS and other investigative bodies revealed the existence of a storage locker in Virginia that may have contained damaging evidence of the Biden family's influence-peddling schemes and Joe Biden's central role in those schemes. The IRS wanted to execute a search warrant on the storage unit. They also wanted to interview Hunter Biden. But the night before December 7, 2020, when this interview was going to happen, Shapley testified that he was informed that FBI headquarters had notified Secret Service headquarters and the Biden presidential transition team about the planned actions of the next day. Shapley and Ziegler were never allowed to search the storage unit, despite strong evidence it contained many potentially damaging documents. The Deep State tip could have allowed the Bidens to relocate or even destroy the documents that would have allowed the IRS to prosecute Hunter and possibly implicate President-elect Joe.

Fourth, Smirnov's FBI form FD-1023, alleging the Bidens took a $10 million bribe, and the Hunter Biden laptop were never shared with the IRS investigators. Despite spending over two years investigating allegations of multiple financial crimes and ever-growing mountains of evidence, the IRS investigators leading the Hunter Biden investigation in conjunction with the FBI were never made aware of the fact that the FBI possessed Hunter's laptop, which had thousands of pages of damaging evidence in the form of emails, text messages, pictures, videos, and bank statements. They were also never made aware of the fact that the FBI possessed Smirnov's FD-1023 form that contained allegations that two Bidens took a $10 million bribe from a Ukrainian oligarch. They also noted that the 1023 was recorded long before the IRS investigation began and the laptop was discovered.

Fifth, Joseph Ziegler outlined how tax investigators were never allowed to talk with various members of the Biden family despite the fact that ten different Biden family members received incremental payments from Hunter Biden lead operations. Ziegler also testified that there were many expenses for Biden family members that were illegally deducted on Hunter Biden's 2018 tax return. Lesley Wolf, an assistant U.S. attorney for Delaware, prevented Ziegler from interviewing any Biden family members even though they received hundreds of thousands of dollars in payments and benefits.

Shapley and Ziegler's testimony confirmed that our federal government was front and center in a massive cover-up of political corruption at the highest levels. They also suggested what I had been saying publicly for months: that Hunter Biden had committed multiple financial crimes that included, at the very least, FARA violations and tax fraud.

Whistleblowers testified to some of the outrageous tax write-offs Hunter turned in to the IRS on his federal returns. He allegedly listed a prostitute as an employee of one of his fake companies and wrote off all his escort services. Imagine, one of President Joe Biden's policy platform positions is to double the size of the IRS to go after tax cheats. I doubt very many families have faced more investigations for tax evasion than his own family.

At the conclusion of the successful hearing, all I could think about was the irony of Joe Biden and his BS about the rich needing to pay their fair share. Hunter, Jim, and Frank Biden have had many well-documented tax problems. Joe's sister, Valerie Biden Owens, along with her husband, John Owens, have been involved in at least five tax liens, according to the *Washington Free Beacon*. This included $229,749 in 1990. Joe's daughter Ashley

Biden owed over $5,000 in federal income taxes, according to Fox News Digital. In reality, Joe believes that his family should be treated like the British royal family was for many years, excluded from paying any taxes. Taxes are not to be paid by the ruling class, only the laborers.

## HUNTER AND JIM BIDEN KNEW THEY WERE DEALING WITH THE CHINESE COMMUNIST PARTY

IRS WHISTLEBLOWERS SHAPLEY and Ziegler had recently turned over to the House Ways and Means Committee their notes from a yearslong IRS federal investigation. In the memorandum of the interview Jim Biden gave to Treasury during a federal investigation, the president's brother said that Hunter "portrayed CEFC to him as Chairman Ye, who was a protégé of President Xi."

Form FD-302 is used by the FBI to record investigative activity, particularly, although not exclusively, the results of an interview. We obtained evidence via an October 23, 2020, FD-302, based on Tony Bobulinski's interviews, that stated:

> CEFC had used its relationship with Hunter Biden and James Biden—and the influence attached to the Biden name—to advance CEFC's interests abroad. Hunter Biden and James Biden did not receive any compensation because Joseph Biden was still VPOTUS during this time period. There was a concern it would be improper for payments to be made to Hunter Biden and James Biden by CEFC due to its close affiliation with the Chinese government. Hunter Biden and James Biden both wanted to be compensated for the assistance they had provided to CEFC's ventures; in particular, they believed CEFC owed them money for the benefits that accrued

to CEFC through its use of the Biden family name to advance their business dealings.[1]

Tony Bobulinski says he explained to the FBI that the Bidens were willing to help China implement China's very dangerous Belt and Road Initiative, a program that is counter to all American blue-collar workers and patriotic businesspeople. Belt and Road is Chinese economic warfare against the West. If true, it shows that our FBI knew about the Bidens' involvement from the start. Our Department of Justice chose to tell every federal agency investigating the Bidens to stand down.

In 2017, Hunter Biden, Rob Walker, and James Gilliar began negotiating with CEFC to form a jointly held company focused on infrastructure projects. Chairman Ye would hold 50 percent in the joint venture and then Hunter Biden, James Biden, Rob Walker, James Gilliar, and Tony Bobulinski would hold the other 50 percent. Then, on May 13, 2017, in what would become the most damning evidence of Joe Biden's direct involvement in the Chinese joint venture, Gilliar described a change of ownership structure in which Hunter would own an additional 10 percent of the holding company for "the big guy."

Multiple sources have corroborated that the phrase "the big guy" was used by the Bidens' business associates to refer to Joe. Additionally, the FD-1023 FD from indicted Alexander Smirnov that the FBI sources turned over to Senator Grassley and me—recorded years before the public had heard the term "big guy"—also referenced Joe as the "big guy" who was implicated in taking a bribe from a corrupt oligarch with the money that was distributed through a series of complex transactions in various banks.[2] That pattern of behavior sure sounded familiar to me when I read that 1023 for the first time! It is all so obvious. Yet there are two holdouts who insist the rest of us must not allow ourselves to believe the conclusion laid out right before our very eyes. Who are those see-no-evil holdouts who don't believe that the sky is blue and that the Biden family got payments from the Chinese government, some of which went to Joe? The FBI. And, of course, the mainstream media.

## THE WHATSAPP FROM HELL

THE ORIGINAL BUSINESS plan for funding the joint venture called for CEFC to transfer $10 million to capitalize the project. The CEFC deal struggled to get the funding from June and July of 2017. Then, on July 30, 2017, Hunter Biden sent a WhatsApp message to CEFC associate Raymond Zhao regarding the $10 million payment:

> Z- Please have the director call me—not James or Tony or Jim—have him call me tonight. I am sitting here with my father and we would like to understand why the commitment made has not been fulfilled. I am very concerned that the Chairman has either changed his mind and broken our deal without telling me or that he is unaware of the promises and assurances that have been made have not been kept. Tell the director that I would like to resolve this now before it gets out of hand, [a]nd now means tonight. And Z if I get a call or text from anyone involved in this other than you, Zhang or the Chairman, I will make certain that between the man sitting next to me and every person he knows and my ability to forever hold a grudge that you will regret not following my direction. All too often people mistake kindness for weakness—and all too often I am standing over top of them saying I warned you. From this moment until whenever he reaches me. It I [*sic*] 9:45 AM here and I assume 9:45 PM there so night is running out.[3]

The following day, Hunter worked to reshape the ownership arrangement of the joint venture by removing Gilliar, Walker, and Bobulinski and shifted to working with CEFC solely with his uncle Jim Biden. All of this was done without informing Bobulinski they were stiff-arming him. Once they realized Bobulinski inconveniently wanted to run an actual, aboveboard investment business, the Bidens ditched him.

In a WhatsApp message dated July 31, 2017, Hunter said to Raymond Zhao:

> Z- I reached out to K and he declined my call and has not returned my text. I assume he knows that our plan to speak is highly confidential. I just hope he isn't talking to Tony or J—if he is we have a real problem. If I can reshape this partnership to what the chairman intended then James and Rob will be well taken care of but I will not have Tony dictating to me nor the director what we can and cannot do.

Zhao responded the same day via WhatsApp:

> CEFC is willing to cooperate with the family.

Four days later, on August 3, Hunter wrote to another CEFC associate, Gongwen Dong:

> If you think it is about money it's not. The Biden's [*sic*] are the best I know at doing exactly what the Chairman [Ye] wants from this partnership. Please let's not quibble over peanuts.

Those four WhatsApp messages paint a pretty accurate picture of what Hunter Biden's objectives were, how he operated, and what he was willing to do for dirty money from the Chinese.

The first message from Hunter to Zhao was an extortion threat to Zhao to fulfill the commitments that the Bidens made with China while Joe was VP. The second message from Hunter to Zhao showed how disloyal and greedy Hunter could be. He did not want any part of a business relationship with Tony Bobulinski, the one guy who openly questioned Hunter on the ethics of how he was doing business with the Chinese.

The third message from Zhao to Hunter showed that the CEFC was in fact willing to pay the "family," a recognition that the Chinese were only interested in the Biden Brand, and that brand consisted not primarily of Hunter and his uncle Jim, who were only relatives of the big guy with the real power.

The fourth message from Hunter Biden to Gongwen Dong—and the most troubling message of all—clearly stated that the Bidens were the best at doing whatever China wanted. And if China's goals were in direct conflict with those of the United States? The Bidens would be obedient to China in exchange for payment. Maybe that admission from Hunter to Dong would explain why President Biden has consistently implemented a China-first, America-last platform in the Far East.[4] The quid pro quo is ongoing.

In his testimony, Hunter responded: "My addiction is not an excuse, but I can tell you this: I am more embarrassed of this text message, if it actually did come from me, than any text message I've ever sent. The fact of the matter is, is that there's no other text message that you have in which I say anything remotely to this. And I was out of my mind. I can also tell you this: My father was not sitting next to me. My father had no awareness."

Nonetheless, one example of Joe Biden giving China what they wanted: while he was vice president and highly influential in Obama administration China policy (Obama famously disliked dealing with foreign policy), China built a series of military bases on contested islands and systematically cordoned off the South China Sea in contravention of international law and the rights of its neighbors while the United States stood down and made *tsk-tsk* noises. It was an enormous territory grab, a blow against the security of the Far East democracies, and a debacle for the peace established by the international law of the sea as enforced by the U.S. Navy.[5]

The navy kicked Hunter Biden out for testing positive for cocaine, but they should have court-martialed him in absentia.[6]

As I've noted, on August 3, 2017, Hunter Biden opened a bank account for Hudson West III LLC, a joint venture formed between Hunter and CEFC's Gongwen Dong that served as a cash spigot leading directly into Biden family coffers. James Biden's recollection of the deal in his investigative interview was "that Dong was dealing with Chairman Ye and then was speaking with Hunter." Hudson West III was 50 percent owned by Owasco PC, Hunter's "law firm," and 50 percent owned by Hudson West V, which was Dong's company, an affiliate of CEFC.

Five days after opening the new bank account, on August 8, Hunter Biden received a $5 million deposit into Hudson West III from Northern International Capital, yet another Chinese company affiliated with CEFC. On that particular day, the wire from the CCP-backed entity Northern International was the only money in Hunter's newest bank account. The same day, Hunter transferred $400,000 of this fresh Chinese money to his professional corporation, Owasco PC. Curiously, on that same day, when Hunter received the $5 million and made the $400,000 deposit into his older Owasco account, the latter had a balance of $500,832.55.

Why does this matter? Because $100,000 of the balance that had been sitting there before was *also* Chinese money.

## TRACING THE MONEY FLOW

THE OVERSIGHT COMMITTEE staff was able to verify that the Owasco PC account was funded by *two* CEFC affiliates. CEFC Infrastructure wired $100,000 on August 4, 2017, and then four days later Northern International Capital wired the $400,000. That comprised 99.9 percent of the cash in the account. Then over the next week Hunter made transfers to his Rosemont Seneca Advisors LLC account, another account named "Biden R Resource Cash," and his "Robert H Biden" account. After those three transfers, Hunter had $366,557.04 in his Owasco PC account.

On August 14, when Hunter made the last of these transfers into his own accounts, he also made a significant transfer to his uncle Jim and aunt Sara Biden's business account, an account belonging to James Biden's longtime company, Lion Hall Group. I subpoenaed both the Lion Hall Group account and Jim and Sara Biden's personal bank accounts over nine years and personally examined every single transaction. The two things that stuck out to me about the transactions in their so-called business account is that most of the expenses appeared to be strictly personal in nature (living expenses like groceries, dog grooming, and beauty shop visits). The Lion Hall Group account transparently served as a personal piggy bank for Jim Biden's family. I also noticed that they had received a ridiculous number of very suspicious "loans."

As for the "loans" recorded there, this is how they are listed in deposits, but I very seldom saw any payments on those loans. Some of their "loans" existed for at least nine years, and the Bidens never made a single interest or principal payment on them. A loan is only a loan if you are going to pay it back. If you receive a loan and do not pay it back, then it is either taxable as income to the borrower or taxable as a gift from the person making the loan. I saw millions of dollars of loans that appear never to have been paid back. This would in turn indicate that Jim and Sara Biden could owe hundreds of thousands of dollars to the IRS, not to mention be subject to legal liabilities for knowingly receiving payments from corrupt characters and characterizing them as "loans," but without the intention (or any action taken) ever to repay them.

On the day that Owasco PC wired Jim and Sara Biden $150,000, the balance of their Lion Hall Group bank account after the deposit was $151,964.62. So before the transfer, Jim and Sara had $1,964.62 in their account! Over the next ten days they made a series of payments and their balance fell to $115,822.13. Then, on August 28, Sara Biden signed a ticket to withdraw $50,000 in cash from the Lion Hall Group Account. After the $50,000 withdrawal, she immediately deposited the same amount into their Sara and James Biden personal account. That is a very strange way to transfer money, directly from a business to a personal account. Any IRS auditor would have a lot of questions about their odd transfer process, and those questions would all revolve around potential tax evasion and/or money-laundering themes.

Prior to the deposit, the personal account only had a balance of $46.88. Again, for the media who have struggled immensely with the concept of tracing money, after the $50,000 deposit, James and Sara Biden had a $50,046.88 checking account balance.

Jim and Sara Biden had $50,000 ultimately traceable back to Chinese government sources sitting in their personal bank account.

The Sara and James Biden personal account received no more deposits over the next week. Then, on September 3, Sara Biden wrote out and signed a check to Joseph R. Biden Jr. The check was for $40,000. On the memo line Sara listed "loan repayment."

## THE "LOAN" THAT WASN'T

I'LL ADMIT THAT when I first saw the check to Joe Biden, the full implications didn't sink in immediately. My first thought was "Wow, that's the first time I've seen that they actually paid a 'loan' back!"

Then I realized that I had never seen a deposit from Joe Biden to Sara or Jim Biden that would account for that $40,000.

I knew that if someone pays an individual a loan back, then that individual should have a check to the borrower for the original loan amount prior to being paid back. That, after all, is what a loan is.

Jim and Sara Biden did not have a check from Joe, and as of this writing, Joe Biden has never shown compelling proof that he actually loaned Jim and Sara Biden any money.

James Mandolfo, Jake Greenberg, and Clark Abourisk of the Oversight Committee staff met with me the next morning after the discovery of the $40,000 check to Joe Biden and pointed out the most damning aspect of all.

It was traceable directly back to China.

The money from the Chinese Community Party–aligned CEFC made exactly five transfers from China's Northern International Capital to Hunter's Hudson West to Hunter's Owasco to Jim and Sara Biden's Lion Hall Group to Jim and Sara Biden's personal account to Joe Biden's back pocket. As I've detailed, none of the accounts had significant money in them prior to the Chinese infusion. When the accounts are laid out in this way, it is not difficult to trace money through its maze of diverse bank accounts when all the accounts are practically empty to start with.

Could that $40,000 have been, not a loan, but rather a payment from the Chinese routed through byzantine channels for services rendered? As the Magic 8 Ball says, "Signs point to yes."

The Democrats on the Oversight Committee were quick to obey their masters at the White House and on the Biden legal team and incorrectly claim that this was just a loan repayment.

## THE PERCENTAGES ADD UP

TO DIVE EVEN further into the $40,000 Chinese payment that Joe Biden received, it is interesting to note that the original Bobulinski-headed SinoHawk deal with CEFC called for Joe or "the big guy" to receive a 10 percent stake in the business. This seemed to be a common Biden family understanding.

Consider the fact that Hunter Biden took out his apparent "professional fee" of $400,000 from the $5 million wire, and Joe Biden ended up with $40,000—well, $40,000 is exactly 10 percent of $400,000. Jim Biden was also set to receive a larger ownership stake in the revised ownership structure that cut Bobulinski, Schwerin, and Walker out of the deal. Jim got $150,000, which would amount to a 37.5 percent stake.[7]

## DEMOCRATS IGNORE ANOTHER SMOKING GUN

I THINK THE only thing that would convince the Oversight Democrats would be if Sara Biden had written "Chinese payment for Spratly Island military expansion, Most Favored Nation Status, etc." on the memo line.

For proof, the Democrats highlighted a wire that came from a Delaware law firm's trust account into the account of Sara and Jim Biden. That firm did a majority of the legal work setting up the Biden family companies, including Hunter Biden's quiver of LLCs. These companies had accounts in at least six different banks, which had collectively issued 170 of those Suspicious Activity Reports filed with Treasury. Suspicious Activity Reports are required when certain unusual transactions occur that could indicate fraud or money laundering.

That law firm never sent any letter or statement to the committee with evidence that Joe had in fact loaned the money to his brother and sister-in-law. At the end of the day, it really does not matter that much whether Joe actually loaned Sara and Jim Biden the $40,000 (although he most certainly did *not* or else he or his lackeys would quickly have produced evidence showing that he'd made such a loan).

The fact remains that Jim and Sara Biden had practically no money in their account before they got the wire deriving ultimately from China. The money they "paid back" to Joe Biden was not owed to anyone, but was simply money paid. We had our first direct paper trail of Joe directly benefiting from his family's shady business schemes.

It's also important to recognize that the entire series of transfers from China to Joe Biden occurred right after Hunter Biden sent the WhatsApp message to Raymond Zhao in China threatening him if he did not pay up.

In that message demanding money from Zhao, Hunter said his father was sitting right beside him and was equally unhappy.

Assuming Hunter Biden is the truthful if misunderstood scion of a noble family that the Democrats on Oversight and the mainstream media always claim him to be, then even they cannot doubt that in that WhatsApp message, Hunter was saying exactly what he meant to say. It's hardly necessary to paraphrase, but I'll give it a try.

*I am not pleased because my father—who was recently vice president of the U.S., I need not remind you—is not pleased. We Bidens are family. We've done a lot for you and will do more in the future. Don't mess with us.*

*Pay up or else.*

So Joe Biden was the central figure who jump-started the entire series of wire transfers that ended with $40,000 of Chinese money going right into Joe's own pocket. Not Hunter. Not Jim.

Joe Biden. President of the United States. Chinese stooge.

# Chapter 8

## FORWARD MOTION

Right from opening gavel of the 118th Congress, we faced mounting obstacles to getting to the truth about the Bidens. Any time we juked past the White House and congressional Democrats' defense, we found the Deep State and the media hot on our heels. But too many times our conference also fumbled the ball on the snap.

On every opening day for the past century, Congress has adopted its rules package and elected its Speaker. Not only were both parties' entire leadership teams always elected in closed-door conference meetings in November and December prior to opening day, but their staffs were hired as well. A general agreement had already been made between the leaders of the two parties on committee population size, budgets, and the schedule or calendar.

But this day was not like every other opening day in the past. Not only were we unable to elect a Speaker because of around a dozen holdouts in our new majority, but by not completing the many normal pre–opening day agreements, the new Republican majority was at least three weeks behind, assuming we even elected a Speaker the next day.

After a record fifteen floor votes for Speaker, Kevin McCarthy finally secured the votes needed.[1] I was the one who gave the thirteenth nominating speech for Kevin. I will always believe that he was the right guy for the very difficult job. Having a razor-thin majority that only allowed us to lose three Republican votes when we also had a dozen members who held hostage nearly every major piece of legislation in exchange for an often unachievable ransom made leading our conference a Herculean task. Kevin spent many years climbing the leadership ladder gaining much-needed experience. He worked harder than anyone doing the things needed to regain a majority, such as recruiting candidates who could win and raising money so candidates can have what they need to win. What's more important than a leader who knows how to win?

Over the first week of Congress, I was on nearly every TV network that covered politics. *Meet the Press*. Fox News. Newsmax. CBS. *Hannity*. CNN. Many more*—and at least a dozen local TV shows across Kentucky. Every interviewer asked about the Biden influence-peddling investigation. I knew that a big part of any congressional investigation is messaging. The picture I wanted to paint was that of a committee chairman who sincerely wanted to get to the truth and would only present hard evidence of any wrongdoing in my investigation of public corruption at the highest levels. My plan of being fully transparent with the entire press corps seemed, at the time, to be working.

## HURRY UP AND WAIT

THE SECOND FULL week—and the first full week with a Speaker—did not go as I and my Oversight staff might have wished. Ours was one of the very few committees that was ready to go. I had the entire staff hired, prepped, and ready to work for the taxpayers. We were set to hold committee hearings and already had witnesses committed to participate.

Most important of all, I was about to exercise my newfound sub-

* The list also includes *CBS Morning Show* and *The Faulkner Focus* on Fox.

poena power on a Biden associate's bank records. I could not hold a hearing before McCarthy and Minority Leader Hakeem Jeffries from New York sat down and agreed to terms such as committee population size, committee budgets, and the official calendar. And *that* meeting could not occur before our Steering Committee elected all the other committee chairs. The Steering Committee had not yet met because the Speaker nominates most of the Steering Committee, and we hadn't had a Speaker. Once McCarthy and Jeffries finally got together, the committees could hire staffs. These meetings were customarily finalized before Christmas.

Then a worse realization sank in. I would likely not have subpoena power before February. I had already lost a month in a race against the clock to get the information required from a hostile administration and corrupt family who were determined to obstruct my requests.

If anything, my press coverage and interview requests stepped up over the second week of January 2023. I sat down for over twenty appearances, including a historic prime-time Fox interview that Sean Hannity did in the Rayburn Room of the U.S. Capitol with Speaker McCarthy, Jim Jordan, and myself to discuss the Biden investigation.[2] I am pretty sure that was some type of congressional record. Some of my ambitious House colleagues probably did not like my investigation getting that much attention, but the truth of the matter was the Oversight Committee investigation of the Biden family was the only show in town. No other major committee was anywhere near ready to go due to the delay from the Speaker election saga.

On Sunday, January 15, I did my fourth major Sunday show over the course of six weeks with Jake Tapper on CNN. At the time, I liked Tapper, much as I liked Chris Cuomo, whom CNN had previously terminated. I sincerely wanted to develop a relationship with CNN like I had with Fox in order to speak the truth to a more liberal audience than my two regular networks of choice, Fox and Newsmax.

At the beginning of the investigation, my Oversight staff and I regularly communicated with Tapper, even inviting him to come into our committee staff office to see for himself the mountains of evidence we had accumulated against the Bidens. Unfortunately, the relationship with Tapper, like the relationship with every other CNN host, turned toxic after their constant misreporting of the facts of our evidence.

CNN is a network lost in the wilderness. They do not know whether they want to be fair and balanced or a liberal Democratic National Committee propaganda dispenser. Their disinformation campaign against the truth in our investigation, coupled with their strange obsession with Donald Trump, is what in my opinion has led to record-low ratings for the once powerful network that so many of us grew up watching as kids.

## POPULATING OVERSIGHT

WHILE MUCH OF Congress sat around twiddling its thumbs waiting for the committees to be populated and the staffs to be hired, my television interview schedule intensified.* In addition, I went on countless podcasts and increased my sit-down interviews with newspapers and other news outlets such as the *Washington Examiner*, Daily Caller, *Wall Street Journal*, and Breitbart.

The media was interested in the investigation for varying rea-

---

* To give just a partial list from my calendar: I did nearly every TV and newspaper interview I had done over the two previous weeks plus *The Story with Martha MacCallum* on Fox News, an Associated Press interview with Farnoush Amiri, Kennedy on Fox Business, *Jesse Watters Primetime* on Fox News, Bloomberg, *America Reports* with John Roberts and Sandra Smith on Fox News, *The Count* on Newsmax, *Washington Watch with Tony Perkins* on the Family Research Network, Greta van Susteren on Newsmax, and *PBS NewsHour*. I expanded my communications outreach to also include many national radio outlets like *The Todd Starnes Show*, Jimmy Failla's *Fox Across America* radio show, and *The Joe Pags Show* on iHeart Radio.

sons. Most of the mainstream media had decided it was a foregone conclusion that I would never obtain anything useful for the investigation (and after three weeks sitting around powerless without subpoena power and without the ability to call a committee hearing, I was beginning to wonder myself) while the conservative outlets were excited at the prospect of actually holding someone accountable for once.

## THE PRESEASON SHUFFLE

THE HIGHLY ANTICIPATED committee population day had finally arrived, albeit two months later than usual as a result of the Speaker holdouts. Signs of progress finally emerged. I walked into the House Republican Steering Committee ready to lead the voyage with my new soldiers at my side.

The Steering Committee is composed of various members of the Republican conference tasked with the responsibility of putting members on all of the standing committees. The membership of the Steering Committee is traditionally very leadership-heavy, and Speaker Kevin McCarthy had a notoriously tight grip on the committee and its recommendations. (Of course, so did Nancy Pelosi before him.) Any congressman or congresswoman seeking membership onto a House committee had to campaign with the Steering Committee to get the appointment. Members would often run extensive campaigns using mailers and other printed materials, and offer swag and gimmicks to the Steering members in order to sway them to support their requests.

I had put a lot of thought into how I wanted to run the Oversight Committee as chairman. I also thought a lot about who I wanted as members on my committee. I wanted to have the best and most credible members in the Republican conference at my side. I already had some of the most high-profile firebrands, like Jim Jordan, Byron

Donalds, Andy Biggs, and Nancy Mace, on board. I also knew that just about every demanding and potentially troublesome firebrand in our conference wanted a seat once we took the gavel. The fact was that few of the other committee chairs wanted these hard-line conservatives who had reputations for not being team players.

Knowing this, I asked for a couple more of the more controversial members. These were representatives I felt would not only add value to the committee, but were people I could work with. Firebrands are drawn to the Oversight Committee like a duck is to water.

Enter Marjorie Taylor Greene and Scott Perry.

I was always frustrated as the ranking member under Chairwoman Carolyn Maloney that the typical Oversight Committee hearing would last over five hours. I had a simple solution to those painfully long hearings. I would shrink the size of the committee. I decided to request that there be twenty Republicans and fifteen Democrats. I made my sales pitch to Speaker-elect McCarthy in December 2022 to reduce the population. He agreed. However, during those six painful days of waiting to get started on all the investigations and accountability that we promised the American people we would deliver, many side deals with the Speaker's holdouts were being made, unbeknownst to me. Most of those deals involved obtaining a spot on the Oversight Committee.

I ended up with twenty-six Republicans and would later learn that I would get twenty-one Democrats. That was a whopping twelve more members than the lower limit I was promised.*

This in turn meant that my five-hour hearings would now be six and a half hours long. Sigh. I did not know it at the time, but that

---

* The six extra members whom I received without any prior knowledge or my own vetting were Lauren Boebert, Tim Burchett, Anna Paulina Luna, and Eric Burlison, who all were holdouts on Kevin McCarthy for Speaker, as well as Mike Turner and Kelly Armstrong, who were close to McCarthy.

development was a sign of many things to come for our conference over the next year and a half. Deals would change at the last minute due to threats from the farthest-right members, and no matter how meticulously things might be worked out, it seemed nothing would ever go according to plan.

All six of my surprise Republican committee additions proved to be productive at times, but unfortunately often disruptive in others. I lost count of the number of committee hearings I had where Lauren Boebert and MTG tangled, or where Anna Paulina Luna made some crazy non-germane motion, or where a combination of the three got into a heated exchange with several of the female Oversight Democratic members like AOC, Jasmine Crockett, or Rashida Tlaib over ridiculous things ranging from fake eyelashes to butch bodies to fat butts (yes, they really did disparage each other that bad much like some middle school female drama).

In the end, I worked with all of the six surprise additions to my committee in some form or fashion. However, as a result of how those six were added to the committee without my knowledge or consent, I was very gun-shy about making future deals with Speaker McCarthy or his staff.

## JOE BIDEN'S WEAPONIZED FEDERAL GOVERNMENT

MY NORMAL SCHEDULE was often full of meetings with private sector executives who were being harassed by nearly every agency in the Biden administration—and, believe me, there are a *lot* of federal agencies. Part of my platform as chairman was to get the government off the backs of the private sector job creators. These are the people who captain the companies and enterprises that enable the rest of us to work hard, pay taxes, and keep our economy humming. I often sent letters to government agency heads and specific bureaucrats who unjustly targeted different industries—and in some cases specific businesses within those industries—to demand explanations for the often questionable tactics they employed.

The Deep State had greatly expanded under Joe Biden, and that meant unelected bureaucrats were interpreting laws and court cases in an extreme left-wing manner. These bureaucrats, empowered as never before under Biden, essentially served as the judge, jury, and jailer in all things related to regulations and compliance. I was happy to assist private industry when I felt they were wronged, but I always tried to avoid wading into their disagreements with other private entities. The one exception was the clandestine effort to shut down a private conservative news network in which Joe Biden's Deep State actors secretly encouraged the censorship from behind the scenes.

After some preliminary research, I agreed to sit down with Chris Ruddy, the CEO and majority owner of Newsmax Media. Newsmax and One America News Network (OANN) were popular conservative cable TV networks that were being deplatformed by various cable providers and by the gigantic DirecTV multichannel video programming distributor. DirecTV is owned by AT&T, and they had recently pulled both conservative networks from their entire platforms. I believed this was done in coordination with left-wing pressure groups that were ultimately puppets of the Biden administration. This administration, like few before, had a love affair with press censorship. And what they seemed to want more than life itself was to silence fast-growing conservative alternatives to the dishonest liberal mainstream media. I was not pleased that this was happening at the very beginning of the Biden influence-peddling investigation. Proper messaging was going to be essential as I moved forward and faced the inevitable obstacles lying in wait.

Days after meeting with Chris Ruddy, I had a meeting with the Washington lobbyists for DirecTV. They were very professional.

They knew I was not happy with what many conservatives viewed as another form of conservative censorship, much like what Facebook and Twitter had been engaged in for years. After a few weeks of "tough love" negotiations between myself and DirecTV—I threatened to subpoena their executives and drag them in front of the House Oversight Committee for a full committee hearing—DirecTV announced a new distribution agreement that restored Newsmax to the programming lineup for all of their satellite TV customers. This was not only an early win for me as a new chair, but also underlined for me a truth that two previous Oversight chairs—Jason Chaffetz and Darrell Issa—had shared with me about the job. Nobody wants their dirty laundry aired. The threat of a subpoena is often better than the actual subpoena.

## PARLIAMENTARY OUTPATIENT SURGERY

THE HOUSE GOP Leadership Conference was held in Jacksonville, Florida, on January 21 to 22, 2023. This was where Speaker McCarthy, Majority Leader Steve Scalise, Conference Chair Elise Stefanik, and Majority Whip Tom Emmer would join all of the brand-new committee chairs to discuss legislative goals and set timelines to accomplish those goals over the next two years. I felt like the rest of Congress was finally ready to do the things that we promised the American voters during the midterm elections.*

---

* The conference served as a much-needed team-building moment for the newly elected leaders of the 118th Congress majority, and we agreed to a very aggressive legislative agenda. Yet for a bill to become a law, it must pass both the House and the Senate in the exact same written form and then be signed into law by the president. We knew well that the U.S. Senate, controlled by the Democrats, would go along with little if anything that we passed out of the House. The president was a Democrat and the Senate was controlled by Democrats (along with at least six Republicans who meet the definition of being a RINO—Republican In Name Only). That gave the Democrats a two-thirds advantage. Nevertheless, we would push forward our conservative agenda

Immediately following the leadership conference in Jacksonville, we had the full House Republican Planning Conference down the road in Amelia Island. All 222 members were asked to attend. Overall, this went exceptionally well and the hard feelings from the first week seemed to subside. One red flag for me did emerge. It was a worry that would only grow throughout the in-

---

and try to negotiate what we could with the Senate when we faced what are commonly referred to as "must pass" bills. Those bills would include items like the National Defense Authorization Act (NDAA) and Water Resources Development Act (WRDA) or the annual spending bills, to name a few.

Our agenda included several major policy objectives for committees.

- Appropriations—twelve individual appropriations bills like Congress is supposed to do
- Ways and Means—major tax reform legislation
- Energy and Commerce—energy reform, social media reform, and medical billing reform
- Financial Services—cryptocurrency reform
- Homeland Security—border security
- Judiciary—FISA (Foreign Intelligence Surveillance Act) and patent reforms and immigration
- Agriculture—Farm Bill to be completed by September 20, 2023
- Oversight—provide oversight of every major cabinet and investigate Biden influence peddling

With respect to Oversight, not one time was the word *impeachment* spoken. The House Democrats had been in charge of Oversight for the first two years of the Biden administration and had not provided one ounce of actual executive branch oversight. Deep State bureaucrats were running the show without any accountability. That needed to change. Oversight also had a large policy jurisdiction. This included areas like the federal workforce (which still had not returned to the office after COVID), the U.S. Postal Service, cybersecurity, and Washington, DC. I pledged to everyone in attendance that a bold policy legislative agenda—in addition to our very aggressive investigative agenda—would flow through the Oversight Committee. At the end of the 118th Congress, we had passed an exemplary number of bills and much quality legislation through the committee. Unfortunately, many other congressional committees were gross underachievers. I put this down to several factors. We experienced wild swings in leadership. We were often stuck with the firebrands' refusal to agree to any compromise needed to obtain the required 218 votes for a bill's passage. And sometimes the committee itself was torn with needless contention.

vestigation. This was the creation of many new oversight subcommittees within various standing committees.

In part, this was understandable. Our House Republicans' Commitment to America revolved around providing much-needed oversight and accountability to the unchecked Biden administration. Kevin McCarthy had made a bargain with several conservative firebrands to grant them more oversight authority. He promised them gavels as chairs of second- and third-tier subcommittees within most of the House standing committees. This was much in keeping with the way the Democrats in the previous Congress had created "civil rights subcommittees" to impose their awful, race-baiting diversity, equity, and inclusion (DEI) initiatives on every executive cabinet and every piece of liberal legislation they passed.

Many of these soon-to-be-announced subcommittee chairs planned to use their newfound authority to subpoena every wild conspiracy theory, from proving Michelle Obama was really a man to finding out if the government was hiding the existence of UFOs! The realization that we had a turf battle on our hands emerged when Jim Jordan and I presented at the conference.

Jordan and I led a session titled "Oversight and Accountability" where we went over in detail the areas in which he and I would lead. The Oversight Committee would take up the Biden financial crimes trail while the Judiciary Committee would investigate the Department of Justice's illegal involvement in the same. McCarthy's newly appointed COVID Select Committee would investigate all things related to Dr. Anthony Fauci's antics, and the new Select Committee on the Weaponization of Government would investigate the cover-ups of previous investigations of Biden shenanigans, as well as the clearly forming battle plan of the administration to use lawfare and legal attacks to nullify Joe Biden's political nemesis, Donald Trump. We also indicated that the House

Administration Committee, led by Bryan Steil, would be the place for matters pertaining to election fraud or the ongoing January 6th excesses and politically motivated oppression carried out by the executive branch.

## FIREBRAND SHOCK

AFTER OUR PRESENTATION, I could see the shock, confusion, and disappointment in some of the firebrands' eyes. I would learn in the days ahead that many of them had been under the impression that *they* would be leading hearings on controversial issues ranging from the stolen 2020 election to the COVID vaccines. They expected to bring in controversial figures such as Rudy Giuliani or Sidney Powell to discuss election fraud, or call for testimony from the most controversial critics in the healthcare world on vaccine concerns.

I would be approached time and again by many of these subcommittee chairs who would tell me that this or that issue that my Oversight Committee was probing was one they were in fact investigating too, so I should give them the lead. I would tell them to take it up with McCarthy. I believed that many of my disgruntled colleagues had either been misled or had just plain misunderstood the roles of each full committee and each subcommittee. Furthermore, I think their displeasure powered several of the mainstream media's hit pieces on me, the Oversight Committee, and our investigation.

Perhaps this misunderstanding was the fault of the firebrands, or perhaps it was a communication breakdown with leadership, but whatever the case, it was an unnecessary problem. Many of my colleagues who were under the impression they would be the next "Trey Gowdy in Benghazi" did not have subpoena authority or a staff larger than one person—and their staffer was often not an attorney. To issue successful subpoenas takes writing numerous legal letters requesting extremely detailed and particular information. Everything has to be perfect and accurate or else the whole thing will be dismissed in court. The information requested, after all, would come from cabinet secretaries and law enforcement agencies with huge legal teams of their own—legal teams that had the sole purpose of obstructing and denying any Republican requests. Any investigatory matter not done to the highest legal standards would simply die after a day or so, leaving only a trail of retweets on Twitter and a few thousand dollars in online fundraising. In other words, it would be for show.

The House Oversight Committee had seventy employees, most of whom were attorneys. We were committed to getting results, and we did. One reason the mainstream media grossly underestimated our ability to obtain the Biden family bank records and successfully haul the family and their associates in for depositions was that they assumed I would run the committee for show and self-promotion. Not so. But unfortunately for me, accurately obtaining facts and proving criminality that leads to real accountability takes time.

## ELON MUSK STOPS BY

BACK IN WASHINGTON during the last week in January, I participated in a fascinating meeting. Speaker McCarthy, Leader Scalise, Jim Jordan, Cathy McMorris Rodgers, and I met with Elon Musk. Musk and McCarthy were old friends from California. Musk was seemingly front and center in the news every day for fascinating issues ranging from humans landing on Mars to the world's only electric vehicle that was successful with consumers, to social media liability reform—and all three issues were likewise at the top of the legislative agenda in Congress. Musk had our undivided attention and I confess I found myself mesmerized by his vast knowledge and experience in some of the most fascinating subjects in the world. Elon Musk was definitely the most interesting person with whom I have ever had a conversation.

My first six years in Congress I was what I often referred to as a "backbencher," a member with little influence and no name identification outside Kentucky. I knew that had changed when I introduced myself to Elon Musk and he said that he had watched several of my television interviews and wanted to discuss my upcoming investigation. Musk remained interested in the investigation and would occasionally retweet some of my tweets, and comment on others.

Elon Musk had just purchased Twitter (which he would later rename as X) and had released the damning Twitter Files through quality journalists like Matt Taibbi. The Twitter Files were documents that proved beyond a doubt that the federal government was coordinating with a social media company (and presumably others) to censure conservative speech. They also provided the first evidence that the FBI had a full team dedicated to nothing but trolling conservatives and then contacting Twitter to either censor the tweet or deplatform the entire account. This was government overreach at its worst. It was exactly what many former Republicans in Congress from Devin Nunes to Jason Chaffetz had accurately labeled as Deep State involvement. It was direct evidence that our federal government had been weaponized, and that the U.S. government itself was at war with conservatives and their ideas.

Elon Musk is not only a genius, he's a patriot. He provided the evidence that every conservative, Fox News–watching American knew to be true, that the government was violating the First Amendment to the Constitution, which guarantees the right to free speech. Prior to purchasing Twitter, Musk was beloved by the liberal mainstream media because his electric cars and scientific achievements seemed to benefit progressives. The media loved Musk's other companies, such as Tesla, which was the leader in electric vehicles (EVs), and SpaceX, a leader in commercial spaceflight. But when Musk bought Twitter and revealed the media's direct coordination with the Deep State and social media companies to indoctrinate unknowing Americans with liberal propaganda, the mainstream media turned on Musk like a pack of seriously displeased spider monkeys. Now for the mainstream media Musk was the second-worst person in the world—next to Donald Trump. For that reason, along with his brilliant mind and many accomplishments, Musk was someone I liked and wanted to work with.

Elon Musk encouraged Jordan and me to hold a hearing with the former Twitter executives to get them on record concerning the illegal and highly unethical behavior our own federal government had engaged in by censoring conservatives and spreading unscientific government-endorsed propaganda about COVID as well as flogging the hoax that was Trump-Russia collusion. I told Musk that we would definitely have one of our first Oversight Committee hearings with the exact witnesses he mentioned. One of my goals for that hearing would be to prove to the world that Hunter Biden's laptop was not Russian disinformation, as the fifty Democratic intelligence community apparatchiks had falsely claimed. It was a claim the corrupt media had originally taken as the absolute truth, so terrified were they that their man might be felled by an "October Surprise," upsetting their carefully orchestrated 2020 election effort.[3]

Musk applauded my plans and said there was evidence that government played a direct role in getting Twitter to censure the *New York Post* story that had accurately reported the evidence of criminal influence peddling laced throughout the hard drive of Hunter Biden's porn-laden laptop. At that moment, the first Biden influence-peddling investigation committee hearing was born.

# Chapter 9

## BLUEPRINT FOR A DEBACLE

On the Sunday night before returning to Congress after the long August recess, I received a call from Speaker McCarthy. He told me that he had decided that I was going to move forward in the investigation to the impeachment inquiry phase. Not having any advance notice and not knowing exactly what that entailed, I simply replied, "Okay."

McCarthy then detailed how he wanted the inquiry structured. He said that I would lead, as chairman of the Oversight Committee, but that Jim Jordan and the Judiciary Committee, as well as Jason Smith and his Ways and Means Committee, would all be equal partners.

"You mean that three committees with over one hundred members are going to be in charge of the same investigation? Who will staff it?" I asked, stunned at the idea of the massive coordination involved.

McCarthy told me to work that out with Jordan and Smith, but that I was the boss.

### "DON'T WORRY, THEY WILL SUPPORT IT"

I WAS, TO put it mildly, not as confident as the Speaker about the potential success of that arrangement, but I told him I would do what he asked. That's how Congress is supposed to work, after all.

I did point out that I doubted the staffs would get along at first. I loved and respected Jim Jordan. What's more, I often needed to call on his vast experience, his tremendous skill set, and his credibility with the conservative media.

Jordan's staff on Judiciary was another thing.

I personally liked them. I knew they were smart. But they had a vastly different communications style and were notorious leakers to their preferred conservative outlets.

I certainly respect Jason Smith, but why bring in Ways and Means? What the heck was the purpose of that?

Plus, there was the messaging disconnect. I had gone to great lengths over the past ten months to emphasize that my role was to *investigate*, not impeach.

I did not want to get people's hopes up. No American president has ever been removed from office directly by an impeachment conviction. Neither Andrew Johnson, Richard Nixon, Bill Clinton, nor Donald Trump. Impeachment was the end of the line. The Senate had to convict. And this Senate was never going to do that. Even Republican Senate leaders such as Mitch McConnell and John Thune had already stated they did not favor impeaching Biden.

A conviction and removal was never going to happen.

What's more, I knew that once the news broke that we were proceeding to an impeachment inquiry, the mainstream media would go apoplectic.

Finally, it was quite possible, maybe even likely, that such a move would doom my Oversight investigation.

McCarthy said the vote would take place during the last week in September. That would give me only two full weeks to get 218 votes lined up to pass anything—a resolution, an authorization—through the House. There were at least a dozen House Republicans who were more than hesitant about voting to impeach. They didn't want to do it.

McCarthy was confident we would have the votes.

How could he be so sure? He had a plan. He was going to insert the language implementing the impeachment inquiry into a short-term budgetary continuing resolution.

This should split the difference between the hard-liners and the squishy moderates. The Freedom Caucus members would get their Joe Biden impeachment. The moderates, who were mainly Republican because they were fiscal conservatives, would get a spending bill that did not shut down the government.

A government shutdown scares every senior citizen into thinking they will not get their monthly Social Security check. It infuriates every veteran who worries their VA benefits will be disrupted.

When Trump was president, he let then-representative Mark Meadows talk him into a government shutdown, but after a few days of nothing but grief from most Americans, Trump himself reopened the government.

I was shocked at McCarthy's strategy, because I knew that not only would Matt Gaetz, Bob Good, and their followers never buy into it, but in fact they would use McCarthy's plan against him with their base.

The Speaker confidently brushed off my concerns and simply said, "They will support it."

## LET'S PLAY BALL

THE FOLLOWING MONDAY, I called my two chiefs of staff, Mark Marin with Oversight and Caroline Cash with my congressional office. We agreed to put our heads together and try somehow to make lemonade out of a bunch of rotten lemons.

The next day was the long-awaited return to Washington by all the members of the U.S. House of Representatives. Prior to boarding my plane in Louisville, I received a phone call from Speaker

McCarthy. He told me he had *changed his mind* from two days ago. We would not put impeachment inquiry language in a continuing resolution. Instead, he decided that he was just going to announce the inquiry at his noon press conference.

I looked at the time and quickly responded, "But that is in *one hour*!"

"Don't worry," McCarthy replied. "I'll handle it. It will be fine."

But I *was* worried because I knew that it would not be well received by my members or the press, and I had never even spoken to Jordan or Smith about a framework. *That* meeting was scheduled to take place later in the week.

Before ending the call and heading to his press conference, McCarthy repeated a phrase that had been a theme of his tenure as Speaker.

"We will worry about that later!"

I genuinely liked Kevin McCarthy, and really believe that he was the best person to lead our very challenging conference. However, he often made important decisions with a very short-term goal of "fighting to live another day."

The problem with that philosophy is that if you don't win every battle, you lose the war.

All I could think about on my flight from Louisville to Washington was how difficult my oversight investigation was going to be moving forward. I doubted we had the votes to formalize the impeachment inquiry. Biden's lead counsel, Abbe Lowell, would be grinning from ear to ear because he could simply send a paralegal intern to court to get our subpoenas kicked out for being part of an "illegitimate" impeachment inquiry. Most of all, the media narrative would shift from "investigation" to "impeachment" and it would be difficult if not impossible to direct it back.

The only reason in the world for Kevin McCarthy to make such a drastic change on the spur of the moment to what was a very successful and historical investigation was that he was in a pissing match with the right-wing flank of our Republican conference led by Matt Gaetz.

## FACING THE VULTURES AND CROWS

ONCE I LANDED and walked up the steps of the Capitol, the Washington, DC, press corps were waiting for me like a bunch of hungry buzzards in the desert flying in circles over a wounded animal.

They surrounded me, and I had a sea of microphones and recorders in my face. They were unusually happy and cordial to me too, which creeped me out. They obviously smelled blood.

The press was happy on several fronts. First, they believed this would be the end of my Biden influence-peddling investigation—which they secretly considered a public relations success for their enemy, the hated Republicans. Second, anyone with any sense already knew the Bidens were dirty (I mean, even Bob Woodward, no friend to Republicans, knew it). Believe me, public relations (the narrative) is *all* the mainstream press corps cares about. Truth is a concept foreign to their ilk.

Finally, they couldn't wait to cover a nasty Republican feeding frenzy.

## THE DEEP STATE ARCHIVIST

AFTER WE RETURNED from the recess, one of the important meetings I had pertaining to the investigation was with Colleen Shogan, the new head archivist of the U.S. National Archives and Records Administration (NARA). The Oversight Committee has legislative jurisdiction over NARA. In my previous six years in Congress, NARA was one of the many little-known government agencies that either responded to an annual committee request or made a crosstown trek to testify briefly in front of an Oversight subcommittee. NARA was just another sleepy government agency until two major events in late 2022 changed everything: the FBI raid of Donald Trump's Mar-a-Lago property in Palm Beach, Florida, and my formal announcement of the Biden influence-peddling investigation.

After seven months of seemingly peaceful negotiations between representatives of NARA and former president Trump's legal team over who legally owned a stash of documents from the previous administration, and whether Trump had declassified some of the classified documents in his possession while he was president (as he had the authority to do), the FBI implemented an unprecedented raid on the former president's home in Palm Beach to retrieve the documents. Unsurprisingly, certain mainstream media outlets somehow knew in advance of the raid and were already set up to record it live. The search warrant was authorized by Biden's attorney general, Merrick Garland. The warrant was granted as a result of a criminal referral by NARA.

That meant NARA had gone political and thrown in its lot with the Deep State.

Immediately following the August 8, 2022, FBI action, I requested a great deal of information from NARA pertaining to the raid. They said that they would comply with the chairman of the Oversight Committee, who at the time was a Democrat.

Two months later, the Republicans won the midterm elections and I was determined to hold them to their word.

Meanwhile, Merrick Garland opened a DOJ investigation of Donald Trump's role in both the mishandling of government records and the January 6, 2021, attack on the U.S. Capitol. He named Jack Smith as special counsel.

I have always been against the appointment of special counsels and special prosecutors. They never work out the way they are intended, and they *always* extend their investigations beyond the initial scope, sucking up tons of taxpayer money in the process. But, more importantly, *special counsels and special prosecutors are not subject to congressional oversight. There are no checks and balances.*

Merrick Garland knew this, which is one reason he appointed Smith. The appointment of the special counsel blocked my ability to obtain the information I requested from NARA about the raid on Mar-a-Lago. With the stroke of a pen, Attorney General Garland obstructed a legitimate investigation of mine for the first time. It would be only the first of many such examples of obstruction over my upcoming two years as chairman.

Smith's appointment also set a precedent for what the DOJ would do when a president mishandled classified documents. Little could he or I have known that in a few months, I would discover during my Biden influence-peddling investigation that Joe Biden also mishandled classified documents. History will show that Garland destroyed the reputation of the Department of Justice in the exact same way Adam Schiff did irreparable damage to congressional investigations.

With several of my top Oversight staff legal team by my side, I explained to Shogan exactly why I needed to know exactly which classified documents Joe Biden had in his possession. She was very nice and undoubtedly intelligent, but to be America's newest historian, she knew very little about the investigation (a sure sign that she got her news from the *Washington Post*, MSNBC, or some other useless liberal outlet). I explained to her that several Bidens had mysteriously received tens of millions of dollars from foreign nationals in rogue countries around the world, and we feared that the president's son not only had access to the classified documents but also may have shared some of them with certain foreign oligarchs.

Shogan was polite, but she made sure that I knew that her hands were tied as a result of Garland appointing Robert Hur as special counsel to investigate Biden's mishandling of classified documents. It was the classic Deep State mentality. For these bureaucrats, Congress is just a pothole to avoid along the road to business as usual.

They know they can snub their noses at us because they usually get away with it.

## WITNESS FOR THE PROSECUTION

AFTER THE MCCARTHY surprise announcement of the hurry-up impeachment inquiry, I had been working closely with our Republican whip, Tom Emmer, to find enough votes. By mid-September at least ten Republicans would not commit to voting yes on the House floor. Since I could only lose three, I had work to do. We had dozens of quality witnesses who would testify under oath that Oversight had enough evidence to investigate. But to impeach?

One huge problem kept arising with each and every prospective witness: nobody wanted to go in front of the Democrat goons on Oversight to be heckled and derided on national TV.

People had seen clips from previous hearings, most recently of the IRS whistleblowers where Dan Goldman, Jared Moskowitz, Jamie Raskin, and their middle row of hoodlums spat vitriol. They also knew that after the media would inevitably distort their testimony, they would be harassed by demented liberals on social media. After many unsuccessful attempts, I finally nailed down the first witness.

Legal scholar Jonathan Turley, a well-known middle-right-leaning professor at George Washington University Law School, agreed to be a witness. I messaged Speaker McCarthy's team that we had one witness down and two more to go.

After many unsuccessful attempts to settle on who these would be, the Speaker's office called to say that they had nailed down two more witnesses.

We were set to go, and we needed to move quickly to make McCarthy's deadline.

Our two other witnesses were Eileen O'Connor and Bruce Dubinsky. The Democrats' stalking-horse witness was Michael Gerhardt, a liberal law professor at the University of North Carolina.

O'Connor was a former U.S. attorney in the DOJ's Tax Fraud Division. Dubinsky was the founder of Dubinsky Consulting and is a world-class forensic accountant. The next few days, my Oversight staff worked frantically to produce the committee guidance and brief the witnesses on what would inevitably be a barrage of hostile attacks from the Democrats. This committee hearing was going to be televised live on every major network.

And I still needed to somehow wrangle another eight Republican votes.

On September 28, 2023, I gaveled in the Oversight hearing. After opening statements, I swore in the witnesses and asked Turley to deliver his five-minute opening statement. Boy was it a doozy. Midway through, he seemed to pause, then headed off on a tangent for which none of us—members, staff, anybody—were prepared.

> It is important to emphasize what this hearing is not. It is not a hearing on articles of impeachment. The House has launched an impeachment inquiry, and I am appearing to discuss the history and purpose of such inquiries. I have previously stated that, while I believe that an impeachment inquiry is warranted, *I do not believe that the evidence currently meets the standard of a high crime and misdemeanor needed for an article of impeachment.* The purpose of my testimony today is to discuss how past inquiries pursued evidence of potentially impeachable conduct.[1]

If a nurse could have taken my blood pressure at the moment Turley volunteered his oh-so-scholarly opinion, I would no doubt have been on the next ambulance to the closest critical care facility.

As it was, I went numb and all sound seemed to be blurred. To my left, my Republican members were staring at me in utter confusion and anger, and to my right the Democrats were fist-bumping and grinning from ear to ear.

I think I mumbled something like "Oh, my Lord."

I peeked at the media in the back of the hearing room, and they were tweeting like a pack of hyenas smelling the blood of an injured water buffalo.

This was all my fault. Turley was *my witness.*

I have tried to understand Jonathan Turley's motives since then. On one hand, the purpose of the hearing was to prove the need to move to an impeachment inquiry, and he did state that we had met that threshold. Had someone in House leadership told Turley to emphasize that we were not impeaching Joe Biden at this time, but merely moving to the next phase, in order to ease the concerns of the moderate members who were still undecided on the upcoming floor vote? Did Turley not know that his opening statement could destroy a whole year's worth of careful work by countless individuals documenting the obvious unscrupulousness of the Biden family?

Turley has since written a number of spot-on op-eds and tweets about Biden wrongdoing. He has also given hundreds of interviews about their potential crimes, and the overwhelming evidence that Oversight uncovered that merits further review. Jonathan Turley is a much better tweeter and interviewer than he was a testifier!

But in that moment I knew I didn't have the votes. This proceeding would fail.

Which also meant that Kevin McCarthy's political doom was sealed.

Of course, I was also in deep trouble. In an instant, I had gone from the House investigative golden boy to the toxic goofball chairman of a clown-car hearing. The media hits over the course of the next seven days were vicious. Whereas before the hearing I would be asked on a near-daily basis by some House colleague or some Republican Party official somewhere in America to speak at an event, in the days following the hearing my requests went dark. That old saying I learned as a young man when entering politics in Kentucky came back to haunt me: if you want a friend in politics, then get a dog.

# Chapter 10

## TEN PERCENT FOR THE BIG GUY

October 3, 2023, turned out to be a historic day in Congress. On that day, Matt Gaetz led seven other Republicans (three of whom were members of Oversight) along with all 208 Democrats in passing the motion to vacate the chair, an action that instantly created a vacancy in the position that was second in line to the presidency, behind the vice president. Kevin McCarthy, who had worked so hard to do all the difficult and time-consuming things to lead the effort to flip the House from Democrat to Republican, was officially out.

This critical moment had been building within our caucus ever since an ill-fated conference call in August wherein McCarthy announced that we would be going forward with a continuing resolution (CR) for the U.S. budget. Now it was October, and we'd actually passed the CR. Everyone in Congress knew that the rebels might pull the trigger, but few thought it would happen.

After the initial shock of the successful parliamentary motion, everyone quickly realized that those leading the coup had no strategy. In fact, they had had only one plan—fire Kevin McCarthy—and now we were all marinating in the aftermath.

McCarthy is an experienced political strategist. You do not remain in politics that long and climb that high over that many years without being smart and savvy. He knew that Gaetz was going to make the motion. Gaetz had been threatening it to the aggressively right-leaning base for weeks. McCarthy had even gone so far as to publicly dare Gaetz to go for it.

I knew McCarthy believed he had a plan to defeat the motion. But he made two huge miscalculations. First, he assumed that there would be fewer than five Republican votes for Gaetz's motion, and second, he assumed that if more Republicans on the assertive right did in fact vote to remove McCarthy, then Nancy Pelosi would honor a promise she had made McCarthy at the beginning of the conference and assist him in retaining the speakership in order to protect the integrity of the institution.

I wish that Kevin had asked me my opinion of his backup plan prior to relying on that because I would have told him (1) no, you'd better assume a dozen no votes and (2) you cannot believe one thing that Pelosi promises.

I was beyond furious myself. I'd been caught in the pissing contest between Gaetz and McCarthy for months, and it had a very negative effect on my investigation.

To make matters worse, immediately after the passage on the floor, Patrick McHenry—who was the Speaker pro tem and became the acting Speaker until a new one was selected—called for a Republican conference meeting and after explaining that nobody knew exactly what the rules were after this unprecedented parliamentary stunt, he had decided to send everyone home for several days so he could figure out what steps to take next.

Upon hearing this decision, my immediate thought was, There really is no backup plan. What about my investigation?

Conservatives cheering this on at home knew this put a temporary stop to any bills the Democrats wanted passed. They may not have realized that this also put a stop to the investigations they wanted.

The Speaker's counsel, a staff position, represented me in court on any disputed subpoenas. I had a bunch of important subpoenas out. Would I have nobody at all to represent them? How long before Hunter Biden's attorney Abbe Lowell—who bears a striking resemblance to the wily Saul Goodman of *Breaking Bad* and *Better Call Saul* in more ways than mere looks—figured this out and moved to dismiss all my subpoenas and requests?

McHenry's decision was met with boos and moans, but he was correct in bringing into focus the obvious fact that we could not just elect someone to be second in line to the presidency without a serious campaign. GOP conference rules stated that everyone must be given three days' notice before voting on anything.

I sat, stunned, in the conference room as everyone slowly filed out. I could not understand how we could have that many people make that big a mistake. I wondered how long it would take to elect a new Speaker. Surely, we'd do that soon.

As confused and upset as I was, I never in my wildest dreams would have imagined that it would take three long and painful weeks to elect the next Speaker. And if you had given me twenty guesses as to who that eventual Speaker would be, I would have not guessed correctly.

## GLEEFUL MEDIA

THE MEDIA HAD a field day. Two hundred and eight Democrats (100 percent of their conference) joined with just eight Republicans (which was only 3.6 percent of our conference) to vacate the chair. Sadly, many in the conservative media praised the move. I thought this was rich, considering that they themselves often trashed moderates like Mitt Romney and Susan Collins in the Senate and Don Bacon and Mike Lawler in the House for joining Democrats to pass bills. Now that some of their own had foolishly teamed up with the "Devil Incarnate," all I heard were crickets.*

Over the next three weeks, our conference struggled to elect a replacement for Kevin McCarthy.[1] Steve Scalise was the first to try for a few days. Steve would have made an excellent Speaker, and I proudly supported him. Unfortunately, Steve could never get the required 218 votes. Next up was Jim Jordan, whom I often refer to as the GOAT (greatest of all time). Jim was the overwhelming favorite of the conservative base. He tried for over a week to gather support but failed several times to reach the necessary vote total on the House floor. The next guy up was Tom Emmer. He also failed. I believe that Tom would have been an effective Speaker.

After a grueling and very embarrassing three weeks of failed efforts, Mike Johnson just happened to be in the right place at the right time.[2]

## CRUCIAL LOST TIME FOR THE INVESTIGATION

THROUGHOUT THE INVESTIGATION there were many highs and lows. The highs came around when my team discovered new evidence of wrongdoing. The lows would occur when the media grossly mischaracterized something I did or simply printed a downright false and malicious hit piece on me, or my family and my friends, for the sole purpose of intimidation. But the three weeks we wasted

---

* The entire basis for the motion to vacate was that McCarthy had been forced to work with Democrats to pass a spending bill (albeit a continuing resolution) in order to prevent a government shutdown. Matt Gaetz, Bob Good, Andy Biggs, Eli Crane, Nancy Mace, Ken Buck, Matt Rosendale, and Tim Burchett joined with Cori Bush, Rashida Tlaib, Ilhan Omar, Nancy Pelosi, Jamie Raskin, Adam Schiff, Alexandria Ocasio-Cortez, Maxine Waters, and every other liberal Democrat in Congress to create chaos in the Republican majority. At the very least, I did not think that should have been celebrated by any Republican or any conservative-leaning outlet.

trying to elect a new Speaker was the lowest of the lows. Although I repeatedly told the media that my investigation was full speed ahead, the truth was that I was paralyzed.

The rules stated that the Speaker had to sign off on my subpoenas. Since we did not have a Speaker, I could not issue any. Also, since I had several subpoenas outstanding and tons of information requested, I feared every second that Biden lawyers would take me to court and get everything thrown out on some technicality I had no representation to oppose—maybe even the technicality of not having a functioning House of Representatives!

The stress and worry were overwhelming. The reality that the recent three weeks without a Speaker, combined with the wasted month of January 2023 when we struggled to get Kevin McCarthy as Speaker and get organized, cost the Biden influence-peddling investigation seven valuable weeks. Since I was in a race against the clock of a two-year congressional term, as well as the upcoming presidential election, those lost seven weeks could be devastating.

But there was good news too, during these depressing days. We continued to analyze the bank records we'd received. It was so clear what the Bidens were doing, but we wanted a smoking gun, something so obvious it couldn't be spun away to oblivion by our Democrat-loving press.

In November, my staff found something.

## THE INEVITABLE PARTISAN PRESS REACTION

I WAS WORRIED that the White House and/or the Biden legal team would have found the $40,000 from James Biden to Joe Biden too, and they would be ready with an explanation that sounded plausible, but was so much horse hockey. Jamie Raskin, who couldn't help himself, always acted as if he were a key part of the Biden legal team, even though he was about as mentally high-powered as a 10-

watt refrigerator bulb. But I always assumed that he shared any and all documents with his masters at the White House. It would be exactly like Raskin to, say, leave documents in a trash can beside a park bench and then some errand boy would come along and pick them up, and they would finally miraculously end up in the Biden lawyers' possession. Plausible deniability.

My fears turned out to be justified. The mainstream media were ready for the revelation of the check.

They had been pre-warned from the White House war room that the check existed, and that it was "simply a loan repayment."

Even though I disclosed the perfectly clear evidence in bank records that traced the money from China to Joe Biden's back pocket, and even though the media never saw any payment directly from Joe Biden to Jim Biden that could have served as a loan, "No, no, no!" the corrupt mockingbird media cackled.

It was a loan repayment. Said so right there on the check, after all.

They knew, as every adult American human with a bank account knows, that you can write whatever you like on a check memo line. You can write something meaningless like "elephant," "Brooklyn Bridge," whatever. Or you can write something misleading or that's a flat-out lie, such as "loan repayment." It's a space for your use, not the bank's.

The one goalpost that the media had set was that I had to find a direct payment to Joe Biden from a foreign or corrupt entity. I never accepted such a goal as necessary, but now we had done something close to that. We'd found a $40,000 payment through one of the LLCs.

So the media moved the goalpost.

There was hardly any money in Jim and Sara Biden's account, then there was a cash infusion, then the money went out to Joe.

Nevertheless, the establishment media decided that my discovery did not count. I am pretty sure that if the roles had been reversed and the same scenario were in place for Donald Trump, the media would have demanded to see an earlier deposit from Trump to prove that this was indeed a loan repayment.

Of course, such rules do not apply to Bidens.

## "MADE IN CHINA" STAMPED ON THE MONEY

THE TRUTH OF the payment to Joe Biden is this: it came, via a front company, from the coffers of the People's Republic of China.

It did not matter whether the $40,000 was actually a loan. What mattered was that the money that Jim Biden paid Joe Biden came from Jim Biden's cut of a $5 million wire transfer from China that was the direct result of Hunter Biden cutting a deal with a shady former CCP spy leader.

Without Hunter saying that his father was sitting beside him, Joe Biden would never have been paid that $40,000.

Even if we go along with the false media narrative that the $40,000 was a loan repayment, it's still true that Joe Biden never would have been paid back his $40,000 without the Chinese funds. Jim Biden did not have anywhere close to that in his account. In fact, Jim's personal bank account was overdrawn before he got the money from Hunter. Joe would have lost $40,000 were it not for the shady influence-peddling scheme with our nation's biggest enemy, China.

## A RESPITE, THEN BACK TO THE FRAY

I LEFT DC that week on a high note despite the media mischaracterization of what we'd found and presented.

I knew the average American had enough sense to see through the mainstream media's fake news. I traveled from DC to Key West, Florida, where I participated in a fundraiser and spoke to

GOP stalwarts. Everywhere I went in airports, restaurants, and hotels along the trip, people would come up to me to say thank you and that I should keep fighting.

In Key West I was surrounded by smart, successful people who knew the facts of the investigation. They also understood financial terms like *SARs* and *money laundering*, and they definitely understood the fundamental principle that if you get paid back for a loan, you had to first *make* the loan to begin with.

It was refreshing to see firsthand that smart people were not buying what the corrupt mainstream media were selling.

After dotting every *i* and crossing every *t* to armor up and win against the toughest competition imaginable in court, on November 8, 2023, I issued two major subpoenas. One was to Hunter Biden[3] and the other was for Jim Biden.[4] As was my right and duty as chairman, these subpoenas required them to come in to the United States House Oversight Committee for legal depositions as part of our investigation. Our cover letters made no bones about why we wanted to talk to these men. We suspected them of wrongdoing, and we laid out our reasons.

# Chapter 11

## REVELATIONS AND RECEIPTS

On November 15, joined by Jim Jordan, Jason Smith, and our committee staffs, I held my very first meeting with the new Speaker of the House, Mike Johnson. I knew that Mike was all in on the inquiry as a rank-and-file member of the House Judiciary Committee, but I was eager to learn his position now that he was the new Speaker.

Right out of the gate, Johnson declared that he supported a full impeachment of Joe Biden. He indicated that it was our constitutional responsibility to do so, because President Biden had clearly checked every judicial box for impeachment.

Mike, a scholarly fellow in appearance, asked Jim Jordan and me what our timeline was. Even though he looked at Jim while asking the question, I popped in and answered. I said that considering that you definitely want to impeach, and assuming that you will help us get the votes to pass a resolution to do so, I would like to wrap up within the next ninety days. I explained that Oversight had scheduled over a dozen important transcribed interviews and depositions with the key witnesses, and that once we wrapped them up and assuming we got the information we needed, I would issue a report with the many criminal referrals for members of the Biden family, including Joe Biden.

In that report, I would recommend impeachment and then hand it off to Jim and Judiciary for the formal impeachment phase.

Mike asked Jim for his thoughts on my plan. Jim in turn had several questions for Mike. The most pressing was about what exactly Marjorie Taylor Greene was doing with her newly filed privileged resolution to impeach Department of Homeland Security secretary Alejandro Mayorkas. MTG had become especially unruly during that time because she had been close to McCarthy and was *not* happy with the circumstances of McCarthy's ouster and Johnson's ascension. Mike told Jim that he'd spoken with MTG and assured her we were going to impeach Mayorkas first.

I was surprised. My first thought was, Wait, we are going to have *two* impeachments going on? That didn't seem legislatively possible, considering there were so many in our conference who did not want to vote on any controversial issues that they knew would never see the light of day in the Senate.

The ten-minute meeting wrapped up. It was a strategy setting huddle between leadership. I wondered if that was the first meeting of that level Mike Johnson had conducted since becoming Speaker. Mike is considered one of the smartest and most morally decent members of Congress, but before this he had never been in leadership of any type. He had never tried to push through a major bill, whip the needed votes to pass a bill, or endure the internal drama that accompanies every single bill that goes to the House floor for a vote. In any case, lots of calls were made in a very short period of time, which is exactly what I like in a meeting. I thought afterward, Wow, I never had this type of clarity from McCarthy. Mike might not be that bad after all!

Of course, Mike Johnson's position would later evolve on several conservative issues, ranging from reforming FISA to require warrants for American citizens, cutting funding for the FBI and other Deep State agencies, and ending foreign aid blank checks to countries like Ukraine. For some unknown reason, Johnson became much less interested in impeachment and much more interested in working with President Biden.

## ENTER SUGAR BROTHER

ON NOVEMBER 17, the news hit that Kevin Morris had loaned Hunter Biden over $6 million while Joe Biden was president. We waited three long weeks for John Solomon, editor in chief of Just The News, to finish corroborating and drop this bombshell evidence.

John had been shopping his big story with CBS News in order to gain wider press with the story, perhaps simultaneously breaking it with a mainstream network. But after weeks of negotiating, CBS refused to air it. They did not want any part of a story that depicted the president of the United States' only living son living lavishly off a big Democrat donor—a donor who also was paying his son's child support payments, his back taxes with the IRS, and his many legal defense fees. But of course, CBS was at the same time running story after story about Supreme Court justice Clarence Thomas supposedly accepting free or discounted fishing trips with a conservative donor.

CBS News was a prime and pathetic example of the current state of the corrupt mainstream media, wearing their clear bias against conservatives on their sleeves while constantly turning a blind eye toward the blatantly bad behavior of liberals.

With CBS out, Fox and Newsmax took Solomon's story and ran with it. The conservative newspaper and online outlets also printed great follow-up stories. But absolutely no mention of this egregious nonsense on the part of Hunter Biden was anywhere in the mainstream media. I asked one of the pathetic DC press corps reporters why they refused to run the story. They replied that they needed more evidence first, and then, since the whole matter did not include Joe, they really were not interested anyway.

It was the president's *son* being given millions by a donor to his father, Joe Biden!

Can you even imagine if the president in question had been Trump? We'd be in for months of "reporting," I can assure you.

As for more evidence, why not *ask Kevin Morris*! There's a journalistic task fit for the graduate of an Ivy League J-school, right?

Couldn't be bothered.

A few weeks later I did interview Morris. He admitted that everything John Solomon had first discovered about the unethical loan to Hunter Biden was in fact true.

## MOVING THE GOALPOSTS YET AGAIN

MY STRUGGLE WITH the mainstream media was never-ending. In the third week of November, *Politico* signaled that the White House had moved the goalposts a few miles for what would constitute a successful Biden corruption investigation. The DC press corps followed the leader. The First Fish in the school was whatever outlet happened to get an exclusive from the war room the White House had set up to attack and discredit me.

*Politico* got the dump on November 21 and declared that there was no "smoking gun" on Joe Biden. It was obvious that investigation would only be successful if he was impeached in the House and convicted in the Senate. Proof didn't matter. Since the Senate was not in the hands of Republicans, what was the point of all this rigmarole? they asked.

It did not matter that we had already proved that Joe's family was living it up on deals with our enemies to the tune of tens of millions of dollars. No, *Politico* stated that the only possible smoking gun would be a direct payment to Joe (which apparently the Biden legal team had assured the White House legal team had never happened) with a subject line something like "People's Republic of

China bribe payment for supporting Chinese demand for airline overflight registration in the East China Sea," or some such.

As bad as the press was over the first ten months of the investigation, the one saving grace for me was viewing the polling data as it accumulated. During presidential years the amount of polling done is ridiculous. Since the investigation was one of the biggest political stories all year, most pollsters would include some type of question about it. Polls were averaging out at 60 percent of Americans thinking the Bidens did something either unethical or illegal. And that was with 100 percent of the corrupt mainstream media trumpeting daily that I had no evidence, there was no smoking gun, etc. Couple this with the fact that Congress as a whole had a dismal 17 percent approval rating, and 60 percent looked pretty darn good. I will always wonder what the polls would have read if the media gave the investigation one ounce of fair coverage. Regardless, despite losing every day to the corrupt mainstream media, I was winning with the American people.

## THE CATHAY CONNECTION

WE HAD ANOTHER discovery to announce that November concerning the Biden bank accounts. In a June 26, 2018, email from a Cathay Bank investigator to his bank fraud examiner superior within the bank we came across this attachment to the SAR.[1]

> We have been monitoring the subject customer due to the PEP designation and observations on the account activity, as well as recent negative news, indicate this entity to be high risk.
>
> Since the initial funding of $5 million from Northern international holdings (HK) Limited on 8/8/17 as a business loan, it was noted that there was no loan agreement docu-

ment submitted. The funds in the account have primarily funded 16 wires ranging from $157,494.19 to $400,000 totaling 2,915,375.25 to Owasco PC–Law Firm in DC [this is Hunter Biden's so-called legal firm]. These payments were indicated as management fees and reimbursements. We find it unusual that approximately 58% of the funds were transferred to the law firm in a few months, and the frequency of payments appear erratic. It was also previously indicated that Hudson West III LLC does not currently have any investment projects at this time, which raises further concerns, as millions and fees are being paid, but does not appear to have any services rendered by Owasco, PC, Robert Hunter Biden (son of former U.S. vice president Joe Biden) regarding allegations by his ex-wife, that there were financial concerns about his extravagant spending on his own interests (drugs, strip clubs, prostitutes, etc.) which may put his family in a deep financial hole. More recent negative news, indicate China targeting children of politicians and purchases of political influence through "sweetheart deals." Specifically, Hunter Biden's $1.5 billion deal with the Chinese state to establish a private equity firm in which they manage the funds over time and make huge fees. The management companies' purpose is to invest in companies that benefit Chinese government. Thus, the activity on the account appears unusual with no current business purpose, and along with the recent negative news (along with the negative news regarding Dr. Patrick Ho Chi Ping's trial in the below email) may require reevaluation of Cathay's café relationship with the customer.[2]

This email from the bank investigator raised seven major red flags:

*One*, prior to issuing a potential SAR on an influential customer, most banks will first call their client to ask specific questions about the transaction or transactions in order to avoid actually filing the SAR. It appears that Hunter Biden claimed to the bank investigator/compliance officer that the unusual $5 million wire from China was actually a *loan*. Then the bank investigator would request to have a copy of the loan documentation on file for the state and federal bank examiners. Hunter told the investigator that *he had no loan documents*. No bank compliance officer in the world would believe that anyone—much less a foreign entity—would loan anybody $5 million without loan documentation.

*Two*, Hunter transferred $2,915,375.25 from his investment company (Hudson West III) to his law firm (Owasco PC). The bank investigator/compliance officer asked Hunter what the $2.9 million wire would have been for, and he told them that it was for "fees." The typical legal/management fees for an investment fund of that size would be 4–6 percent ($250,000). Hunter apparently charged 58 percent—or *eleven times* the standard rate—*fees for no services rendered.*

*Three*, federal bank compliance requires that every business account summarize its business type. Hunter told the bank that Hudson West III was an investment company. The bank investigator/compliance officer noted that Hudson West III had no investments. In other words, *Hunter's investment company had no investments*. Nevertheless, Hunter's one-man, do-nothing "firm" was still paid nearly $3 million.

*Four*, press accounts cited Hunter's ex-wife saying that Hunter was in financial trouble and addicted to drugs and prostitutes.

*Five*, being a Chinese American bank that specialized in Chinese commerce, Cathay Bank knew full well that *China targeted children of politicians* for political influence.

*Six*, Cathay Bank knew that Northern International Holdings was not a private company, but rather a state-owned entity. *Hunter Biden's $5 million came from the Chinese government.*

And finally, *seven*, Hunter Biden's business associate Patrick Ho was convicted in the Southern District of New York for bribery and FARA violations. The bank knew that Hunter might very well be under the federal investigation that swept up Ho since Ho and Hunter worked for the same company and were close associates.

Not only did this email validate every financial concern that I had spoken publicly about, but it was also a snapshot of the thought process that the bank investigators used to make the decision to file those 170 SARs against the entities associated with members of the Biden family. Specifically, six different U.S. banks filed 170 SARs against the Bidens (primarily Hunter Biden) that indicated potential financial crimes ranging from money laundering to tax evasion to bribes.

With that revelation, the momentum at least temporarily shifted back in my favor, that is, the favor of justice. The email proved everything that I had been saying all along. It was evidence of wrongdoing in the eyes of a bank regulator whose main job was to identify and report financial crimes to the Department of the Treasury. This particular bank investigator did everything right.

I went on Greg Kelly's show on Newsmax, and he seemed happy to report Oversight's discovery. It seemed that, after a few bad stories and quotes on Newsmax over my not bowing to Hunter Biden's demands, everything appeared to be back on track with this key conservative outlet.

It truly had been a roller-coaster week. It would not be the last.

## ATTACK OF THE SMURFS

ON NOVEMBER 14, 2023, Oversight had a full committee hearing on wasteful spending. It focused on all the empty federal government office space around the country, particularly in DC. Since

President Biden had come into office, he kept extending his work-from-home policies in order to be popular with federal employees. After all, the bureaucrats were, for the most part, running his administration.

I had the General Services Administration (GSA) director in to testify about substantive ways we could disperse some excess government property in order to save taxpayer dollars. It cost the same to maintain government office buildings whether there were people occupying them or not. We learned at the substantive hearing that some office buildings only had an 8 percent occupancy rate, and the average was in the mid–30 percent range. But the taxpayers were paying maintenance costs as if they were 100 percent occupied. Even Washington, DC, Mayor Muriel Bowser strongly supported what I was doing. There were so many empty buildings downtown that many of the restaurants and retailers had shut down because of a huge drop in customers. She wanted to redevelop those underutilized buildings, and I agreed with her.

Unfortunately, and regardless of the topic of any committee hearing, whether it be about reducing waste, eliminating fraud, or holding people accountable for abuse, the Democrats on Oversight inevitably attempted to show their butts. They reveled in disruption. They could not have cared less about the frustrated American taxpayers who desperately want Congress off their backs. For the Democrats, it was just a game of political theater. And the audience they were aiming to entertain was their liberal base. Their "best" showman-exhibitionist was Representative Jared Moskowitz of Florida's limousine-liberal 23rd District.

Moskowitz was a small guy with a big mouth. He was the kind of guy who thought he was funny and charming when in fact he was annoying. People were just humoring him because, for some unfathomable reason, they felt sorry for him. He constantly did things to disrupt substantive hearings and expressed great joy if any Republican member of my committee took his bait to initiate a combative rant.

In this particular hearing, *I* was the Republican who took his bait—but only after he yielded me time to respond to a flat-out lie that he was repeating about my family.

The *Daily Beast* had just published a libelous story implying that I loaned my brother $200,000.[3] This was, coincidentally, the exact same amount that Jim claimed Joe wrote out to him. The dumb liberals were elated at such a story because in their simple minds I had lost the moral authority to speak about anything pertaining to a "loan" or "$200,000 check." Otherwise, according to them, I would be a hypocrite.

The problem with the *Daily Beast* story was that it was a bald-faced lie.

My brother, Chad Comer, is the only person I know who has never, at any time in his entire life, had a real loan. My brother graduated from high school and moved straight into our farmhouse in Gamaliel, Kentucky, the night of his graduation. He began farming full-time the day after he graduated from high school and he farms to this day. The farmhouse was built by my grandfather Harlin Comer, and it did not have a mortgage. He did not go to college, so he did not have any student loans.

And I certainly never loaned him any money. He was like most rural red-blooded, hardworking, God-fearing patriots in that he would likely starve to death before he asked anyone for money. He earned his own by farming.

My brother has never done anything bad or questionable to anybody. He was neither in politics nor a public figure. He did not deserve to be mentioned in that tabloid *Daily Beast* story, and he did not deserve to be slandered by a little smart-ass like Jared Moskowitz. Where I come from, family and friends stick together, and I was not going to let that lie stand.

Moskowitz quoted the dishonest story, which has since been "stealth edited" to take the word *loan* out—although they never issued a correction like an ethical outlet would do. Instead, they edited it (literally) in the dark of night in hopes that my brother would not sue them.

Moskowitz spoke his piece, then offered to yield time to me to respond.

I took his time and responded with the facts. Once he figured out that I was serious, and that the story was dishonest, he tried to reclaim his time. He was yelling, "Reclaim my time! Reclaim my time!" As I gazed in contempt at his desperate pleas to get the microphone back, I stated the obvious to everyone in the room.

I declared to Moskowitz, who was wearing a blue suit, blue tie, and white high-top tennis shoes, "You look like a Smurf over there flapping your wings."[4]

Thankfully, Jamie Raskin was not sitting in the ranking member's chair. Kweisi Mfume was serving as the ranking member. Kweisi looked at me and whispered calmly, "Just let it go." Kweisi was always a gentleman, and one of the very few Democrats on the committee whom I respected.

He was right, and I regained order.

Predictably, the media had a meltdown. As the old farmers used to say when referring to the *Farmers' Almanac*, the "sign was bad" that day. Two other skirmishes much more severe than mine also took place at the same time. Markwayne Mullin got into it with the head of the Teamsters union in a Senate committee hearing, and Kevin McCarthy had allegedly "elbowed" Tim Burchett in the hallway.

All I did was call a lying little loudmouth a Smurf.

But to the DC press corps, the three Republican villains (McCarthy, Mullin, and me) had crossed the line and created havoc and chaos. I had never seen so much drama from the press corps.

In the eyes of the DC press, you can have your family receive tens of millions of dollars from adversarial countries for no apparent reason (like the Bidens had done), you can sleep with a Chinese spy while serving on the House Intelligence Committee (as Eric Swalwell is accused of doing), you can receive gold bars from Egypt while serving as chairman of the Senate Foreign Relations Committee (as Senator Robert Menendez is accused of), you can pay your boyfriend out of our office budget account (as Cori Bush is accused of), you can make millions of dollars trading stocks and options (as Nancy Pelosi is accused of), but under absolutely no circumstances can you ever accuse a little blue man of looking like a Smurf!

# Chapter 12

## THE HIT PIECE THAT WASN'T

Unlike many lawmakers, I am not an attorney. And thank goodness for that.

Starting out as a farmer, banker, and general businessman gave me the savvy to understand the complex banking schemes and other financial shenanigans the Biden family has used to mislead the IRS and other federal investigators. My political upbringing and business experience have seen me through other perils in Congress as well. Chief among these developed skills is the ability to surround oneself with stellar team members working toward a common goal.

From my earliest memories I wanted to be involved in the American political process. It runs in the family. My paternal grandfather, Harlin Comer, was a larger-than-life figure in Monroe County, Kentucky. He was a businessman first and a politico second, what used to be called the "political boss" of his community. Granddad Comer was chairman of the Republican Party in Monroe County, a county located southeast of Bowling Green and nestled against the Tennessee border. At the time, Monroe had the largest percentage of Republicans of all 120 counties in Kentucky, and Harlin Comer was the person whom any aspiring politician would have to meet with first if they wanted to do well there. Granddad Comer died when I was in college, so I knew him well when I was a young man. He never wanted me to be in politics. He advised me to become a successful businessman, because he believed they were the ones who controlled the politicians.

My maternal grandfather, Kenneth Witcher, was also a businessman, but he did serve in elected offices. He was a Tennessee state representative in Nashville, was for many years chairman of the Macon County Board of Education, and served on the Tennessee State Board of Education. In fact, my grandfather Witcher ran for office twenty-five times and won every election.

Both of my grandfathers served as delegates to several Republican national conventions, Harlin representing Kentucky and Kenneth representing Tennessee. I used to gaze in fascination at the many pictures they had of themselves posing with high-ranking politicians. But the pictures that meant the most to both grandfathers were photos of themselves with U.S. presidents. My grandfather Witcher had a shot of himself with President Nixon and President Ford. My grandfather Comer had photos with President Ford and President Bush. All of these are now prominently displayed in my Washington congressional office—beside *my* pictures with all of the presidents I've met. At first glance, this may seem a bit vain, but whenever I look at them they remind me of who I am and where I came from. They help me recall the legacy I am forever striving to live up to and carry forward.

## DOWN ON THE FARM

GROWING UP IN rural Kentucky, I set my goal to be like my grandfathers, successful in both business and politics. My grandfather Comer owned a construction company. He also served on the board of directors of five different small banks in Kentucky and Tennessee. His son Sam, my father, was a dentist. Together Granddad Comer and my dad also owned a beef cattle farm. Grandfather Witcher owned a lumber mill in Red Boiling Springs, Tennessee.

With beef farming and agriculture in my blood, I decided prior to college that I would be in business and my business would be beef cattle. I also knew that once I was established in business, I would become involved in the political process in some way.

Every big-time politician I met growing up gave me similar advice: "Make money first, because you cannot make any money as a politician."

I guess those old-time politicians never met Joe Biden.

If they had, they might have amended their advice. "You cannot make any money in politics—unless you are a Biden!"

I graduated from Monroe County High School and attended Western Kentucky University, where, true to my plan, I majored in agriculture. While in college I served as state president of Kentucky Future Farmers of America. The FFA is a tremendous leadership development organization that helped prepare me for the future. I hurried through college, eager to make my mark, and graduated from Western in just over three years. Once I got back to Monroe County, I hit the ground running. I established myself as a young entrepreneur and aspiring leader in my community. In what felt like record time, I was elected president of the Monroe County Chamber of Commerce, vice president of the Monroe County Farm Bureau, and put on the board of directors of my local community bank, South Central Bank. At the time I was the youngest director of a bank board in Kentucky. All of this came out of a singular drive to achieve my vision.

Yet mostly what I did was farm full-time. Farming is tough, and a low-margin affair even in the best of times. It didn't take me long to realize that the only way to generate wealth by farming was to accumulate real estate. So over the first fifteen years of farming, I borrowed from the banks as much money as I could afford to purchase farmland. I was a tightwad when it came to profits and I took every hard-earned penny I made and reinvested it in more farmland.

I was a responsible risk taker who worked hard and, by the grace of God, accumulated enough equity to set sail on an amazing political journey. That journey would lead me to the chairmanship of the high-profile House Oversight Committee. As chairman of that committee, I would lead the investigation of what I consider to be the biggest political scandal in the history of America—bar none.

But, of course, I didn't start out as a congressional committee chair. At twenty-seven I ran for my first public office, and won! I served two terms as the youngest Kentucky state representative in our capital of Frankfort. I served eleven years total in the Kentucky General Assembly, representing the four south-central Kentucky counties of Cumberland, Green, Metcalfe, and Monroe. I was elected to the statewide office of Kentucky commissioner of agriculture in 2012. Kentucky was still a state largely controlled by Democrats, and at the time I was the only elected statewide Republican officeholder. In 2016, I was elected to Congress from Kentucky's 1st Congressional District.

I share this to give you a sense of where I'm from, so you can see why the press came after my hometown, and why that didn't work.

On December 7, 2023, I hosted my Oversight senior staff for Christmas lunch in DC on the congressional fly-out day. I felt like we had a lot to celebrate. We did it. Every single fact Americans learned about the 170 Suspicious Activity Reports, the twenty shell companies, the $20 million–plus the Biden family raked in from our enemies around the world, we had uncovered. We had thrown light on the Biden family's dirty money and their shady deals, which all mostly occurred while Joe Biden was vice president. We'd confirmed the fact that Joe Biden had in fact met with nearly every person who wired his family money—this despite assuring the American voters that he had never met such people or done such things.

All of it was the result of my staff's hard work.

The Biden influence-peddling investigation was a success, but we were not done yet, not by a long shot. We had uncovered evidence of immoral, unpatriotic, and possibly illegal activities, but the next challenge would be determining how to hold the Bidens accountable for their behavior, and how to hold the Deep State accountable for its cover-ups.

As I was flying home from DC to Louisville, Hunter Biden was indicted by Special Counsel David Weiss. As usual, my American Airlines plane had no Wi-Fi, so I was completely out of pocket. Then, just as the plane hit the runway, my cell phone started blowing up with messages. The messages were a mix between congratulations from friends and requests from the press for interviews and statements. I declined to do any interviews until my legal staff thoroughly read the charges and I digested the news. On its surface the news seemed good, but nothing was ever as it seemed with the Biden family, or David Weiss, who had proved himself far more beholden to the Biden power machine in Delaware than to the U.S. president who had appointed him.

I also had come to expect that whenever a really juicy Biden corruption story emerged, some mainstream media outlet would have a hit piece on me lying in wait. I'd be contacted with a list of demands to answer ahead of some kind of made-up, slanderous garbage story against me that they hoped would strike a note of moral equivalency or even get me in real trouble.

The problem for them was, I was just some guy from Kentucky. My family and I weren't anything like the Bidens.

## YET ANOTHER SLEAZY, BIASED "NEWS SERVICE"

THIS TIME IT was the Associated Press doing a profile piece on my allegedly corrupt private business. My business is farming. What in the hell would the AP find corrupt about a farm?

In the private sector (or in the real world, as I like to think of it) I am a farmer. I grew up exhibiting Charolais beef cattle at shows all over Kentucky and Tennessee. As I mentioned, I was the Kentucky Future Farmers of America (FFA) state president. I *majored* in the subject at college. I received an agriculture degree from Western Kentucky University.

Upon graduation, as I've also said, I became a full-time farmer. My first big elected office was that of Kentucky commissioner of agriculture. I was and am as legitimate a farmer as you can be. I am also proud of that. No occupation on the planet is more important than that of the farmer. A safe, healthy, and abundant food supply is essential to everyone's survival. Farmers are hardworking, God-fearing, business-savvy, salt-of-the-earth people. I am very proud to be one of them.

After having served fifteen years in Kentucky politics, I arrived at the U.S. Congress maybe a trifle naïve. I felt like the only legitimate news service in America was the Associated Press. I had good reason for thinking so, however. Two of the best, most respected journalists in Kentucky were Bruce Shriner and Adam Beam, both AP reporters. They did not always write flattering stories about me, but I don't remember them writing anything untrue or unfair. That is the way journalism is supposed to be, and when I was in Kentucky, that is how the AP was.

Today's AP is not what I grew up relying on for accurate information. Today's AP political team is liberal swamp people doing whatever it takes to get on TV. Most of them act almost like paid political operatives, since their goal is creating a scandal CNN will care about. The AP in Washington, DC, is weaponized against any conservative leader or conservative cause. I rate the AP today below the *Washington Post* and *New York Times*, both basically being charcoal-grill starters. I cannot name a single AP reporter in DC whom I trust or for whom I have an ounce of respect.

The AP reporter who sent his list of unbelievable demands to me this time was Brian Slodysko. I have never met Slodysko or even spoken to him. But he has spent a lot of time in Monroe County digging, interviewing, and harassing my lifelong friends and family. People had run him out of their houses and even called the sheriff on him.

This list demands answers to an entire list of questions about ludicrous things:

> What is Farm Team Properties LLC?
> What is a hunting lease?
> Does your farmland have oil wells?
> Why haven't you sold the various properties you have publicly listed for sale that are owned by Farm Team Properties LLC?
> How did you acquire your house?

On December 14, 2023, the AP website and wire service put out an egregious bundle of lies and half-truths with the headline "The Republican leading the probe of Hunter Biden has his own Shell company and complicated friends."[1]

In the AP false narrative, my personal LLC (Farm Team Properties LLC) was a shell company on the order of an international money-laundering operation.

## A LEGITIMATE BUSINESS, NOT A SHELL GAME

FARM TEAM (NOTICE the subtle play on words!) is in fact an LLC that my wife and I formed a few years ago as an added layer of liability protection to administer all of the hunting leases I do on my 1,500 acres of farmland in Kentucky and Tennessee.

That is exactly how it is (properly) listed on my very thorough

Congressional Financial Disclosure Form. Every year I have about seventy-five hunters from six different states in seventy-five deer stands in trees scattered all over my farmland. If you are not familiar with deer hunting, the hunter places a deer stand in a tree, usually anywhere from ten to thirty feet off the ground, and the hunter climbs into the deer stand before sunup. He climbs in complete darkness to begin his hunting.

Sound like a situation where people can take a tumble if they aren't careful? It is.

From a potential liability standpoint, a lot could go wrong for the landowner, and that is why most landowners who lease out a significant amount of land for hunting do so through an LLC. Every accountant in America would advise his client to do the leases through an LLC. A limited liability company (LLC) is exactly what it says it is. It is an independent entity that limits the owner's liability. If somebody sued me, they could perhaps take the company's assets, but they couldn't bankrupt me and leave my kids on the hard pack.

The reason farmers use LLCs is the Trial Lawyers of America and the liberal trial-lawyer-friendly legislation they lobby for. Nowadays LLCs are used frequently in anything outdoor-related.

I also own some speculative properties in my Farm Team LLC—properties I hope to develop one day if it ever makes sense—which makes Farm Team above average in size for a small business in Kentucky. So my LLC has both assets and the known purpose of administering hunting leases on my private farmland.

By contrast, the twenty Biden shell companies had no assets and no concrete purpose. Hunter and Jim's LLCs served to pass money from China and Romania to Joe Biden's relatives.

The Associated Press should be ashamed for writing a story about my businesses that someone with the slightest financial literacy would agree is false. But no, the AP persisted with their garbage. The AP's sole purpose was to create a false narrative that I did the same thing as the Bidens, when in fact I most certainly did not.

In addition, in falsely stating that I had a shell company, they also personally attacked four of my lifelong friends.

## THE AP ATTACKS MY FRIENDS AND FAMILY

DARREN CLEARY, WHO is married to my cousin, is Monroe County's biggest private employer and biggest local philanthropist. He and I purchased 6.5 acres of land in front of my beloved Tompkinsville Walmart when I was a private citizen and prior to my getting elected to Congress. It has been publicly listed for sale for almost thirteen years.

One of these days, some smart developer will see the potential. So much traffic on the way to Walmart! Location, location, location!

At least that is our reasoning. My 50 percent of that property is owned by my LLC. The AP said it was a shady deal because Darren and his wife (whose maiden name was Comer) had made donations to my campaign. There was nothing inappropriate about that. He's my cousin-in-law, yes. So what? He has every right, as do you, to make political donations under a certain amount to whomever he wishes.

Furthermore, everything about the asset and the effort to sell the property was legally and correctly listed. As for donors, I have around 350 political donors in Monroe County, whose population is less than 11,000. I am proud of that number.

The Clearys are good people who have helped many of my friends and family back home when they needed it most. They did not deserve to be written about by the AP as if they had done something wrong.

The next friend the AP took a slug at was my best friend growing up, Billy Proffitt. Billy and I played basketball and showed cattle all through school. When I am in Monroe County, I almost always visit Billy, and we either have dinner at a local restaurant or at my house with a few of our other high school classmates. Billy was attacked for simply working at the real estate company that had my LLC properties for sale. Again, if an LLC has assets, it is not a shell. A shell company has *no* assets by definition, or at least no legal assets. That's why you call it a shell.

The last people attacked were Mitchell Page and Larry Pitcock. They were two old Monroe County politicos whom I grew up around, and whose children I went to school with. The AP never even mentioned them to me in their demand letter for commentary. In the story, they were referred to as my "political mentors." The only person in the outside world to whom I had ever mentioned Page and Pitcock was the *New York Times*' Jonathan Swan, back nine months earlier when he was in Tompkinsville working on *his* hit piece.[2]

I introduced Swan to them and invited all of them to my house so they could tell stories about what it was like growing up around Monroe County politics. Swan seemed to be coordinating with the AP to further discredit me—proof again that the corrupt mainstream media were engaged in an attempt to intimidate me and warn me away from the truth about the Bidens. The AP reporter—who never met or spoke to me, Mitchell Page, or Larry Pitcock—wrote that I had "complicated" friends and listed Page and Pitcock. Shame on the AP editorial team for instigating, enabling, and abetting such garbage reporting.

I detest being lied about in the corrupt mainstream media. But in today's toxic political environment, populated by an unethical and liberally biased media, it is fair game to slander people just for being conservative or Republican.

A semi-reporter like Brian Slodysko could not operate for long without a great deal of support behind him. But the left's so-called dark money *can* often be traced if one is patient and knows how to follow a financial trail.

Let me tell you the story of Representative Dan Goldman of New York. Goldman, who sits on Oversight, is a Democrat who takes things beyond mere partisan rancor. His tactics harm his opponents' reputations, but also potentially endanger the safety of the families of Republicans in Congress. Goldman bankrolls the Congressional Integrity Project. The CIP, which is little more than a partisan hate group, specializes in deploying underhanded tactics against its target set of conservative Republicans.[3] If you hear about a Republican congressman and his family being cornered and screamed at while trying to have a meal in a restaurant, the CIP and its sister groups have probably paid someone to follow them, supplied the location, and called out one of its semi-affiliated goon squads to deliver the threats.

Who do you think funds the braying mobs of chemically dipped blue-haired haters who sit outside Supreme Court justices' homes trying to intimidate their families? I'll give you one guess. "The project openly states that it also targets the 'friends and family' of the legislators it chooses to attack," reports Influence Watch.[4]

Goldman is a literal trust fund baby, heir to the Levi Strauss blue jeans fortune.[5]

My friend Representative Byron Donalds called Goldman "the leading defense attorney in Congress for the Biden family. He's going to spin and do whatever he needs to do."[6]

Goldman is in general a money spout for leftist causes.[7] He's also linked to a major consultancy that funnels millions of dollars to obstruct, intimidate, and run information operations on the Oversight Committee's Biden family influence-peddling investigation. That funnel feeds right into the monster left-wing dark money mother lode, Arabella Advisors.

The *Wall Street Journal* calls Arabella "the financial behemoth at the center of the left's web of political nonprofits."[8] Arabella Advisors and its group of affiliated political action funds form the largest dark money network in the U.S. Arabella itself receives big dollops of Goldman family foundation cash.[9] And, wouldn't you know it, Arabella Advisors owns the Sixteen Thirty Fund,[10] which bankrolled the CIP.[11]

Every time I see Dan Goldman, I am reminded of the fact that he is using his parents' tens of millions in trust fund money to pay for harassment of my family and friends.

CIP operators were responsible for numerous intimidation tactics against me, including flying an airplane with a banner that read "Investigate Comer" over the 149th Kentucky Derby all afternoon, hiring a disparaging billboard truck to drive around my hometown congressional office, and putting up my picture in the form of a wanted poster all over Capitol Hill. Hilarious, right? Sure. But that's just the side CIP uses to cover up its actual slimy core operation: attempts at personal intimidation and slander against its opponents. For instance, not so hilarious was CIP coordination with corrupt mainstream media outlets to publish false information about my family, friends, and private businesses.

I'm convinced by evidence I've seen that the CIP arranged AP reporter and smear-monger Brian Slodysko's dirt-digging trip to Tompkinsville, Kentucky, for example. Slodysko spent five days in my hometown (population 2,500), where he met with a convicted drug dealer who had also recently pled guilty to assaulting a judge overseeing another drug possession case of his. This dealer had a decades-long political hatred of my family, and the fake news story involving me and my best friend from high school is simply false.

Slodysko didn't stop with our local thug. He met with four other locals whom he tried to get to collaborate with the drug dealer's false story. But it turns out he knocked on the wrong doors. In each instance, the people threw Slodysko out of their houses. Before he even made it to his car at the curb, they called my wife or Sandy Simpson at my congressional office to report that the AP was concocting a fake hit piece.

Alarmed, I immediately hired Garrett Ventry (who represented Brett Kavanaugh during his Supreme Court confirmation, which the Democrats turned into a slanderous witch hunt[12]) to represent me against the Associated Press. Ventry called the AP editor and unloaded upon him about half of the evidence I had accumulated to discredit their nasty attempted ambush.

The AP never ran the story, reporting to Ventry that it had been shelved, for now!

The very fact that they allowed a reporter to become a gateway and mouthpiece for CIP political monkey business is a glaring example of the AP's sheer lack of journalistic integrity (and common sense) these days. I have not the slightest doubt that the libel would have run if Garrett Ventry hadn't made his call. Not long after, Slodysko wrote another fictitious hit piece on a Trump-endorsed Republican (Bernie Moreno) days before Moreno's primary.

If a new president is sworn in in January 2025, and if that president demonstrates a willingness to dismantle the Deep State actors who have protected corrupt Democrat families like the Bidens and Clintons, then I plan on presenting to the new leadership of the FBI exactly what evidence I have of CIP work with that Kentucky drug dealer to conspire to write what could have been a very damaging fake news story that would have, without a doubt, derailed the Biden investigation.

I also won't forget Slodysko's perfidy toward people I care about. I certainly will not overlook Dan Goldman's role in this tawdry matter either. Who is the greater scumbag—the scumbag or the guy who hires the scumbag to do his dirty work?

I am no longer shocked by this, and I even think it's kind of funny how far from the truth these goons actually stray.

*But under no circumstances should my family and friends be attacked for simply being my acquaintances.*

I love my family, and I am very proud of my hometown friends. I am forever sorry that they have been shamelessly attacked by the corrupt mainstream media for simply knowing me. My only sin as far as the mainstream media is concerned is that I am investigating the very public corruption of a Democrat president.

# Chapter 13

## GEARING UP FOR THE IMPEACHMENT VOTE

Speaker Mike Johnson was still settling into his new job at the beginning of December. I learned that he could not hire many of his new staff until January 1 because the budget had been approved for 2023, and many of Kevin McCarthy's employees were given until the end of the year to leave. One of many pressing concerns that Johnson faced was the upcoming vote to formalize the impeachment inquiry. He knew from listening to the whip team that we were still some votes short, so he decided that Jim Jordan, Jason Smith, and I needed to have another special impeachment inquiry conference meeting.

Before the presentation, Jordan and I briefly met with my senior Oversight staff. We spoke about how bad the relationship was between me and Jamie Raskin. I told Jordan that I despised Raskin so much I would trade ranking members with him. "I would rather smell shit for five straight hours than listen to Jamie Raskin lie like a dog!" To properly understand that juxtaposition you need to ride in an elevator for a few floors with Jim Jordan's ranking member, Jerry Nadler.

Despite it being sparsely attended by only around one-third of our conference, the presentation that Jordan, Smith, and I delivered on the impeachment inquiry went well. Starting with me and ending with Smith, the three of us took turns going through the evidence of corruption and criminality we had accumulated against President Biden and his family. I focused on the twenty shell companies, the 170 SARs, the number of times Joe Biden had lied about his knowledge and involvement in his family's influence-peddling schemes, and the two direct payments that Joe received from those schemes. Jim Jordan talked about the Burisma scandal. Jason Smith detailed the damning evidence that IRS whistleblowers Gary Shapley and Joseph Ziegler had turned over to the Ways and Means Committee. We concluded by explaining the necessity of going to the next phase in the investigation. The White House was obstructing the investigation in several ways: first, by not turning over the thousands of emails Joe Biden sent as vice president from his private emails; second, by not listing which countries were included in the classified documents that Joe Biden had mishandled (much more on this later); and finally, by not allowing certain White House aides to come in for interviews.

One tidbit I did learn at the conference was that five New York moderates were not going to vote for anything they deemed controversial unless Mike Johnson put a motion to expel George Santos on the floor for a vote. This was a perfect example of how the Republicans' slight majority could lose three votes on anything and the bill or measure could not pass without Democrat votes. This meant four or five Republicans could band together and be very powerful. That was exactly what happened with Santos. Whatever my opinion of Santos, I was afraid we were going to regret this action. Our numbers were steadily dwindling.

The conference featured about a dozen friendly questions from members. It was obvious that we had the momentum as well as the votes to pass an impeachment inquiry when Tom McClintock from California, who had been a very public impeachment skeptic so far, stood up and said that he believed this was the biggest political corruption scandal in our lifetime. That was exactly what I had been saying for over a year.

We had momentum and the media knew it.

## LEAKS BUILT INTO THE SYSTEM

OUR REPUBLICAN CONFERENCES are legendary for leaks. I often joke that I am not going to bother going to the next conference meeting because I can just sit in my office and follow the Twitter posts of Olivia Beavers and Juliegrace Brufke—basically political gossip columnists with *Politico* and Axios, respectively—to get a play-by-play of every word spoken in the conference. The thing was, Olivia and Juliegrace were about the only two reporters in the DC press corps that most Republicans liked, much less trusted. Members would sometimes clandestinely call straight to their cell phones so they could hear everything said in our closed-door, private conferences.*

As I emerged from the conference briefing, the entire DC press corps seemed to be outside waiting. They looked like a bunch of kids in an orphanage who just watched the Grinch steal all of the presents under their Christmas tree. The mainstream media had been tolling like some mournful bell over the past two and a half months that Republicans didn't have enough votes to impeach. They would never pass an impeachment inquiry because there was "no evidence."

"No evidence, no evidence, no evidence," rang their bells.

---

* The two would then immediately tweet out what they heard. I would be in a conference meeting and looking at their accounts when a member would say something and within five seconds Olivia and Juliegrace would be tweeting exactly word for word what I'd just heard. All of the bad reporters—which accounted for the other 99 percent—would be following them too. They used them to learn what was being said in our private meetings without having to do the legwork.

This whole charade would infuriate Republican leadership, but it was helpful to the members who did not want to sit and listen to all the bullcrap of such conferences. That day was no different. The entire DC press knew what McClintock said just as he said it, and they knew that was a very good sign for me and—even better—a very bad sign for the Democrat–mainstream media complex.

The problem for them was, there *was* evidence now, and plenty of it.

The first (and what would end up being the last) question they asked with their uniformly pouty facial expressions was "We understand you think you have the votes. What changed?"

I answered proudly and honestly, "After being stuck up here for ten straight weeks, the members went home and talked to real people on Main Street and at high school football games, and they quickly realized that everything you guys have been writing over the past eight months is a crock of shit. A majority of Americans are keeping up with this investigation and they realize that something very bad is going on with the president and his corrupt family, and they want to know the truth. So, fortunately for me, the American people aren't buying what y'all are selling. They realize that we have accumulated a mountain of evidence, and that Oversight is the only entity in the world looking into this."

It was a drop-the-mic moment for me and by far the most enjoyable press gaggle I had ever had. For once I walked back to my office with a little pep in my step.

Another reason I had a bounce to my step was the information we discovered pertaining to the money that had moved from foreign companies through multiple bank accounts into Joe Biden's pocket. This was smoking-gun evidence that, if nothing else, proved that Joe did benefit from his family's shady influence-peddling schemes.

## GOING VIRAL

AT THAT POINT in the investigation, I had already given up on the media. Nobody had covered anything properly for months. Even the friendlier, conservative media would take solid issues and either trivialize them or overdramatize them. I had tried a video format for communicating in November but had combined it with traditional press.

This time I decided that a better way to get this bombshell discovery out to the public would be by filming a video with me speaking at my own slow pace, in which I could explain exactly what Joe Biden did and where the money came from. Then I would ask my Oversight members, many of whom had huge numbers of social media followers, to share the video.

My plan was to disrupt the normal communications model—it was obviously not working—and bypass the media altogether. That night I went down to the audio room in the Rayburn House Office Building and taped a two-minute and thirty-nine-second video that detailed exactly how Joe Biden took $40,000 from the family's shady Chinese scheme. I sat on the video all weekend while the Oversight communications staff and I secretly explained to Oversight members exactly what evidence we had uncovered, and how I planned to sidestep the media to deliver the truth.

At noon on December 4, Oversight dropped the video on all of its social media accounts.[1] Within one hour, almost every Republican member of Oversight had shared it. It was, after all, the first direct evidence of Joe Biden receiving a payment from his family, and the payment was traced directly to China.

Within the first hour, my video had over two million views. By the end of the day, it had over ten million views. By the end of the week, the video had over twenty million views. To put that into perspective, Rachel Maddow has around 1.4 million evening viewers on her MSNBC show and Kaitlan Collins has only around 700,000 nightly viewers on her prime-time CNN show. My video easily surpassed their combined nightly viewerships. I had disrupted the dishonest cable TV news media with my new media outreach plan.

They were prepared for the discovery of money going directly to Joe, however, because any time I received subpoenaed information, the Democrats on the committee would receive it too—which meant the White House got the info as well, compliments of the perfidious Oversight Democrats. From there it was parceled out to selected media like so many fish chunks for the penguins. The media came out swinging at the exact same time my video went viral. Their media narrative was consistent: the money Joe got was simply a loan repayment, because written in ink on the memo line were the words "loan repayment." Didn't that prove it was a loan? How could anybody but rubes and yokels doubt it?

Not a single mainstream media outlet covered the fact that the source of the $40,000 was Communist China. Zero.*

That evening, Oversight staff director Marin had a meeting with Speaker Johnson's newly assembled legal staff in order to receive direction from the Speaker's office on how to proceed with the House impeachment inquiry. After all, the inquiry was an idea concocted solely by the Speaker's office, albeit Speaker McCarthy.

Everyone quickly realized that nobody knew anything about appropriate steps forward. It was not Speaker Johnson's fault or the fault of his brand-new staff. They inherited this problem as a result of eight Republicans joining with 208 Democrats to perform a coup and install an inexperienced, unprepared replacement. The new staffers were all nice and supportive and wanted to be helpful,

---

* Of all the horrible explanations for the money Joe Biden received, probably none top Philip Bump's of the *Washington Post*. Nobody wrote more dishonest crap about the investigation than Bump, who never accepted the fact that the Bidens took money from China or even that the laptop was real, even after Hunter Biden himself admitted it was his in court. Philip Bump was the worst of the worst, and even more alarming, Bump was a "fact checker" for the *Post*.

but few (with the exception of my former staffer Ashley Callen, whom Johnson had hired just days before) had any experience or understanding of the investigation, much less the impeachment inquiry process. Instead of the Speaker's staff telling us how to proceed, we realized that *we* would have to figure it out, and then explain it to them. And while we were at it, we would need to figure out how to get 218 votes to pass the inquiry or else the investigation would be over.

On December 5, 2023, I did an early TV interview with NBC News *Meet the Press* host Ryan Nobles, who questioned my evidence of Joe Biden taking money from China. He asked how I came up with such a thing. It seemed not just preposterous, but utterly incomprehensible!

I told him that their bank statements and bank records did not lie.

Nobles went through several contortions that amounted to deliberately misunderstanding me.

He acted confused, oblivious to the English language's plain meaning. He dramatically questioned the comprehensibility of the obvious series of wire transfers from China to Hunter to Jim to Joe. None of this was particularly difficult to understand, but Nobles seemed bewildered. He reminded me of your standard drunk bully hopped up on cheap hooch at a bar who is trying to goad you into a fight.

I told him that he must be "financially illiterate" if he could not understand that simple series of money transfers.[2]

The entire mainstream media was outraged that I would say such a nasty thing to poor Ryan Nobles. I stand by my statement. Either he was (as are most of his media colleagues) indeed financially illiterate or he was flat-out misreporting the obvious truth for partisan purposes. It was a fine example of six of one, a half dozen of the other.

## A RARE BIPARTISAN MOMENT—AND A WIN FOR BOTH SIDES

ON DECEMBER 6, 2023, former Speaker Kevin McCarthy announced he was leaving Congress. So he and Bill Johnson were both resigning. George Santos had also recently been removed. We could now only lose two Republican votes to pass a bill if every Democrat objected. Nothing was getting easier in the business of governing for Mike Johnson or myself.*

---

* One bill I sponsored that was moving though the painfully slow process of becoming law in the 118th Congress was my "Washington, DC–John F Kennedy Stadium Bill." The U.S. Department of the Interior owned the 178-acre property—land and buildings—at the old Washington Redskins football stadium. It was run-down and beyond repair. The site was only being used for drug deals and homeless tents. The new owner of the Washington Commanders, successors to the Redskins, was interested in building a new stadium in the DC limits and that was the only feasible location big enough for the massive project.

Mayor Muriel Bowser (whom I had grown to surprisingly like and work well with since the Oversight Committee had legislative jurisdiction over DC) alerted me about the project months earlier when we had a private meeting to discuss ways to help DC lower crime and battle poverty. She asked if I could help the city obtain a ninety-nine-year lease from the federal government so that the city could sublease the property to the owner of the Commanders. The Commanders would then agree to build a fabulous state-of-the-art football stadium and develop the area for the community. Since the federal government was currently having to maintain the decaying property and Washington, DC, desperately needed new investment in the area, I thought the bill was a good idea and something I should lead. It was a win-win because it not only saved money and generated investment, it also kept the property on the books of the federal government.

Like every single piece of legislation—good or bad—attempting to move through Congress, my bill also faced obstacles. Several members of the Freedom Caucus opposed the bill simply because the District of Columbia government supported it. In one of our legislative strategy sessions, Mayor Bowser said that she felt like the bill was moving along well. I told her that not only were some of the more aggressive Republicans against our bill, but some of the far-left Democrats were as well, because they wanted the old stadium to be turned into some type of homeless shelter.

In addition, Jamie Raskin, a few other Democrats from Maryland, and some Democrats from Virginia were also opposed to the bill because both Virginia and Maryland were making pitches to the new owners of the football team to build a new stadium in their states instead.

Soon Hunter Biden's whip-smart but unscrupulous lawyer Abbe Lowell sent a second letter to me and Jim Jordan stating that Hunter would only testify publicly, and not in a deposition as my subpoena clearly stated. Amazingly, the media once again had their spoonfed stories online before I received his demands. The media narrative was quickly taking shape that Comer did not want Hunter in public because—here's the never-ending false refrain—I had no evidence. But this time the false media narrative was not just being trumpeted by the left; many on the right were also critical of my decision to demand a deposition.

Steve Bannon (who really ought not talk about obeying subpoenas, considering his own checkered history in that regard) roasted me on his show. Sebastian Gorka soon followed on Newsmax. Even my own committee member Anna Paulina Luna (who is a solid presence on the committee, but not exactly a stellar legal mind) joined the right's "legal experts" in attacking me for not letting the Bidens make their own rules.

## THE CONSERVATIVE PRESS IS OUT FOR POLITICAL BLOOD

MY WORST FEAR was always getting bad press from the conservative outlets. People often questioned why I did so many conservative interviews.

---

We needed a few changes to get the Republicans on board, I told Mayor Bowser that I was going to use accurate football terminology to describe the current state of our bill. I said, "You are going against a Republican defense that on paper looks awful because they may give up ninety-nine yards per possession, but they have the best goal-line defense in history. You will not score a touchdown unless you alter the bill!"

She agreed to my proposal to make some simple changes to the bill in order for it to be more palatable to those Republicans in opposition. The bill would later pass through the Oversight Committee, then the Natural Resources Committee, and then the full House floor in the coming year.

It was because, even when they get things wrong, they *listen*. And they let me have my say. Furthermore, I was playing defense. Our conference had been a divided mess throughout the entire 118th Congress. It is the unfortunate truth that, unlike Democrats, Republicans often eat their own. I knew that I could not take incoming missiles from both the left and the right and continue to make progress in the investigation.

I realized that with the Biden deposition, I had a problem with the right side of conservative media. Of all the things to create a problem, it was my standing up to Hunter Biden's demands to set the rules of the investigation that bothered them.

After suffering outrage after outrage for over three years, including online harassment, covert government censorship, and even imprisonment, they were longing to see a Biden, any Biden, in the dock being grilled. It seemed to overcome their reason.

The way to make this thing stick to the Bidens and stick good was to observe the legal proprieties and do it right. Oversight was after long-term results, not bread and circuses.

I was upset, but I did not have time to pout. I had a fire that was starting to spread throughout conservative media outlets. I needed help.

The difference between a regular committee hearing and a formal deposition is huge. During a normal Oversight Committee hearing each member gets five minutes to ask questions. That usually ends up being around two questions on average per member. That means if everything were to go perfectly, we would only be able to ask Hunter Biden around fifty questions during a normal committee hearing. However, during a *deposition*, which typically lasts around eight hours, with Republicans and Democrats each rotating one hour for questions, we could easily get in seven hundred questions for Joe Biden's bagman of a son. This was a huge difference, especially when you considered the thousands of pages of documents that we had obtained and the hundreds of questions that needed to be asked.

Serious investigations require substantive answers. Substantive answers take time. A mere public hearing with Hunter Biden would be limited, besides potentially becoming a complete circus. He had already demonstrated what he was capable of with his stunts, both on the day of his scheduled deposition and on the day that we had a committee markup to hold him in contempt of Congress.

We also knew how the appalling Oversight Democrats would behave. Committee hearings like that only serve as theater or entertainment, and my job was not to entertain the mainstream media or political junkies. It was to lead the investigation and set the truth about the Bidens and their schemes before the American people.

My aim was justice, not showy hogwash.

How to bring them around to my way of thinking?

Then it hit me. What if President Trump issued a statement?

That was it! That would get everyone in line, if anything could.

I knew the perfect person to connect with Trump and explain to him why we needed a deposition instead of a public hearing, as well as to ask him to explain the reasons to his supporters. What's more, she was on my committee.

Marjorie Taylor Greene.

## CALLING IN THE BIG GUN

I CALLED MARJORIE and asked her if I could come to her office and discuss something important with her. She quickly replied and told me her door was always open. I went straight to the Cannon House Office Building and met with her privately in her office. I explained why we needed the deposition and asked her if she agreed.

Yes.

Would she stick with me on this?

Yes.

She asked what she could do to help. I immediately requested that she call President Trump, explain the situation to him, and ask him to issue a statement.

MTG pulled out her cell phone then and there and dialed a number. I asked her who she was calling.

"President Trump, of course."

I had gone to great lengths to avoid communicating with President Trump throughout my investigation because I did not want the Democrats on the committee to claim that I was taking orders from Trump. I was not investigating Joe Biden because of any loyalty or allegiance to Donald Trump. That was a separate matter for me as a Republican.

No, I was investigating Joe Biden for public corruption as a servant of the people. My job—any chairman's job—as the leader of the House Oversight Committee was to investigate just that.

MTG dialed the number and I thought to myself, There's no way Donald Trump would just answer a call right then and there from anyone, including MTG.

On only the second ring, a very familiar voice spoke up loud and clear. "How's my favorite congresswoman?"

"I'm doing just fine," MTG responded. "How's my favorite president?"

It was obvious that both Trump and MTG genuinely liked and respected each other.

After some initial pleasantries were exchanged, MTG proceeded to tell Trump that she had Jamie Comer in her office, and that I needed to explain something to him.

She put the former president on the phone and he said, "Jamie? Jamie, are you there?"

Obviously, I had to reply. "Yes, sir, Mr. President. It's good to hear from you."

Trump exclaimed, "Jamie, everyone loves you. I mean they absolutely love what you are doing." He paused for a brief moment and, after considering what he had just said to me, added the most Trumpy statement ever: "Of course, they love *me*, too!"

It was a funny moment, and I remembered how amusing and charming Donald Trump could be. He was definitely one of a kind, and someone with whom you knew exactly what you were getting. Those character traits are why so many people who hate politics and politicians nonetheless love Trump.

I reminded the president how his own family had had to sit in front of the January 6th Committee for nearly twenty-two hours in closed-door depositions.

Hunter Biden, I told him, should be required to do the same thing.

Trump agreed with me.

Less than an hour later the president issued a statement in support of what I was fighting for. He said I should reject Hunter's request to dodge the deposition.

From that moment on, nobody on the right gave me trouble on the deposition versus public hearing debate.

Hunter Biden would indeed go on to participate in a formal deposition, just as I had demanded all along. Donald Trump is the ultimate spin master. He definitely put out a fire for me before it spread.

# Chapter 14

## THE BAGMAN DOESN'T COMETH

After spending three solid weeks feverishly lobbying my Republican colleagues to get them to support the impeachment inquiry legislation we'd agreed in conference to put forward, I was making solid progress on December 13, the eve of the vote. We could only lose three Republican votes and still pass the bill. Less than twenty-four hours before the vote, my whip count listed Ken Buck as a solid no and Mike Gallagher and Brian Fitzpatrick as undecided. There were also a few disgruntled retiring members who would not tell me one way or the other how they intended to vote, so my fear of the unknown was high.

My frustration was also high. I could not understand how any Republican would not want to advance the investigation of public corruption at the highest levels of our government, especially after all the new evidence that we had discovered in the past year—evidence proving that Joe Biden had peddled access through his family for decades.

I was also in disbelief that anyone elected to the U.S. Congress would not answer a simple question of whether or not they would vote for a major piece of legislation, especially knowing that the exact vote count was essential in our present situation. I halfway respected the undecideds. At least I knew where they were. But the members (many of whom were current committee chairmen still upset over Kevin McCarthy being removed from the speakership) who would not even answer the question as to how they would vote? Well, I felt like telling them to not let the door hit them in the ass on the way out.

Of course, I held my tongue and counted what votes I could.

## BIDEN CONTEMPT FOR CONGRESS AND THE PEOPLE ON FULL DISPLAY

DECEMBER 13, 2023, was also the day my original subpoena to Hunter Biden specified that the president's wayward son was to arrive for his deposition. At 8 a.m. CNN reported that Hunter was coming in for the appointment, but since CNN had not correctly reported much of anything throughout the entire investigation, I did not put much stock in what they said. The deposition was scheduled to begin at 10 a.m. in the Oversight Hearing Room in the Rayburn House Office Building. Hunter Biden's attorney—the crafty Abbe Lowell—would not tell us whether his client was going to show. Lowell had recently been seen on TV pushing his narrative that Hunter would only show for a public hearing. I had countered him, also on TV, saying that Hunter did not set the rules, I did. If Hunter did not show, then I would be forced to hold him in contempt of Congress, just as the Democrats did with Peter Navarro, Mark Meadows, and Steve Bannon when they refused to show up via subpoena from the January 6th Committee's circus of a hearing. Nevertheless, the Oversight staff had to assume that Hunter *would* show and were prepared for the long deposition.

As I entered the hearing room where the deposition was scheduled to take place, counsels from the three House investigative committees were present. Also there were Andy Biggs, Lauren Boebert, Clay Higgins, Scott Perry, Lisa McClain, Byron Donalds, MTG, Nancy Mace, Paul Gosar, and Jim Jordan from my committee. Darrell Issa, Matt Gaetz, and Kelly Armstrong had come from Judiciary.

Of course, the raucous and unserious opposition was represented by Raskin, Sheila Jackson Lee (fresh off her loss in the Houston mayor's race the night before), Goldman, and Smurfkowitz.

Not long after I'd come in, we got word that the press was pulling out of Rayburn and running out to the steps in front of the Senate side of the Capitol for a Hunter Biden press conference.

Wasn't it amazing that the press knew before I did that Hunter was not going to show up for his subpoenaed deposition and instead have a press conference? It was enough to make someone think that Hunter's legal team had a close relationship with the corrupt mainstream media. Close, as in cheek-to-cheek.

So around twenty members of the U.S. Congress and twenty-five highly paid congressional committee staffers sat waiting on the privileged son of the president of the United States—a man who had already consumed hundreds of thousands of dollars in taxpayer expenses incurred from years of justified investigation for a host of crimes, including probes by the IRS, FBI, ATF, SEC, and DOJ. Furthermore, this was a guy who was accused of stiffing the government of unpaid taxes to the tune of millions of dollars.

If anybody in this country was a privileged princeling along the lines of the ancient pharaohs' sons, and the "redblood" brood of the murderous Chinese Communist Party upper class, it was Hunter Biden.

Hunter Biden rolled up to the Senate steps of the U.S. Capitol with an entourage, complete with taxpayer-funded Secret Service protection, his Netflix documentary film crew, his high-priced legal team (which he had never paid one penny of his own money for), and Eric Swalwell.

Hunter Biden walked up to the mic. All of DC liberal mainstream media stood trembling, waiting for his words. What wisdom would their beloved president's prodigal git utter? They felt so sorry for him. Here was Hunter, an unwitting victim of drug abuse and bad judgment. It was a disease, not a choice! At least that's the way it was for Hunter.

He had achieved the highest level of the only cred that mattered to them: victim status. Poor Hunter Biden was being picked on by MAGA world. And here he was, bravely standing up to his bully.

Hunter read a prepared statement and did indeed play the victim card, proclaiming his father's innocence and ending with the phrase "I am here to answer questions."

Yes, that was because he was not in the Rayburn Building to answer questions, as he was legally and morally obligated to do.

As Hunter moved away, his journalist groupies began to yell questions at him. Just as his father had so many times throughout his presidency, Hunter turned his back on the media (oh, no, he doesn't *like* me!), got in his car (did he come in the Porsche? did he come in the Porsche?), and drove away without answering *a single question*.

I am here to answer questions. Right. But I knew these dupes. They would buy it. They would repeat it.

Hunter Biden was not coming to the deposition, that was for sure. Jordan's top counsel, Steve Castor, angrily called an end to the proceedings. Raskin and Goldman took this as a cue and raced each other outside to address the waiting press, eager to declare victory and announce that Comer had been duped. The corrupt mainstream media who were so offended by the Republicans who failed to comply with the January 6th subpoenas were elated at Hunter's audacity. The stories miraculously popped up within seconds after that. "Comer got played by Hunter" and so on.

Jim Jordan, MTG, and I watched Raskin, Goldman, and Sheila Jackson Lee conduct their impromptu press conference. After they had rambled for nearly twenty minutes, Jordan, MTG, and I walked out to hold our own short presser.

Our message was loud and clear. Hunter Biden had defied a lawful subpoena. He would be held accountable through the proper process, namely the U.S. House of Representatives holding him in contempt of Congress.

As we left this impromptu press event, all I could think was that I had the impeachment inquiry vote in a few hours and if that passed, I would have to start all over and convince 218 of my colleagues in this very divisive 118th Congress to hold the president of the United States' son in contempt of Congress. The White House/Oversight Democrat/Biden legal team strategy to obstruct, disrupt, and collude with the mainstream media to create false narratives was on full display. But I believed the American people were not amused.

A few hours later the full House convened for our vote series, which included the legislation to proceed to an impeachment inquiry. The legislation had been sponsored by Kelly Armstrong.

Lo and behold, in what was one of the biggest legislative victories for our conference all year, it passed.

In fact, it passed with unanimous Republican support. Nancy Pelosi's impeachment inquiry vote on Donald Trump had two Democrat defectors. Mine had none. Even Ken Buck, who had previously stated that he would not support the measure, voted in favor. I give Andy Biggs all the credit for getting Ken Buck to vote "yes," because Andy had been lobbying him hard for days.

It was also a huge show of support for all of the hard work Oversight had done over the past tumultuous year. All I could think about was how far I had come since the awful predicament Kevin McCarthy had put me in three months ago when he sprang the necessity of an impeachment inquiry vote on me. Of course, the downside was that many who reluctantly voted to support the inquiry had stated that they would never vote to impeach Joe Biden, regardless of what we uncovered.

Every celebration I experienced throughout the investigation seemed to be short-lived.

Not a single mainstream media outlet acknowledged that I did something that Pelosi (in their minds, the greatest legislator of our lifetimes) had failed to do. I got a unanimous vote. And I did it with what no one could argue was the most divisive Republican conference in recent memory.

It had been a long time since the GOP recorded a unanimous vote on a controversial party-line bill. What I did not know was that it would be the last unanimous vote our conference would achieve on a partisan bill for a very long time.

## THE HUNTER BECOMES THE PREY

WE HAD OUR first weekly GOP conference of the new year at 9 a.m. across the street in the Capitol. I attended the first half of the meeting because I needed to lobby a few of the wafflers on the Hunter Biden contempt-of-Congress vote to see if they had ever made their decisions.

Unlike the Democrats, Republicans began our conferences with a Pledge of Allegiance and a prayer. As the prayer was ending, I received a text from my Oversight staff saying I needed to call them immediately. I stepped out to call and was told that the Secret Service was snooping around in the hearing room prior to the Oversight Committee markup on the contempt vote. My first thought was someone had called in a bomb threat (after all, Jamaal Bowman pulled the fire alarm once, so who knew what Jared Smurfkowitz might do to gain attention). I immediately left the conference to return to the Oversight Hearing Room to see what was happening. Like every other incident I have had with the Secret Service, FBI, DOJ, or IRS throughout the entire investigation, nobody would answer my question as to why they were there. The arrogance of the Deep State knows no bounds.

After a few minutes pondering the Secret Service visit and the fact that they were remaining close to the outside door, it suddenly occurred to me that Hunter Biden might be showing up to the Oversight Committee contempt-of-Congress markup. I told the staff that I would proceed with the contempt committee hearing, but if Hunter insisted that he wanted to break the rules and be deposed at a time of his own choosing, the staff should be prepared to go. My staff had spent countless hours in preparation for the Hunter deposition, and despite the official committee rules that stated that depositions had to be noticed three days in advance and that we had to have a court reporter in place to conduct the official transcript, I wanted to proceed in front of the world.

We were ready.

I told them to start off hot with the bank records and see how he explained all of the shell companies and bank transfers from the foreign nationals. That was not the way substantive investigations were usually handled, but I was not going to get attacked by the conservative media again for letting Hunter Biden slip away.

## A VISITOR AT THE CONTEMPT-OF-CONGRESS MARKUP

I GAVELED IN the Oversight Committee markup on the Hunter Biden contempt-of-Congress vote at exactly 10 a.m. on January 10, 2024. After I went through the formalities of any markup, I delivered my opening statement as chairman. In my statement, I explained in detail why I subpoenaed Hunter Biden and why we were about to hold him accountable for defying my lawful subpoena. After the opener, I yielded time for Jamie Raskin to deliver his first remarks as the ranking member of the committee.

Once the motion to approve the contempt bill was in order, I recognized members who wished to speak on the bill. As with every other contentious bill before the Oversight Committee when there was a roomful of TV cameras, almost every hand on the committee was raised seeking my recognition. I started with Nancy Mace, recognizing her for five minutes.

In the midst of Mace's five minutes of comments, Hunter Biden walked into the Oversight Committee room. With him was his Secret Service detail, his lawyer Abbe Lowell, sugar brother Kevin Morris, his personal documentary crew, and a slew of the national press corps looking more like groupies than reporters.

Nancy incorporated the interruption perfectly in her impromptu remarks. She called Hunter out for his arrogance, entitlement, and sheer lawbreaking. She said that he was the epitome of white privilege, and even said to Hunter as he had just sat down, "You don't have the balls to answer our questions." (I love Nancy, but she does have a potty mouth.)

As is always the case per our committee rules, the majority and minority rotate speakers for up to five minutes each. Normally I ask ranking member Jamie Raskin which Democrat on his side he wants me to recognize next, but this time I picked who I wanted.

And I wanted Jared Moskowitz.

I knew the entire nation was either tuned in watching this political stunt live or would watch clips later on the evening news, and I wanted the biggest fool the Democrats have on Oversight to set the tone.

Moskowitz used every second of his five minutes as pure theater.

He flapped his small wings and declared multiple times, "He's here! He's here! He'll answer your questions publicly."

After Moskowitz pulled his stunt, I realized that I needed to be calm and cool and sure as hell not make mistakes. We were in deep viral moment territory. I felt like a coach, with the Democrats as my competition and the Republican side as my team.

I looked at the faces of all of my players. Most were wondering what play I was going to call. After all, we were facing a dirty team (the Oversight Democrats) in front of a hostile crowd (the media). But one face on my bench stood out. I knew she not only wanted in the game, but that she badly wanted to run with the ball. That person was Marjorie Taylor Greene.

At that very moment Moskowitz concluded his five-minute rant. He said that Hunter Biden was there to answer questions. Well, he'd had his chance.

I instantly recognized MTG as the next questioner. As I recognized her to speak, I looked deep into the eyes of Hunter Biden, who was sitting in the front row, and his eyeballs literally seemed to pop out of socket. Before MTG could speak, he grabbed Abbe Lowell and they flew out of the hearing room, almost knocking several people over along the way.

So much for answering any questions.

Hunter's total time spent in the committee room was less than ten minutes. I can only imagine the questions MTG would have asked him. Storming out of the Oversight hearing room prior to MTG grilling him was the first smart decision Hunter had made in a long time.

After a very long five hours of back-and-forth debate on the merits of the bill, the House Oversight Committee voted 26–20 along party lines to hold Robert Hunter Biden in contempt of Congress for failing to show for his subpoenaed deposition. Within hours of the successful vote, Judiciary and Oversight staff attorneys received a call from Abbe Lowell, who wanted to make a deal on Hunter coming in for a sit-down, closed-door deposition!

Lowell had several asks, including no video recording of the deposition (unlike what the January 6th Committee did to its unfortunate victims). I was also not to ask about the gun or tax evasion charges because of the ongoing investigation by David Weiss, and not to ask about the salacious stuff on the laptop because they disputed its authenticity.[1]

Lowell also asked for a new subpoena to be issued, which would have had to happen anyway because the one Hunter defied was now expired. The last thing he mentioned was not a request so much as a threat. Lowell said that if I continued to talk bad about Hunter or himself, Abbe Lowell, on TV, then he would pull Hunter from the deposition.

I guess it was a kind of gag order request. I agreed to that because I didn't want to give Lowell any reason to blame me for Hunter not showing. The deposition was too important, and I had gotten to the point that I detested doing TV interviews about the investigation anyway. No matter what I said, the corrupt mainstream media continued to report the exact opposite in their never-ending crusade to protect the Bidens. Of course, the second the Hunter Biden deposition concluded, I would return to speaking the truth on TV about both him and his unctuous attorney.

Hunter Biden had caved.

# Chapter 15

## THE SUGAR BROTHER

Of all of the shady characters involved in the Biden influence-peddling schemes, none defined the stereotype of sleaziness better than Kevin Morris. Morris is Hunter Biden's so-called "sugar brother" who also claims to be his attorney. I knew prior to the January 18, 2024, transcribed interview[1] that Morris had loaned Hunter over $6 million. A confidential source who had access to documents that were used in Hunter's child support case had reported this to me, among other facts.

The saga of Hunter Biden's attempt first to deny his own newborn daughter with Lunden Roberts and then to drastically reduce child support has been dealt with plenty in the tabloids.[2] Suffice it to say this was not a case of "the disease of addiction," drugs, booze, or "the tragic shadow of Beau Biden looming over him." Hunter Biden had fathered Navy Roberts while cheating on his then-current girlfriend, Beau Biden's widow, Hallie, with whom he had previously cheated on his first wife, Kathleen. More than all the crack cocaine, hookers and escorts, and porn uploads, this tawdry family melodrama showed Hunter Biden for what and who he really is, and it is not a pretty sight. That is between Hunter Biden and his Creator. It becomes important for the American people in its relationship to Hunter's father, Joe Biden. Hunter is not some poor lost Biden sheep. He is instead a key player in selling the Biden name to the highest bidder.

Hunter likes to point out that his father made him everything he is today. Never a truer word was spoken.

As Mollie Hemingway puts it in her book *Rigged*, "Ultimately, the problem for Joe Biden was that Hunter's problems weren't confined to his personal life. Hunter Biden's poor decision-making and track record of dishonesty was an issue of public corruption. No serious person could argue that Hunter hadn't leveraged his father's status as vice president to make a series of lucrative deals with shady foreign entities."[3]

## THE MORRIS MONEY SPIGOT FLOWS

SUGAR BROTHER KEVIN Morris met Hunter and Joe Biden at a political fundraiser in California for Joe's 2020 presidential campaign. Less than five weeks after meeting Hunter for the first time, Morris paid the IRS for all of Hunter's 2017 delinquent federal taxes.[4] This is yet another example of Joe Biden being present and having knowledge of and participating in his family's receipt of large sums of money from odd outside sources. As is always the case, Joe was involved and this time there was no doubt he benefited directly, if nothing else from a political standpoint. After all, it is a huge political gift not to have your son arrested for failure to pay taxes right before an election. That gift from Morris is, in my opinion, a campaign finance violation for Joe Biden for his 2020 presidential campaign. Does anyone doubt that a number of voters would be less likely to vote for a man running for president whose son was *still* attempting to dodge years of federal income taxes?

At the beginning of the transcribed interview, my oversight staff asked Kevin Morris how much money he had loaned Hunter Biden. He said he didn't know. The Democrats in attendance at the interview gasped because they were aware that Morris knew to the penny just how much money he had loaned Hunter. The sole purpose of the transcribed interview was to determine how much money he had given the president's family, and lying to Congress was a felony. After Morris's attorney whispered some legal advice into his ear, Morris "remembered" that it was over $5 million. During the third hour of the Morris interview, he recalled that the amount he loaned to Hunter was $6.2 million.

We asked Morris about the terms of his $6.2 million loan to Hunter. This loan had been accruing principal since right before the 2020 presidential election, when Kevin Morris paid Hunter's delinquent IRS tax bill. From 2020 to January 2024, Hunter was not required to pay one cent of principal or interest on the loan. In fact, the terms called for a balloon payment to be made in 2025, one year after Joe Biden hopefully leaves the presidency. As someone with extensive experience in loans, and as a businessperson and a bank director, I can say with confidence that I have never seen a loan set up that way. One reason loans are not done this way is that real loans by definition are supposed to be *paid back*. Loans also usually come with interest payments. Nobody would ever loan someone a significant amount of money and expect to be paid back years in the future by a borrower who currently has no job, no source of income, and no assets. The IRS would classify the Biden/Kevin Morris "loan" as either a gift or income. Either way, the IRS would require someone to pay taxes on any such so-called loan. The federal taxes would be somewhere in the range of $2 million. Failure to pay them on a gift or income is called tax evasion, and that is a felony.

One line of questioning for Morris revolved around an email he sent to someone in charge of doing Hunter Biden's taxes. In the email, Morris stated that Hunter needed to pay his 2017 delinquent federal tax bill immediately or else they would have a serious political problem. The serious political problem was the 2020 election. Joe Biden did not need his son carted off to prison for failure to pay federal income tax.

That day, Kevin Morris paid Hunter's federal taxes. It was the first of many years of federal income tax that Morris would subsequently pay for Hunter, all while Joe Biden was serving as president. No credible ethics body in American history would approve of the child of a president receiving millions of dollars in gifts for any reason, much less payment of the child's federal income tax, child support, and basic living expenses. Such commonplace rules apparently do not apply to the Biden family.

## SUGAR BRO OR ATTORNEY?

I DO NOT believe that Kevin Morris was an attorney for Hunter. Morris claims he is one of Hunter's attorneys so he can claim "attorney/client privilege" and thus be shielded from having to turn over certain documents or answer certain questions pertaining to our investigation. One perfect example of a document that we could not obtain due to Morris's claim of being Hunter's attorney was the actual loan documents detailing the arrangement of Morris's payment of Hunter's debts and expenses. These documents would be helpful not only to understand the terms of the shady "loan" but also to see if in fact there was any collateral for it.

One of the allegations made by the attorneys representing Lunden Roberts in the child support case was that Hunter was hiding assets in order to reduce his child support payments. The main asset that Morris may possess is Hunter's ownership in the Bank of China–Biden joint investment fund Bohai Harvest Rosemont (BHR) via his company Skaneateles LLC.[5] Morris was said to have purchased this from Hunter during Joe's presidency.[6] One question I have, and that we have not been able to answer, is whether Hunter actually sold this stake or is just hiding it in Morris's name in order to reduce his child support payments and skirt ethics laws prohibiting the president's immediate family from owning anything related to the Chinese Communist Party while in office. Hunter's huge BHR holdings seem to be the remaining nest egg he has not squandered. Before the Devon Archer trial, he tucked this stock away in Skaneateles,[7] and the promised large payout from BHR doesn't seem something that Hunter Biden would give up lightly.

Another reason I don't believe Morris is actually Hunter's attorney is that we asked him if he also represented Melissa Cohen, Hunter Biden's current wife, who is the mother of Hunter's fifth child. Morris responded that *he didn't know* if he represented Melissa Cohen! He then looked at his counsel and asked them if he represented Cohen. Morris's lawyer gazed back, confused, and Morris responded to Oversight that he would find out during the break. But before that, Morris's counsel jumped in and replied that Morris was indeed Cohen's attorney, which meant that he would not be able to answer any questions about her because of attorney-client privilege. How convenient.

Regardless of whether Morris is or is not Hunter Biden's attorney, he still has a major legal and/or ethical dilemma. The California bar states that attorneys are prohibited from loaning their clients money. So, at the very least, Morris has a huge ethics liability to contend with.[8]

In one of the creepier moments I've experienced as a member of Congress, Morris responded to Representative Jasmine Crockett from Texas when asked a simple question from her by grinning profusely from ear to ear and telling her that he was "a huge fan of hers." It seems, at least to me, a salacious come-on. I don't know how Crockett felt, but I didn't like it. It was very apparent to me that Morris liked Crockett's eyelashes much more than Marjorie Taylor Greene did!

In addition to admitting that he loaned Hunter Biden $6.2 million, Morris also admitted to purchasing over $650,000 worth of

Hunter's art. That makes Morris's total, as of January 2024, $7 million paid to Hunter. That is why Kevin Morris has become known as Hunter Biden's sugar brother.

Is it all coming from Morris, or is he perhaps a channel for Hollywood Democratic donors looking to help out Joe Biden? It certainly seems possible.

## THE FREE BOOKKEEPER

ERIC SCHWERIN WAS another former Biden associate we subpoenaed for a transcribed interview and whom I considered to be a hostile witness. He was one of the first Biden family lackeys whom Oversight staff met with in March 2023, shortly after I became chairman. We knew after meeting with him that he was not going to cooperate. In March 2023, he claimed he did not know anything about Biden business schemes—that is, other than the fact that Joe was *definitely* not involved in them.

In the January 30, 2024, transcribed interview,[9] Schwerin delivered an opening statement that read like it came straight from the Biden legal team. Like the other hostile witnesses who coordinated for similar openers—all of which centered on "Joe was not involved"—the media miraculously had these statements in hand and online before the interview even began.

Schwerin did not give the impression that he was a shyster, as so many of the other associates did. He was more on the nerdy side. He testified that he met Hunter Biden while they both worked in the Clinton administration's Commerce Department, and then they both joined a law and lobbying firm.

Schwerin cofounded Rosemont Seneca Partners along with Hunter Biden and others. This was one of the many companies Hunter owned with "Rosemont Seneca" in its title. Schwerin said Rosemont Seneca Partners was a consulting business for a wide range of clients interested in public policy services. In Washington, DC, we call that type of business a lobbying firm.

By my count, Eric Schwerin was involved in some way with five of Hunter's more than twenty-five LLCs. To Schwerin's credit, the five were the more legitimate of the assemblage. But we also learned that Schwerin performed bookkeeping tasks for Joe Biden. This was relevant to the investigation because Joe always said that he kept a wall between his and his family's business dealings. It's hard to have a wall if you share the same bookkeeper.

We further learned that Schwerin did receive pseudonym emails from Joe Biden while Biden was vice president.[10] That admission by Schwerin gave even more credence to my request from NARA for the pseudonym emails for the investigation,[11] such as the infamous "robinware456@gmail.com."[12]

## THE GIFT OUTRIGHT

THROUGH THE COURSE of the interview, Schwerin volunteered the fact that he never charged Joe Biden for any of his bookkeeping services.[13] This was a huge revelation because that meant that Joe received a valuable gift or service for free without ever reporting it.

Remember, Joe Biden's annual salary in the Senate when he ran for vice president in 2008 was $169,300. He'd been making amounts in that range his whole life, with a raise to $230,700 as VP.

It was hard to believe that Schwerin did that job for Joe Biden and never got paid for it. Do you pay the guy who does your taxes? Perhaps one of Hunter's shells somehow paid for it, or perhaps Schwerin got some type of favor in return for his "free" bookkeeping services to Joe while he was vice president and in the private sector, but at any rate, the fact that Joe received that gift was in my opinion a huge ethics violation and even perhaps tax evasion, depending on the value of the gift. I know how much I pay my CPA each year to prepare my books for my farming operation and financial disclosure forms for my banks, and it runs in the thousands of dollars. If Schwerin did that for Joe for several years, that would be a gift well in excess of ten thousand dollars and subject to state and federal taxes.

On December 14, 2015, Eric Schwerin wrote to Kate Bedingfield in the Office of the Vice President, providing quotes to use in response to media outreach regarding Hunter Biden's role in Burisma. Later that day, Bedingfield responded to Schwerin saying, "VP signed off on this." This was evidence that Joe Biden did know exactly what his family's shady schemes were and he coordinated with the characters to spin narratives. There was no wall between Joe's government office and his son's influence-peddling scheme.

An April 11, 2023, Fox News investigation revealed that Hunter Biden's business associates visited the White House more than eighty times when Joe Biden was vice president.[14] Eric Schwerin was one of the most prolific visitors, and logs show he visited thirty-six times,[15] apparently doing lots of accounting work for Joe for free. I cannot overstate how big an ethics violation that was. If a member of Congress was found to have received a gift that large and failed to report it, the congressman would get fined at best, and expelled at worst. Ethics rules—like tax laws, securities fraud, financial crimes, and FARA violations—apparently do not apply to the Bidens.

# Chapter 16

## THE BOBULINSKI BLOCKBUSTER

I recounted earlier the first few hours of Tony Bobulinski's blockbuster testimony of February 13, 2024. Over the final five hours of his transcribed testimony, Bobulinski provided much valuable evidence concerning President Biden's direct knowledge and involvement in Hunter Biden's shady business schemes with China. He also described in detail exactly what CEFC was (the funding arm of the Chinese Belt and Road Initiative), who their real owners were (the Chinese Communist Party), and how they implemented their business model (fool gullible Westerners into thinking they were a normal capital fund with charitable nonprofit subfunds).

CEFC, according to Tony Bobulinski, was a CCP-backed entity whose sole purpose was to initiate their Belt and Road Initiative throughout the world. It was state-funded to the tune of billions by the Chinese government. One way CEFC achieved its goals was through bribing susceptible world leaders to take it up on offers of usurious loans and construction of unnecessary facilities (unnecessary, that is, to all but the Chinese navy). This was going great while President Obama was in charge in America, and opposition to Chinese outrages and aggression took the form of gentle rebukes and lily-livered scolding.

Then along came Donald Trump. He was determined to put a stop to China's reckless and militaristic expansion of its influence. Trump recognized CEFC for what it was, and the Trump Justice

Department began looking into the activities of CEFC's apparatchiks in America. One of those was CEFC's number two guy, Patrick Ho (Chinese name Chi Ping).

Ho had run afoul of the Foreign Corrupt Practices Act, or FCPA. U.S. citizens and, crucially, businesspeople of any country who are active in the United States are not permitted to bribe foreign officials to gain favors, whether inside or outside the U.S. Business officials who reside within our borders are bound to abide by it. Ho, a former Hong Kong home secretary but now a CEFC operative, was cheerfully skipping around Africa bribing one government official after another to make CEFC deals, until he attempted to pay off one man who was not having any. This was President Idriss Déby of Chad, whom Ho attempted to bribe with $2 million in cash stashed in eight gift boxes. The bribe was to allow CEFC to obtain oil rights in Chad. Déby angrily refused and publicized the bribery attempt.[1]

Trump's Justice Department followed up and found even more evidence. Eventually Ho was arrested by federal agents at John F. Kennedy International Airport in New York City and tried in Southern District of New York (SDNY) federal court. According to lead attorneys on the case, Geoffrey S. Berman, U.S. attorney for SDNY, and Assistant Attorney General Brian Benczkowski of the Justice Department's Criminal Division, Ho was sentenced on December 18, 2019, "for his role in a multi-year, multimillion-dollar scheme to bribe top officials of Chad and Uganda in exchange for business advantages for CEFC energy company Limited (CEFC China)." He was convicted of violations of the Foreign Corrupt Practices Act, money laundering, and conspiracy to commit the same.[2]

Patrick Ho was a close associate of Hunter and James Biden. They had *two* ventures going with CEFC. One was called Sino-Hawk. Tony Bobulinski was CEO there. The other was a back-channel deal that Bobulinski was unaware of until later, to "counsel" CEFC executives privately. Could it be that once the Bidens realized straight-arrow Bobulinski was causing a problem channeling Chinese funds (specifically to Joe's relatives), they went behind his back to redirect the CEFC cash spigot? This is certainly what Bobulinski believes. SinoHawk and Bobulinski would never see a dime from China, but Hunter Biden certainly did.[3]

The Bobulinski-avoiding side hustle was set up using a Chinese-owned, Delaware-incorporated shell company called Hudson West III. On August 8, 2017, CEFC wired $5 million to Hudson West III. Quickly Hunter and James Biden began feeding at the trough of Hudson West III as the fund sent "consulting fees" to Hunter's firm Owasco totaling $4,790,375.25 and over $76,000 in "office expense and reimbursement" to Jim Biden's firm, Lion Hall Group.[4]

Also in 2017 there was a $1 million money wire from Hudson West III to Hunter Biden's Owasco marked for "Dr Patrick Ho Chi Ping Representation."[5] After Ho was arrested, the first call he made from the midtown Manhattan lockup was to none other than James Biden, the president's brother.[6] Jim Biden told him to call Hunter. Hunter Biden knew as much about criminal law as he did about energy legalities. On the afternoon of Ho's arrest, Hunter hired attorney Edward Kim of Fifth Avenue white-shoe firm Krieger Kim & Lewin to represent Ho.[7]

On what matters might Hunter and Jim Biden have been consulting Chinese Communist Party–controlled CEFC? The trout fishing in Delaware?

It's generally assumed that Ho expected a Biden to pull strings and get him sprung. Hunter and Jim had sent him back to the U.S. from shelter in Hong Kong by telling him the coast was clear. They may have been acting on faulty information. Or it may have been a setup.

Ho was a central figure whom I desperately wanted and needed to depose in the Biden influence-peddling investigation. Jim Jordan and I are also trying to determine if the Biden name was deliberately kept out of Ho trial transcripts and whether Biden family member names were redacted from evidence presented in the trial.[8]

After Trump's attorney general had succeeded in shutting down CEFC's America play and a deal for Russian gas turned sour, China's Xi Jinping, waved a hand and CEFC's chairman, Ye Jianming, disappeared into a Chinese prison. Patrick Ho similarly went to ground after his release and returned to Hong Kong. He was now behind CCP lines (and is currently suing Hunter Biden for legal malpractice[9]).

It's funny how so many former Biden associates, like Patrick Ho, Jason Galanis, Devon Archer, and CEFC chairman Ye Jianming, went to jail for crimes committed while they were in direct partnership with Hunter Biden, yet Hunter never even got interrogated by law enforcement. And it didn't stop there. Once the committee began looking into such matters, two potential witnesses to possible crimes, Gal Luft, who was on the payroll of CEFC at the same time as Hunter but was paid significantly less, and Alexander Smirnov, who according to Director Wray was one the FBI's most trusted and highest paid informants, were indicted for a FARA violation and lying to the FBI, respectively. Both these indictments occurred right before we were able to interview them for the Biden investigation.[10] How amazingly convenient for the Bidens!

We did talk with Tony Bobulinski, however, and his transcribed interview was a huge success for the investigation. Highlights include Bobulinski affirming that Joe Biden not only knew about his family's business dealings, but he enabled them and participated in them, despite being buffered by a scheme to maintain "plausible deniability." Joe Biden is, in fact, "the big guy" as referenced in the email instructing the Chinese deal to give Joe a 10 percent equity stake. Joe has repeatedly lied to the American people about his knowledge of and participation in family business dealings. CCP-linked energy company CEFC sought to infiltrate and compromise Joe Biden and the Obama-Biden White House. Finally, according to Bobulinski, Joe Biden engaged in misconduct and possible illegal activity. Hunter rejected these allegations. "I had no faith in Mr. Bobulinski. I think that you can see of the documents that were sent to us in preparation for this, there are many instances in which I call Mr. Bobulinski out for his what I would call complete absurdities."

## THE BIDEN ADMINISTRATION'S CROWS BEGIN TO CACKLE

NOT SURPRISINGLY, THE mainstream media had a completely different take on the Bobulinski interview that had proven so damaging to President Biden. CNN was the first out of the gate, even before the interview concluded, with their dishonest summary by partisan hack Annie Grayer under the headline: "Former Biden family business associate recycles unproven allegations to House panels."[11] The CNN story did not interview a single Republican who was in the seven-plus-hours interview. They did not have any transcripts of the interview because those are usually released a few days after the transcribed interview, when both sides and their attorneys have had time to review them for any errors. Furthermore, she had seen no copies of the dozens of official examples of evidence that Bobulinski and Oversight staff presented, which included text messages, emails, organizational charts, and proof of meetings. CNN just published a story that either, as we say in Monroe County, they pulled out of their ass, or that someone gave them to copy and paste on their stationery. Either way it was fake news. And that report could have served as the anchor for all the other corrupt mainstream media outlets to distort the truth in the hours to follow. Annie Grayer demonstrated zero journalistic integrity with that story and, unfortunately, many more.

Washington-based Grayer was a regular on the Biden investigation beat. I don't lightly call Grayer a partisan operative. I often texted her in the beginning to try to keep her informed on all new evidence we acquired. But as with nearly every other mainstream media reporter, the more Biden corruption we found and revealed, the more hostile she would get. Toward the end of the investigation, Annie, like her CNN counterparts Jake Tapper and Pam Brown (whom I had also tried to work closely with and give special access to), had, almost as if they'd received orders from above, turned hostile and did not cover the investigation in a fair or accurate manner.

Shortly before Eric Schwerin's transcribed interview, a Democrat staffer on the Oversight Committee announced in a room (where she did not realize one of the Republican Oversight staffers was present) that they had leaked his opening statement to "their" press. Minutes later and just before the actual beginning of the interview, CNN went up with a story falsely summarizing that the transcribed interview just revealed that Joe Biden had no knowledge of Hunter's deals. First, the interview had not even begun, and second, Schwerin's testimony actually revealed more damaging evidence of Joe's involvement.

We soon found out which faithful Democrat press apparatchiks the Democrat staffer was referring to. The very next day, Annie Grayer wrote a CNN attack piece on me saying, among other things, that I leaked transcripts to certain media. I have never leaked any transcripts ever, and she wrote a completely false story the day before from information unethically leaked to her by a Jamie Raskin staffer. Later, ratings poison[12] Jake Tapper made the false claim that I leaked tapes. It takes a special kind of "journalist" to blatantly and dishonestly speak whatever their political betters tell them to without attempting to verify those false claims. We know who two of them are.

Tapper has been on a long, well-documented decline from being a mediocre real-life journalist to his present role as yet another yes-man for the left. Perhaps the lowest point of many was in 2020 when Tapper suggested to the *New York Post* that they cave to censorship and delete their bombshell Hunter Biden laptop story on Twitter.[13] Nice look for a so-called journalist to cheerlead for censorship! In December 2023, Grayer was named to the Forbes 30 Under 30 list.[14] This was a list of the nation's top leaders who were thirty years old or younger. Annie was the only reporter on it. Of course, if you changed the title to "Democratic Party public relations shill," *Forbes* might have a point. If Grayer is the top young journalist in America, then journalism is doomed.

# Chapter 17

## THE SMIRNOV DISTRACTION

Aside from a disastrous and abortive impeachment inquiry hearing on September 28, 2023,[1] where our three witnesses performed extremely poorly, February 15, 2024, was the worst day of the entire investigation.

I took the blame for September 2023's botched House inquiry hearing (even though I could have pointed to House leadership for finding two of our three witnesses, or to Professor Jonathan Turley for deciding a committee hearing was just the place to pull out surprising, contradictory statements and irrelevant constitutional theories[2]). Some conservative outlets pointed out the obvious—that the White House engaged a willing mainstream media in an information operation to squelch the September impeachment and supplant what actually happened with their own narrative,[3] but, as I've said, overall the hearing was not a success.[4]

But there was no way I was going to take the blame for the massive, coordinated offensive that came compliments of our very corrupt FBI.

I don't know when the FBI went from being heroic officers of law enforcement to a gathering of partisan blackguards, but this was a Deep State operation of the most blatant, arrogant, and devious sort.

## HERRIDGE HARASSED AND EVIDENCE SNATCHED

ON FEBRUARY 13, 2024, veteran CBS reporter Catherine Herridge, who had been notified a few weeks earlier that she was being terminated, watched as network security entered her office and took possession of files from her yearslong investigative work of Biden schemes. They also took her copy of the Hunter Biden laptop hard drive, the one that she used to work with forensic auditors to verify its authenticity.[5]

Stalwart Jim Jordan launched a probe via Judiciary[6] and eventually the material was returned[7]—but not before CBS had plenty of opportunity to rifle through and copy it.

I knew that the Biden legal team had been trying to get that from CBS for months. I have no doubt the CBS move resulted from pressure from the Biden administration. The level of corruption that had been uncovered on the Bidens over the past year of my investigation was staggering, but the strong-arm tactics that would appear over the coming weeks were downright scary. The DOJ, FBI, and the corrupt mainstream media all worked together to intimidate, indict, obstruct, and disinform everyone from an honest reporter, to witnesses about to be interviewed by Oversight staff, to trusted FBI informants, to me in my personal life (as I discussed in chapter 12). The collection of bad actors performing bad acts to sabotage my investigation was the media equivalent of what my dad, who served in Vietnam, knew as the Tet Offensive.

## SMIRNOV INDICTED AND SMEARED

"GOP SUFFERS MOST spectacular embarrassment imaginable in anti-Biden case," by the always unctuous MSNBC mouthpiece Steve Benen,[8] was one of the nicer headlines after the DOJ indicted and arrested the FBI informant—Alexander Smirnov—for allegedly lying to the FBI by providing false and derogatory information about Joe Biden accepting a $5 million bribe from the Ukrainian oligarch owner of Burisma.[9] This, according to the FBI, was the mysterious paid informant named in the FBI form FD-1023. The same guy who six months earlier FBI Director Wray had named to Senator Grassley, Jim Jordan, and myself as one of the Bureau's most trusted and highly paid informants, an informant they had used in the past to successfully convict others of fraud.[10]

From the day I announced it after the midterm election, my Biden family influence-peddling investigation had always been about following the money by obtaining bank records. Mine was an investigation of potential financial crimes as outlined in the 170 SARs filed by six different banks, mentioned prominently in dozens of emails and text messages from both the Biden associates and the laptop, and confirmed under oath by the dozens of shady characters I was interviewing and deposing during the final phase of the investigation.

The DOJ indicted Alexander Smirnov on February 22, 2024. Coverage of the indictment was spread over all the news shows on every mainstream channel every hour. We were now at a full week of coverage and Thursday was the biggest, most coordinated effort yet by the White House war room and the corrupt mainstream media to not only discredit the investigation but also create the newest false narrative. Yes, that's right. They were pulling out Old Faithful. James Comer and Jim Jordan are actually working with the evil Vladimir Putin to disseminate Russian propaganda!

Never mind the very shady circumstances of the arrest and indictment of Smirnov, and never mind the fact that we had no idea who this guy even was beyond what FBI Director Wray had told us. Wray said he was one of the FBI's most trusted and highly paid informants. Funny that they would suddenly slap him in chains then. The fact is that Smirnov was never going to be an important part of our investigation. We could never locate him, much less identify him and send him a subpoena.

Besides, we already had real evidence in the form of bank records. Despite all this, the media continued to hammer home the fairy tale that the Biden influence-peddling investigation must end due to a tarnished witness being indicted by the DOJ as a spy working in Russia—which, of course, was exactly what the FBI had apparently been paying him hundreds of thousands of dollars over the past decade to do.

It seemed like madness. What sane person could believe such stuff? But it was madness with a method. Throw mud and send out smoke screens, and hope enough will stick and confuse everyone.

And for what?

To protect a tawdry empire of backdoor payments and underworld networking built around a weak president who was showing every sign of age-related mental decline, that's what. That's what the FBI and DOJ were doing with their taxpayer money when they weren't holding DEI education conferences.

Russia Collusion Hoax 2.0!

The sacred bonds of the U.S. intelligence community? The untarnished brand of the FBI?

The righteous legacy of the U.S. Department of Justice?

Gone.

I have a message for this cabal of Deep State actors: You are all just a bunch of political fixers working for a petty crook, and you ought to turn in your badges and get out of Dodge. You are no longer fit to be the sheriffs of this town.

All I ever knew about the 1023 was that Senator Grassley claimed that he had two FBI sources who gave him the document because the FBI had never investigated it. The agents felt that the part where Joe Biden was referred to as "the big guy" and reference was made to hiding the bribe in a complex maze of bank accounts was very consistent with what I had already uncovered from China and Romania, despite the fact that the 1023 was written several years before the discovery of the Hunter Biden laptop. Senator Grassley asked me to subpoena it, and I did, because in a credible investigation, you always investigate every tip. This was Chuck Grassley's tip.[11]

As I clearly stated in hundreds of interviews when asked about the 1023, I had no idea whether the allegation was true. I had no idea whether any tapes actually existed. And I had no idea of the identity of the informant. I would state that "the informant is one of the FBI's most trusted and highest paid informants in the entire Bureau" because that is exactly—word for word—what FBI Director Wray told me. The FBI briefers also said the exact same thing as Wray when I was in the SCIF being briefed on the 1023.

Never was the 1023 bribe allegation an important part of the evidence from my investigation. It was a mystery that would have always been difficult to prove because all the witnesses were very shady individuals supposedly living in war-torn Ukraine. I investigated the 1023, as I should have, but never could find anything. Whether or not the FBI was telling the truth about the informant actually lying did not have any impact on my full investigation, because I could not obtain sufficient evidence to corroborate the allegation (much as I had to abandon the probe I led into the cocaine found at the Biden White House because the Secret Service destroyed the little plastic bag that contained the cocaine a few days after it was discovered, and the tapes in the White House—amazingly—did not show the particular location of the discovery).

I also stated hundreds of times in seemingly countless media interviews that I (Oversight) was investigating the financial crimes and Jim Jordan (Judiciary and/or Weaponization Select) was investigating the Deep State cover-up. The FBI 1023 fell under Judiciary's jurisdiction in the investigation because Judiciary led on anything pertaining to the DOJ and FBI.

I do not know who the FBI agents were who gave Senator Grassley the 1023. I never met these people despite being in an adjoining room in their law firm when I first viewed the 1023 with Grassley. I do not know whether the agents were sincere, or whether they were part of a coordinated Deep State setup to make the investigation look bad. As the *Wall Street Journal*'s Kimberley Strassel says while decrying the FBI's partisan political maneuverings around Smirnov and others, "If you are going to lie to the Federal Bureau of Investigation, make sure it's a lie the FBI wants to hear."[12] I don't know if the FBI is lying about the informant. I don't even know if that was the real informant mentioned in the 1023.[13]

In the final analysis, it didn't matter. I did not need to prove whether or not the FBI was corrupt. This was a self-evident truth to anyone keeping up with the Biden investigation.[14] My investigation would not be deterred by a sudden, unexpected, and completely inconsistent FBI stunt that came out of left field and happened less than forty-eight hours after President Biden reportedly criticized Attorney General Merrick Garland for letting Robert Hur publish the report on Biden's mishandling of classified documents.[15] I would continue to move forward. Our much-anticipated transcribed interview with Jim Biden was rapidly approaching, and after that—the deposition of Hunter Biden.

## IT'S ABOUT THE BRIBERY, STUPID

OF COURSE, THE corrupt mainstream media piled on me. Just me. And they falsely reported that the investigation was over because my "star witness" had been indicted (ironically, they said the same thing months earlier when I was about to subpoena Gal Luft in relation to his knowledge of Biden involvement in the Chinese front company CEFC). Here the DOJ did exactly the same thing and, out of the blue, indicted a witness who might possess first-hand knowledge of the Biden crimes.[16] Luft, by the way, catching wind of the DOJ witch hunt, subsequently disappeared down some Middle Eastern spy hole. I suppose I might subpoena him again, but Luft is one of the many Biden crime family witnesses who are currently "missing."

The ensuing twenty-four hours brought a scorched-earth attack on me by the mainstream media, intended to discredit the investigation and deflect a cascade of godawful news for the Democrats that had hit like a storm over the past couple of days. First, the president had received the long-awaited report from the Department of Justice's Special Counsel Robert K. Hur on Joe Biden's retention of classified documents in his residence (actually his garage), and in his collected papers at the Penn Biden Center, affiliated with the University of Pennsylvania and located in Washington, DC.[17] Hur recommended against prosecuting Biden for hoarding secret documents (big surprise), but his reason for not charging the president was a classic. In the report, Hur says, "Biden would likely present himself to the jury, as he did during our interview with him, as a sympathetic, well-meaning, elderly man with a poor memory."[18]

The obvious interpretation was that Biden was a mental invalid, and no jury would vote to convict such a doddering fool. Just so there would be no doubt as to his meaning, Hur laid it out in black and white. "It would be difficult to convince a jury that they should convict him—by then a former president well into his eighties—of a serious felony that requires a mental state of willfulness."[19]

Biden—perhaps in a state of dementia-laden "sun-downing"—apparently got steamed and decided to put on an early evening presser to claim the report exonerated him. He ended up tripping over his words, calling Egypt Mexico, and cursing Hur for a mean old bully. Total disaster. And it validated Hur's assessment.

Then there was our committee's damning Tony Bobulinski interview,[20] the bad inflation numbers,[21] the demise of the ill-starred Schumer-Langford Immigration Bill,[22] the wide-open southern border,[23] and all the unrest around the world as a result of Biden's failed foreign policy. I received dozens of calls from my colleagues in Congress. Several of my committee members and a few Republican moderates (those Republicans representing House districts won by Biden in the 2020 presidential election) were constantly being harassed by the media.

The Smirnov story gave them a way to cover a story that didn't make Dems look bad.

Lucky for the Democrats, the FBI just happened to announce their indictment right then.

## A MISERABLE TWO DAYS

IT WAS A miserable two days following the Smirnov affair. My office staff asked if I really wanted all of my daily press mentions, a report they usually put together around 10 a.m. each day so I could keep track of the media. I knew it must be bad, because on any given day for weeks I'd had a ton of negative press mentions in the *Washington Post*, MSNBC, and *New York Times* for having the gall to investigate public corruption. My staff had never before asked me if I simply didn't want to look at them.

## UNCLE JIMMY

WHEN HE ENTERED the room on February 21, 2024, for his interview,[24] my first thought was that—minus a few inches in height—Jim Biden looked and sounded exactly like his brother Joe. As the interview progressed, his mannerisms proved to be the same as well.

Unlike the other witnesses, who had strikingly similar opening statements, Jim Biden did not read his, but rather just turned it in for the record. He didn't have to. The press (as was always the case) miraculously had his statement online before the interview even started. Like other hostile witnesses, Jim clearly stated that his brother was not involved in the businesses. Jim would even go so far as to say that in his fifty-plus years in business he never once discussed business with Joe, and that Joe had never even asked him what he did for a living.[25] Perhaps Jim's pride, or more likely his vanity, wouldn't let it rest at that. He went on to admit that he and his brother talked nearly every day of his seventy-five years of existence.

But apparently never once about business.

## CROOKED JIM AND HIS PACK OF DENIAL

OF ALL THE shady characters I have interviewed and deposed, Jim Biden was by far the *least* believable. He was unbelievable to the point that his prevarications and smoke screens were downright offensive. His testimony was contradicted by evidence numerous times.

For example, Jim Biden initially said that Tony Bobulinski lied during his testimony when he claimed that Jim was part of a deal with Rob Walker, Hunter Biden, James Gilliar, and Bobulinski. But when presented with the documentation of the Oneida Holdings LLC charter agreement that Bobulinski had earlier presented as evidence—there were the five principals' signatures right there on the incorporating papers, including Jim Biden's—Jim then changed his story. As a matter of fact, he played the famous Biden "forgetful old man card" and claimed that he did not remember signing the agreement, despite admitting that it was in fact his signature.

Of course, Jim Biden had done much more than that, including traipsing all over Hong Kong at CEFC chairman Ye's behest and assuring CEFC sacrificial patsy Patrick Ho that the coast was clear back in America (it wasn't).[26]

Jim testified that Joe never met with any business associates, but BlackBerry messages produced by Bobulinski contradicted that claim.

Jim announced that Hunter received a diamond from the Chinese while Joe was VP to entice him to go in business with them. (That brought the total to *two* diamonds Hunter received as gifts from the Chinese, one while Joe was VP and one afterward.) However, Jim said that he took the newly discovered diamond and had it appraised. The appraiser found it to be worthless, so Jim just tossed it in the trash! At that particular moment, I don't think my "bullshit meter" had ever registered higher—and I have been exposed to a lot of bullshitters in my lifetime.

Jim confirmed that there was no loan agreement for the two "loans" that he claimed Joe gave him, one for $200,000 and one for $40,000. Jim claimed that the money was wired to him through the Delaware law firm Monzack Mersky and Browder from Joe's account after Jim called the law firm to request it. If the story Jim told was true, then it would possibly be the first time in the history of America that a reputable law firm sent one quarter of a million dollars to a broke guy with a long history of indebtedness and crooked dealings with others, a quarter of a million with no loan documentation whatsoever listing, say, collateral and a payback date.

It is interesting to note that Monzack Mersky and Browder also represented several of Hunter's companies that were reported for financial shenanigans in the SARs filed by the banks. By my estimation, that law firm represented six LLCs owned by at least three

Biden family members. So even if the money did come from the law firm, there is no guarantee that it actually came from Joe Biden individually.

Suppose that money came from one of Hunter's LLCs and was wired to Jim. Then if Jim subsequently wrote Joe Biden a check, but after cashing the check, Joe failed to report that as income—well, that would be the financial crime of money laundering, right there. It would also be tax evasion by Joe Biden.

One might assume that if Joe Biden or the law firm had actual evidence that Joe did individually loan his brother $240,000, then Joe would have quickly produced it in order to discredit the investigation.

Jim Biden admitted to receiving massive loans from Democrat donors—many of whom have had serious legal issues, such as attempted bribery[27]—but has yet to fully repay them. These loans are in excess of a million dollars. But rest assured, the seventy-five-year-old Biden, who by all accounts is flat broke, testified that he fully intended to pay them back someday in the future.

Jim admitted that investor Michael Lewitt "loaned" him $225,000 but testified that Lewitt forgave every penny of the loan. Lewitt is currently being investigated by the Securities and Exchange Commission for stealing $4.7 million from the Third Friday Total Return Fund.[28] Lewitt would later state in court that Jim Biden was mistaken when he stated that Lewitt had forgiven the $225,000 loan. Lewitt testified under oath that a third party assumed the loan. I'll bet two good Angus-cross cows that the person who paid off Jim Biden's loan was a big Democrat donor who did so to protect Joe Biden during his 2020 presidential campaign. The Democrats and corrupt mainstream media would call something like that "hush money payments" if they were made to a certain Republican presidential candidate.

## RUSSIA HOAX 3.0

JIM BIDEN OBVIOUSLY knew in advance the media spin that was being planted for him. One of his attorneys asked Oversight staffer James Mandolfo (who was leading the interview) the source of an email that Mandolfo had presented as evidence to counter a statement that Jim had made. Mandolfo replied that it was from the Hunter Biden laptop. That prompted an immediate Biden-esque exclamation from Jim, "Oh come on, man, the laptop, really?"

Jim's attorney quickly shut him up, and calmly responded to Mandolfo that they disputed any contents from the so-called laptop.

I thought to myself, How can you dispute the legitimacy of the laptop? Hunter admitted twice in court that it was his.

Furthermore, CBS's Catherine Herridge headed up a forensic audit that confirmed its authenticity. Little did I know that even as we spoke, CBS was seizing the evidence that Herridge had compiled over several years of investigating Biden corruption, *including her copy of the Hunter Biden laptop hard drive*, the copy that was used in the forensic audit.

The Biden legal team, along with the White House war room, were colluding in real time with the corrupt mainstream media to begin a Russia 3.0 narrative on the laptop. It was quite the influence operation. Word had gone out to all outlets.

Within twenty-four hours, MSNBC would be reporting that Jim Jordan and I were working with Russian propaganda to create lies about the Bidens. The "Hunter Biden Laptop Was Russian Disinformation" had worked so well in October 2020, they were trying to rerun it!

Fortunately, that particular spin was so ridiculous and the nation had been so thoroughly inoculated against "Russian collusion" hoaxes, the operation never really got traction.

But that wasn't from lack of furious effort by the Democrats' mainstream media lapdogs.

## THE AMERICORE BLIGHT

THE LAST HOUR of the interview concerned the many questions my staff and I had about what's become known as the Americore healthcare scam. I discussed the basics of that operation in chapter 1.

*Politico* had finally published something useful a few days earlier, putting out a story that extensively detailed the manner in which Jim Biden took advantage of the failing healthcare company headquartered in Florida.[29] Reporter Ben Schreckinger cited two sources who corroborated that Jim Biden told the executives at Americore that Joe Biden was interested in an equity position in the company, as well as a seat on the Americore board.

The *Politico* story was important because the business model Jim Biden used in the Americore Health influence-peddling scheme was the exact one used by Hunter in the CEFC model. The first step was to communicate with both companies to signal "the Biden Brand," and then to lead the companies to believe that Joe would take an ownership stake in the deal. The *Politico* story also confirmed what I had already stated.

Joe Biden profited $200,000 from the Americore Health scheme.

The *Politico* story had extra meaning to me because one of the rural hospitals that were defrauded by Jim and Joe Biden was in Pineville, a small community in Bell County, in eastern Kentucky.[30] Many of the employees lost their health insurance and went without paychecks once government officials rolled in to investigate Americore Health for Medicare fraud, among other infractions.

My entire political life I've fought for rural Kentucky. Time after time I see these big-city cons roll in to economically depressed communities and absolutely rip off the goodhearted, well-intentioned community leaders. Nothing angers me more than seeing small-town elected leaders, hospital administrators, school superintendents, and economic development directors getting crooked. Seeing what Jim Biden did in Pineville made me even more determined to hold their entitled and corrupt family to account.

# Chapter 18

## LEAN INTO THE HARVEST

On February 23, 2024, Oversight and Judiciary staff traveled to the federal penitentiary in Montgomery, Alabama, to conduct a transcribed interview of convicted financial felon Jason Galanis.[1] This interview was negotiated in large part by Oversight Committee member Andy Biggs, who played a huge role in the investigation.

Galanis was a former business associate of Hunter Biden and Devon Archer from 2014 to 2015 via their company Burnham & Company, in a merger deal with Harvest Fund Management. Harvest was a sovereign investment firm represented by the Bank of China and communist official Henry Zhao. In 2013, Zhao helped create and poured money into Hunter Biden–linked LLC Bohai Harvest RST. Zhao's interest in doing business with the three partners was based solely on the Biden Brand and all the influence that would bring, according to Galanis.

As Peter Schweizer puts it in his masterful *Secret Empires,* "In short, the Chinese government was literally funding a business that it co-owned along with the sons of two of America's most powerful decision makers."[2]

Those sons were Chris Heinz, the stepson of then–secretary of state John Kerry, and Hunter Biden, the son of the current vice president.

In his book, Schweizer lays out all the gritty details of how the massive influence operation worked, concluding, "So during a critical eighteen-month period of diplomatic negotiations between Washington and Beijing, the Biden and Kerry families and friends pocketed major cash from companies connected to the Chinese government. The consequences of those deals are as surprising as the fact that they were conducted in the first place."[3]

It's important to realize that the Bohai Harvest shenanigans occurred *before* the CEFC Chinese operation. So there were *two* massive Biden influence-peddling schemes in China. Bohai Harvest first, CEFC second. One might imagine that the Bidens found Bohai Harvest so lucrative, they wanted to run the same play again but on an even larger scale, with the Belt and Road money available to CEFC.

But make no mistake, the Bohai Harvest scheme brought enormous wealth into the coffers of the associated Hunter Biden LLC shells, to be distributed to interested parties.

Yet of course it wasn't enough. With crooks and swindlers, it never is. Galanis and his colluders decided to use some of the lucre to fund a gigantic con job by bilking an entire Lakota Native American tribe in South Dakota, and bringing in a cash haul for their personal use.

Galanis testified that he, Hunter Biden's best friend, Devon Archer, and *Hunter Biden himself* were partners in a scam to defraud a tribal union pension fund by having it issue overpriced bonds, then buying the bonds with BHR investment funds. The idea was that money from the bonds would be invested toward eventually building a community center for the tribe and in other projects.

That did not happen. Instead the whole operation proved to be an elaborate scheme to make the BHR money from China washed, fungible, and immediately usable.

In short, the money went straight into Galanis's and Archer's pockets. Whether or not some or most ended up in Hunter Biden's pocket? Curiously that did not come up at the trial. Galanis says it did.

In all, Hunter's and Devon's companies received $15 million from the tribal bonds sale. Hunter would testify that he had no ownership in the Rosemont Seneca Bohai deal, when in fact he had been on the board of Harvest in China.

Even though all three were equal partners, Galanis received the maximum sentence, Archer received the minimum federal sentence, and as usual, Hunter Biden walked away scot-free. Documents I subpoenaed from Archer would later reveal that the Securities and Exchange Commission wanted to subpoena Hunter during the Obama-Biden administration, but then nothing ever happened. Jason Galanis felt firsthand the two-tier system of justice in America that always seems to protect the Democrat ruling class as highlighted by the Clintons and the Bidens.

As Galanis said in his opening statement, "The entire value-add of Hunter Biden to our business was his family name, and his access to his father, Vice President Joe Biden. Because of this access, I agreed to contribute equity ownership to them—Hunter and Devon—for no out-of-pocket cost from them in exchange for their 'relationship capital.'"[4]

This deal was consistent with the other "business deals" the Bidens participated in where they never put up a penny of capital but still demanded large equity ownership stakes. It was also consistent with the other shady deals in that the only tangible asset the Bidens had in the deal was Joe Biden, the Biden Brand.

Hunter and Jim never produced a good or service, they never manufactured anything, they did not have any intellectual property to offer, they weren't licensed to sell anything or even registered to lobby; they were simply immediate Biden family members with unlimited access to "the big guy," Joe Biden. The overall goal of my investigation was to prevent that from ever happening again.

Galanis continued:

> My lawyer has provided to the committee a draft email dated August 23, 2014, from Hunter Biden that reflects this understanding. It states: "Michael, please also, remind Henry [Zhao] of our conversation about a board seat for a certain relation of mine. Devon and I golfed with that relation earlier last week and we discussed this very idea again, and as always, he remains very keen on the opportunity." This section of the email was struck from the final version. It was drafted with an understanding of what had transpired regarding this effort.
>
> Devon Archer forwarded this email to me, with the words "FYI . . . example of lean in on Henry from Hunter . . . this is email drafted for him to send to Henry."
>
> The words "lean in" were used often by Devon and Hunter in our business dealings as a term for access to Vice President Biden's political influence. As Devon Archer is mentioned as a direct party to the conversation with the vice president on the golf course, it is clear from his email that Devon believed this was an accurate representation of that conversation.
>
> I am certain that the phrase "a certain relation of mine" refers to Vice President Biden, and Devon told me about this conversation on the golf course shortly after it happened. And it was one of many conversations that I understood the vice president had expressing his willingness to join the Harvest board after his vice presidency.[5]

This was the second former Biden associate to testify that Joe Biden was going to join the Harvest board. Bobulinski had testified that Joe was to be the 10 percent owned by "the big guy" referenced in the email about the Chinese-related entity CEFC, and now Galanis testified that Joe was interested in being on the board of Harvest, the Chinese partner of Bohai Harvest RST. The interviews and depositions paint a clear picture of how the Biden family conducted its influence-peddling schemes. They would dangle Joe as being interested in joining the board of the shady entity once he became a private citizen and would also take a free equity ownership stake. In order to prove Joe's interest, the Biden family would tell the interested party that they had to keep it quiet until Joe left office and enough time had passed so nobody would claim it was unethical to jump into business so soon after he left the vice presidency in January 2017.

Galanis further stated:

> I recall being with Hunter Biden and Devon Archer at the Peninsula bar in New York, where Hunter took a call from his father. He told his father things were going well with Henry and Harvest, and that he might need a little help getting it across the finish line. Hunter did not put the call on speaker as we were at this bar, but I am certain that Hunter was discussing our business efforts on the Burnham Harvest partnership, and that the vice president was aware of these efforts.
>
> It was not the only time I heard Hunter call his father regarding business matters. I was present when Hunter Biden called his father on a cell phone and put the call on speaker. Present for the call where Yelena Baturina, an investor in Rosemont projects, her husband Yuri Luzhkov, the former mayor of Moscow, and Devon Archer.
>
> This took place on May 4, 2014, during a gathering hosted by a Ukrainian associate of Ms. Baturina and a business partner of ours, at Romanoff's, a restaurant in Brooklyn New York.[6]

This was more evidence that Joe Biden knew full well who his family was in business with, and that he often spoke to all the shady characters who wired millions of dollars to his family, despite denying that he ever met them.

Galanis also testified that he tried hard to help get Yelena Baturina a bank account in the U.S., but because of numerous reports of her ties to criminal figures in Russia and corruption allegations related to her husband, the former mayor of Moscow, Galanis was unsuccessful. This meant that no American bank would take the Russian billionaire's business because of the inevitable compliance nightmare that would accompany Baturina's money.

But it was just fine for Hunter Biden to receive $3.5 million from her.

In December 2020, before Donald Trump was set to leave office, Galanis applied for a pardon from the Trump administration. He based his legitimate pardon request on the obvious unequal treatment that he received compared to both Archer and especially Hunter Biden for the exact same crime. Galanis, unfortunately, never heard back from anyone in the administration, despite the fact that many in Trump World, including Rudy Giuliani, had referenced the obvious mistreatment that Galanis received in the courts compared to Hunter Biden. Not only was Galanis abandoned by the Bidens to rot in prison while his former business partners were living the high life, but he had just poked the bear of the incoming Biden administration, who wanted nothing more than Galanis to remain silent in prison forever.

Galanis recalled during his interview that Hunter's primary goal with their initial deal was to make billions, not just millions.[7] This is an important insight into the mindset of the president's son. He truly desired to make the *Forbes* magazine Billionaire List, but unlike every other billionaire on the list, Hunter did not invent anything unique or work tirelessly to develop an amazing product into a major corporation like Bill Gates, Elon Musk, Mark Zuckerberg, Michael Bloomberg, Phil Knight, or Jeff Bezos—six of the top fifteen billionaires in the U.S. Hunter was not a great investor like Warren Buffett, who spent decades slowly compounding his steady investments. And Hunter was not a successful CEO of a major corporation like Oracle's Larry Ellison or Google's Larry Page, who received hefty stock options based on their leadership performance. Hunter sincerely wanted to be a billionaire by influence-peddling to our adversaries around the world or through some investment scheme that he knew (if caught) he could get out of simply by virtue of being the son of the vice president of the United States.

Hunter's blind ambition and unethical pursuit of it pales in comparison to the fact that his father was entirely willing to exploit that ambition in his son and make money off it. This is one reason that most Republican members of Congress fear that President Joe Biden is a national security risk. The shady schemes with the shady people in the shady countries that his family was privy to make him so.

Galanis testified that on February 4, 2023, he applied for home confinement based on language in the Cares Act that encouraged more home confinement of nonviolent criminals versus institutional confinement. This resulted in massive savings to the taxpayers, and after a lengthy hearing process, on June 9, 2023, he was approved for home confinement by the Pensacola, Florida, federal prison warden and referred to the California Bureau of Placements.

But that never happened.

On June 12, I issued a subpoena for Devon Archer to testify before the Oversight Committee. The next day, Galanis's home incarceration was denied. It was Galanis's understanding from a high-ranking Bureau of Prisons official he spoke to that someone with the Justice Department's Southern District of New York opposed the release from the prison in Pensacola to home confinement in California.

In June 2023, after his home incarceration had been denied,

Galanis testified that he was sexually assaulted by a prison guard. This sexual assaults lasted until August 2023, when the chaplain for the prison intervened and brought the female warden of the prison in for a thirty-minute counseling session. She determined that there was merit in the allegation, and after a quick investigation, Galanis was transferred to the federal prison in Montgomery, Alabama.

The details of the sexual assault and subsequent constant harassment were horrific and difficult to listen to.

All I could think about when I read the transcript from the Jason Galanis interview was the many years of trauma that he had gone through. Yes, he committed an awful financial crime, but he paid dearly for it. The fact is, his business partner, Hunter Biden, would never suffer such consequences. Instead, Hunter would go on to enjoy driving his $142,300 Porsche compliments of the Kazakhstani oligarch, revel in two expensive diamonds compliments of a Chinese-government-linked entity, earn $5 million sitting on the board of a corrupt Ukrainian energy company despite having no experience in energy whatsoever, enjoy all the trashy escorts and cocaine that foreign money can buy, and live in a fabulous $42,000-per-month California condo compliments of his Hollywood attorney and sugar brother, Kevin Morris.

What's more, Hunter frequently traveled on Air Force One at taxpayer expense and participated in formal state dinners at the White House with our president, the wellspring of Hunter Biden's wealth, and the man who happened to be his daddy.

Coincidence?

I think not.

# Chapter 19

## THE BEGINNING OF THE END

We held the fourth hearing of our investigation, "Influence Peddling: Examining Joe Biden's Influence of Public Office," on March 20, 2024. This hearing was after the major interviews and depositions with all of the former Biden associates. There were many discrepancies between what three of the associates (Bobulinski, Archer, and Galanis) said pertaining to Joe Biden's knowledge of, involvement with, and benefit from his family's clear influence-peddling schemes. There were discrepancies in what both Hunter Biden and Jim Biden testified under oath. Finally, there were discrepancies in what Joe Biden had said publicly.

The hearing was called to determine for both the committee as well as the American public who exactly was telling the truth. It would be the Biden family associates either with or against Hunter Biden.

Despite Hunter Biden demanding for months that he wanted a public hearing, he did not show.

I was not surprised at all.

Despite a barrage of claims by the media that I did not want to be transparent or that I was too scared to question Hunter Biden in front of a national audience, when Hunter did not show up, the mainstream media went silent.

In addition to Hunter Biden's absence, Devon Archer failed to appear.* Matthew Schwartz was as big an obstacle to the investigation as anyone at the DOJ, FBI, IRS, or any other Deep State institution. According to multiple credible Oversight sources, Archer never paid Schwartz for his many years of intense legal services. But somebody did.

Archer had other attorneys who would agree to certain testimonies and document releases, and then on multiple occasions we would get a call from Schwartz, who would renege. On more than one occasion, Archer would tell us he had a new attorney and express a willingness to cooperate, but then we would receive a call from Schwartz putting a halt to whatever new avenue we tried to work out with Archer.

Archer was a huge disappointment. Everyone familiar with the inner workings of the Biden schemes suspected that he possessed many more documents and much more damning information on Joe Biden's involvement, especially with Burisma.

According to two witnesses in the investigation, Archer told them privately that *Joe* had called into a Burisma board meeting once. According to another witness, Archer was contacted by a longtime Biden family moneyman and arranger to see if he was interested in negotiating a future pardon from President Biden.

Jeff Cooper is another person whom Joe Biden mentioned in an email to Hunter that he should do business with.[1] Cooper, who had a preternatural ability to curry favor with the rich and powerful, had long been a Biden family friend and supporter. After an abortive 2020 congressional run in the Illinois 20th District as a Dem-

---

* Archer's attorney Ed Haug called us two months before to tell us that Mark Schwartz (who we thought to be Archer's attorney) was no longer on the case, and he, Haug, would now lead his legal team. But days before the hearing and weeks after we had notified Archer of the date of the hearing with all of the associates (which his attorneys confirmed he would attend), we got a letter from Mark Schwartz—at the exact same time as the media—that Archer would not attend due to the lack of time for "planning."

ocrat, Cooper made his fortune in asbestos litigation,[2] then found his true calling in international influence peddling.[3]

Cooper had deep connections among the old-money families of Mexico and Latin America and worked with Hunter to connect on various business deals in Central and South America. In 2014, Hunter, Cooper, Vice President Biden, and two Mexican business executives—Miguel Aleman Velasco (whose father was president of Mexico from 1946 to 1952) and his son Miguel Aleman Magnani—met to discuss "business opportunities."[4]

In 2015, Hunter set up a breakfast at the Naval Observatory with the same group plus Mexican billionaire Carlos Slim. In 2016, Jeff Cooper joined Hunter and Vice President Biden on Air Force Two for a trip to Mexico City.[5] Today Cooper, who communicates often with the Bidens and is a major political donor to both American political parties, owns a thriving law firm with offices in Illinois and Mexico City.

So, after his old buddy Jeff Cooper's possible intervention, Archer and his attorney played both sides. This was a frustration for me. But you know what they say about those who share soup with the devil—use a long spoon. The Bidens have already had Archer for dinner once, and I'm afraid they're going to try to serve him up again before all is said and done.

Archer is and always will be a Biden family stooge, it seems. I wouldn't be totally shocked if he receives a pardon at the end of the Biden administration. Of course, what I really expect is that Joe Biden will screw Devon Archer, fail to provide him a pardon after all, and leave him and his family twisting in the wind.

One thing about working for the Bidens: if your last name *isn't* Biden, you're expendable.

Nevertheless, I believe Archer believes in his heart, God bless him, that Joe Biden will reward his silence with a pardon. Archer always knew more, had more damaging information, and lied to more people than anyone in the investigation whose last name was not Biden.

He can come clean to the committee at any time. My door is open.

## GO WITH YOUR BEST HITTERS

WITH BIDEN AND Archer failing to show, that left me with two witnesses: Tony Bobulinski, who was present, and Jason Galanis, who unfortunately had to appear via Zoom from his Alabama prison.

As much as I admire Tony Bobulinski, I was pretty put out when he wanted to postpone the March 20 Oversight hearing. First he was alarmed that Devon Archer would not be appearing. Bobulinski always sincerely believed that Archer shared his desire to speak the truth about the Biden corruption. It was a touching, if misplaced, sentiment.

The rest of us all knew Archer would not show up. You only have to look into his unblinking, empty eyes to see the man is a natural-born equivocator, always trying to play both sides to his advantage. I'd sooner trust a crumbling old railroad bridge over the Cumberland River than a promise from Devon Archer. Down on the farm in Kentucky we call people who always promise big things but never deliver an "Indian giver" . . . which seems appropriate for someone who went to prison for committing fraud promising to pay a Lakota community big dividends on their Native American bond fund investment and then pocketing the money.[6]

Most of all, I think what Bobulinski wanted very much was to be able to confront Hunter Biden, the man who had wasted so much of his time and energy and casually tried to put him in deep ethical jeopardy. After Hunter's slippery lawyer Abbe Lowell sent word that his client was not going to show, Bobulinski was considering backing out himself.

This would, of course, have been a PR disaster for the investigation, registering at least a 6.0 on the Turley-witness-screwup scale. But far more importantly, the country needed Bobulinski to be there surrounded by those empty seats. No Hunter Biden. No Devon Archer. Just stalwart Tony Bobulinski (and poor Jason Galanis via video) willing to testify openly—that the Biden family had sold their own country out, including its string-pulling patriarch, the current president of the United States, who had full knowledge of all its doings.

After a bit more hemming and hawing, Bobulinski put aside his misgivings, entered "the arena" as he called it, and fought like Russell Crowe versus the emperor Commodus in *Gladiator.*

Bobulinski's performance was one for the ages. Other than Joseph Ziegler, no witness we had throughout the entire investigation provided more value. Any time the Oversight Democrats attack dogs like Goldman or Robert Garcia (D-CA) tried to rattle Tony, he gave it right back to them, and he did it in a polite manner that played well on TV. The hearing was going so well that CNN and MSNBC cut it off, and most of the mainstream media did not even mention the hearing in their nightly newscasts.

Over on the right, the hearing was made for conservative TV, with red-meat clips of Congresswoman Alexandria Ocasio-Cortez (AOC) arguing with Bobulinski and then incorrectly stating that RICO was not a crime.

"And what crime has he committed?" AOC asked, referring to Joe Biden.

"How much time do I have to go through it?" Bobulinski answered.

Bobulinski also stated in his opening comments that Jamie Raskin was a liar. Raskin lost his cool with Bobulinski and interrupted the opening statement to get me to rule on whether calling him a liar would be allowed.

I allowed it because it was a factual statement.

The most significant part of the hearing was Bobulinski describing his realization that the Bidens weren't interested in actual business.

Tony Bobulinski was the one clean guy in the Biden orbit. He made his own money legally in successful and credible business ventures around the world. He testified that what Hunter and Jim Biden were after was personal money from Communist China. He said that the Bidens' only motive was to be paid, and they thought they were entitled to their $9 million from China because they were Bidens.

## THE MAINSTREAM MEDIA ROLLS OVER AND PLAYS DEAD YET AGAIN

THE ALLEGATION THAT the president of the United States' family received a bribe from the People's Republic of China should have been a major news story. A bribe to a family member is clearly the basis for violations of the Foreign Corrupt Practices Act.

One legal question is whether the timeline of the bribe's being given would implicate Joe Biden, since the payment was received while he was out of office. In other words, it was payment for services rendered or, perhaps, to be rendered.

The deals were negotiated while Joe Biden was VP (as Tony Bobulinski and Devon Archer previously testified). The results were manifestly apparent. Biden, who had direct responsibility in the area, stayed out of China's way in the Far East.

Bobulinski had never previously put it in such stark terms, even in his deposition. So his allegation that the Bidens were taking bribes should have been covered wire to wire on every network in America. But like every other news story throughout the investigation that would have been major in other circumstances, it received virtually no coverage. Even conservative media failed to pick up on the bribery allegation and were instead bedazzled by the theater of the heated exchange between Bobulinski and AOC, or his withering exchanges with Raskin and Goldman. I don't blame them. It was great stuff. But ultimately unimportant.

## GALANIS BOMBSHELLS AND AUTHENTICITY

OUR OTHER WITNESS was Jason Galanis. We had a deal worked out with the Bureau of Prisons to allow Galanis to be extradited from his Alabama prison to the Oversight hearing, but, like clockwork, four days before the hearing we received a call back from the bureau declaring that the DOJ had blocked their request to allow Galanis to testify in person. If we wanted to have Galanis as a witness, we had to do it in the much less effective virtual method of Zoom.

I have literally lost count of the times that Merrick Garland's DOJ has obstructed the Oversight Committee's investigation. I also felt sorry for Galanis. Because of my investigation, he was denied home incarceration, raped in prison, and denied his awaited opportunity to set the record straight in person to a national audience on how he (and, to a certain extent, Devon Archer) took the fall for a scheme in which Hunter Biden was not only a partner, but on which Hunter Biden made significant profit. The claim that Hunter knew nothing about the tribal bond scam is impossible to believe.

I worry about other unthinkable consequences Galanis might face as a result of my investigation. One day I hope to find whoever did this to the guy and make their life extremely uncomfortable. It's the least I can do.

Galanis testified that Hunter's ultimate goal was to make billions, not just millions, off the schemes. This showcased the audacity of this entitled son of a vice president, a "café artist" who believed he was entitled to such a ridiculous sum just because of his last name.

Galanis also testified that Joe was set to be an equity partner in a deal with Hunter and Galanis. This marked the third time that someone affiliated with the Bidens said that Hunter or Jim used Joe as a potential equity partner on a scheme (the others being Bobulinski on the China deal where Joe was "the big guy" and the Americore Health scheme where Jim told the owners of the failing healthcare company that Joe wanted a board seat and an equity ownership stake).

## THE GREASEBALL ON THE LEFT

THE DEMOCRATS CHOSE as their witness Lev Parnas, a Soviet-born American scoundrel who was found guilty in 2021 in federal court on six counts related to illegal donations to the 2020 campaign of Donald Trump.[7] Parnas also pled guilty to a fraud charge pertaining to receiving money from Russia in a marijuana scheme. The Democrats could have asked another Biden associate we'd deposed to be their witness (say, one who they falsely claimed exonerated Joe Biden, such as Eric Schwerin or Rob Walker), but they chose instead a Russian criminal.

Parnas was such a slimy character that after sitting in front of him for the miserably long six-hour hearing, I felt I needed a bath with bleach. The facial expressions, the constant nodding of his head, and the remarkable taunting of Tony Bobulinski while he was testifying were scenes I had never seen before from a witness. Parnas had no knowledge or experience with Biden influence-peddling schemes.

His claim to fame was accompanying Rudy Giuliani looking for answers in the Burisma scheme. Parnas was there to instigate yet another Russia hoax operation and to try to get Bobulinski rattled so the media could write that our witness was crazy and my hearing was a circus.

You might as well try to rattle Plymouth Rock.

"You're a liar and a fraud," Bobulinski replied to Parnas's whispered taunts.

Parnas kept hissing jabs. Finally, Bobulinski turned to him. "Is that a threat?" he asked.

"If you keep lying, you're going to end up in prison," Parnas commented out of the side of his mouth, looking for all the world like a stereotype of a 1930s low-level gangster.

"You're the one who went to prison for lying," Bobulinski replied evenly.[8]

## ENTER THE CLOWNS

AS USUAL, THE unserious members of Congress performed immature stunts for their pitiful, partisan DC press corps following. Jared Moskowitz wore a Vladimir Putin mask[9] (symbolizing their favorite theme of Russian disinformation) and Eric Swalwell held up a chalkboard to declare the impeachment "time of death." All three DC press insider publications (*Hill*, *Politico*, Punchbowl —aka Toilet Bowl—and *Roll Call*) covered the two stunts as if they were the real show. Meanwhile, they ignored the presentation and elaboration of evidence of Biden wrongdoing.

Punchbowl even stated in its newsletter that we did not present any evidence of wrongdoing "other than emails, text messages and a bank statement that was difficult to understand." That reference prompted me to tell its author, Max Cohen, that if he couldn't understand a simple bank statement, perhaps he should stop writing about financial wrongdoing and just write Dr. Seuss fan fiction.

# Chapter 20

## THE CLOSER'S KID

On February 28, 2024, Hunter Biden entered the Rayburn conference room with his high-powered attorney, Abbe Lowell, to give his deposition to the Oversight Committee.

There is a metaphysical slouch to Hunter Biden. He somehow always manages to make even his smartly tailored suits look shabby, like he's leaking shame into them. He wore a tie whose color might as well have been a symbol for his soul. Puce.

Also present were curious Republican members from the Oversight and Judiciary Committees, as well as plenty of adoring fans from within the Democrat ranks.

### BRINGING ORDER TO THE ZOO

IMMEDIATELY—EVEN BEFORE the court reporter could get her typewriter set up—Lowell and my Oversight counsel started going at it. Of course, with a room full of firebrands, that arguing would quickly spread, and the Democrats were determined to turn the proceedings into a sideshow spectacle in any case.

Eric Swalwell yelled from the back of the room to ask when I would release the transcripts. Dan Goldman chimed in, followed by a half-dozen other backbench Democrats who wanted to be able to suck up to their MSNBC mothership later, like monstrous little children of the night bragging that they yelled at the evil chair-human who had the audacity to throw sunshine on all the Biden misconduct. I seldom speak in depositions. I hired a top-notch staff who are very experienced in these proceedings and, like a good coach, I want the best players on the court. But I immediately pounded my fist on the table and said that I would not tolerate further outbursts. I said that the majority would ask questions—uninterrupted—for one hour, then the minority would get the same.

Swalwell stood up in the rear of the room, pointed his finger at me, and yelled at the top of his lungs, demanding to know when I would release the transcript.

I replied in a normal voice, "As I have always done, we will release the transcript as soon as both sides approve it, as is standard process; so, it could be one to three days."

Swalwell then popped off one of his usual smart-ass remarks demanding the terms he wanted and I quickly snapped back, "I don't care what you want, Eric." As I was attempting to restore order, Judiciary ranking member Jerry Nadler, who had already filled the room with his signature essence, Eau de Truck Stop Restroom, swelled with emotion (or something equally noxious) and cried forth, "Well, I care!"

I knew going into the deposition that the Democrats did not want Hunter Biden to answer our questions. They knew perfectly well that the president's son might provide evidence of committed serious financial crimes ranging from money laundering to tax evasion. Their strategy was to disrupt, get my members to take their bait, and turn the Oversight hearing into a circus. I was tempted to respond in kind, but I did not want to open the floodgates in what I needed to be a substantive deposition that would get Hunter on the record lying about both his financial transactions and his father's involvement.

Abbe Lowell turned pompously to the back of the room and assured Swalwell that the transcripts would be released as soon as possible. Swalwell uttered his last smart-ass remark for the time being: "Will it be written in Russian?"

He must have spent hours thinking up that one.

I restrained myself.

The objective of the deposition was to get Hunter Biden on the record lying as much as possible so we could have as many criminal referrals as possible when we had a Republican DOJ to hold him accountable.

Jordan's Judiciary staffer Steve Castor had negotiated the terms of the deposition with Lowell. Castor had been the lead staffer for the Republicans during both Trump impeachments, and he was an old hand at depositions. The agreement was that Oversight staff would get the first hour, Judiciary staff would get the next hour, and then the individual members would conclude the questioning. The Democrats (and later, their ally in personal rancor, Steve Doocy) criticized me for not personally asking questions. I did not. Neither did Jim Jordan. Instead Jordan and I had both spent hours with each of our staffs preparing the precise questions for them to ask. That is how formal depositions usually work, and both Swalwell and Doocy knew it.

## WHAT WE LEARNED

AFTER ALL THE dust settled and both staff and conservative media had ample time to digest[1] the transcript from the deposition,[2] I believed Oversight's Hunter Biden deposition was an overwhelming success in making our legal case against the Biden influence-peddling schemes.

A future DOJ with true justice in mind should note Hunter Biden's telling contradictions and admissions.

One, Hunter Biden admitted receiving millions of dollars from China and a $250,000 wire from the CEO of a state-backed investment fund. He declared these payments from China to be "incredibly ethical."

Two, Hunter Biden admitted that he traveled with then–vice president Biden on Air Force Two to Beijing, where he introduced his father to his Chinese business partner, Jonathan Li. Vice President Biden went on to write a college letter of recommendation for Li's son.

Three, Hunter Biden confirmed that CEFC chairman Ye Jianming gave him a diamond.

As he explained it, "Well, if anyone has been to China, in particular, and other parts of Asia, it's commonplace to exchange gifts at the beginning of any relationship and introduction."

Yes, I'm sure readers are quite familiar with Chinese friends showering you with diamonds whenever they come over to watch March Madness with you. Or maybe Hunter Biden's explanation just sounds crazy to you.

Whatever its ultimate worth, the diamond came from a PRC intermediary. We've already established that CEFC chairman Ye had close ties to the Chinese government. After all, CEFC had sprung from nowhere. The magic of third-way capitalism? Hardly. It was the Chinese Communist Party's sovereign wealth fund created for use by the Belt and Road Initiative. Of course it didn't advertise itself as a state-operated entity, but only a fool would think it was anything else.

Four, when asked about sending a threatening WhatsApp message in July 2017 to a CEFC functionary demanding payment from the CEFC, Hunter Biden said he was on drugs, yet he knew his father was somehow not sitting next to him, although in the message he says Joe Biden is there. Furthermore, dated laptop photos prove Hunter was at Joe's Delaware home the day he sent his message.[3] The CEFC money poured into Hunter's joint account days later.

Dad was there.

Five, Hunter Biden admitted he attempted to set up a lunch between his father and CEFC associates. This is consistent with a pattern the investigation had already uncovered. Joe Biden always played some role (usually the role of the closer of the deals) in the Bidens' influence schemes.

Six, Hunter Biden confirmed that his father, then–vice president Biden, dined with Kenes Rakishev, a Kazakhstani oligarch, at Cafe Milano.

Devon Archer confirmed this was around the same time the Kazakhstan oligarch sent money for Hunter Biden's expensive sports car. Hunter was evasive about that payment during his testimony.

Seven, Hunter Biden admitted he put his father on speakerphone many times in front of business associates and invited his father to lunches, dinners, or other social events with dubious associates and shady international figures. This was more evidence that Joe Biden's main role in the influence peddling schemes was "closer" of the deal.

Eight, Hunter Biden denied any association with Rosemont Seneca Bohai, despite its having his "Rosemont Seneca" branding. He previously received his payments from Burisma into the account and took into the account $142,300 from a Kazakhstani oligarch in payment for his sports car.

It was very interesting how Hunter kept distancing himself from the BHR fund, in which he had partial ownership. I would encourage future DOJ prosecutors to have a look into that fund in depth.

Nine, Hunter Biden confirmed Tony Bobulinski's testimony that he met with Joe and James Biden in California.

Ten, Hunter Biden often claimed he could not recall certain meetings, phone calls, or other forms of communication, but he always remembered specific details about these occurrences when they served his purposes.

## MORE EVASIONS AND WHOPPERS

THE DEPOSITION ALSO generated some downright whoppers from Biden, as well.

Devon Archer in his testimony referenced Hunter making a call to DC after executives at Burisma told Hunter that he needed to call his dad for help in getting the Ukrainian government off their backs. Hunter shook his head and chuckled. Oh, no, this was actually a call to his teenage daughters and not Joe Biden or anyone else in the Obama/Biden administration.

That would mean that during this moment of crisis when the Burisma owners, panicked over legal trouble and with many of their foreign assets frozen overseas, begged the board member they had specifically paid $1 million a year to solve just this sort of problem with his powerful father's influence, Hunter Biden simply ignored them, excused himself, and stepped outside to check in with his teenager.

Hunter Biden said that he did not know who the "big guy" was, but he knew it was not Joe Biden. After that comment he was shown the famous "10% for the big guy" email. Hunter claimed he never read that email—this despite the fact that he responded to it.

Hunter implied that his infamous laptop was compromised by Russia, following a path of explanation that Jim Biden used whenever he did not want to answer a question about an email or text from the laptop.

Hunter also said that he did not remember if he dropped off his laptop at Mac Isaacs's computer repair store in Wilmington, and that he could not remember if he even *had* a laptop during that time period. Playing the drug-addict card is to Hunter what playing the forgetful-old-man card is to Joe. Hunter would say he couldn't remember something because he was high on cocaine or drunk whenever he could not answer the question without perjuring himself, much like Joe Biden grew angry at the questioning when something Special Counsel Robert Hur asked didn't suit him, and blamed his fuzzy answers on the matter being lost in the mists of time.

Hunter Biden ticked off his mediocre résumé.

"I wrote it down because it's long," he commented.

It was filled with ceremonial board seats provided for him because of who his father was, but Hunter used it to imply that he was qualified to be on a Ukrainian energy company's board of directors. It was noteworthy that in Hunter's opening statement when he rattled off his big accomplishments, one accomplishment he did *not* list was being on the board of Burisma.

Hunter claimed during his opening comments that the Biden influence-peddling investigation was just a MAGA-orchestrated conspiracy theory, just before confirming most of the details.

Of all the unbelievable statements made during their depositions, the most ridiculous claim the Bidens and their allies in the media wanted the American people to swallow was that Joe Biden had absolutely no idea what his family did for a living, and that it was pure coincidence that he met and/or spoke with every single person who wired his family tens of millions of dollars.

As the *Wall Street Journal*'s Bill McGurn later joked of the testimony, "I think you're underestimating how often people suffering from a traumatic incident in their life then respond to that by inviting their father into all their business meetings with overseas oligarchs and so forth. Look, it doesn't pass the smell test. It's patently false."[4]

## THE SPORTS CAR FROM HELL

IT IS ALSO hard to imagine that Joe Biden, who by all accounts loves and understands the value of sports cars, would see his son (who was, according to Hunter's own testimony, addicted to drugs) pull up at his Delaware house driving a brand-new Porsche and not ask his son, "Wow, son, how much did that car cost?"

Or, "How did you afford that $142,300 sports car?"

Or how about, "How much is the insurance on that thing?"

Every other father in the world would ask. If I had pulled into my dad's house driving a new Porsche, my dad would have asked all three of those questions, plus questioned me as to whether or not I was actually a Comer. (I have only owned three new vehicles in my entire life, including my current Toyota 4Runner, which has over 370,000 miles.)

## THE COSTS TO THE COUNTRY

THERE WERE SEVERAL additional outbursts by the Democrats during the deposition, as you might expect, as well as combative comments by Hunter Biden himself. Hunter got visibly mad at all the questions pertaining to his many wire transfers from shady foreign sources. He looked at me and asked why I was not investigating Jared Kushner. I responded sincerely and said I would love to have Kushner answer some questions when I focus on passing legislation to ban influence peddling. I glanced over at Abbe Lowell, whose reptilian eyes flashed back at me, and added that maybe Hunter's own attorney, Lowell, would be called to testify at that time, since he had represented both Hunter Biden and Jared Kushner. Lowell leaped into action like a twitching marionette and denied that he represented Kushner *at that moment.* Of course, he had represented Kushner in a very high-profile manner in the past.[5] Another clever Abbe Lowell twisting of the truth.

Kimberley Strassel of the *Wall Street Journal* sums it up succinctly. "To really understand the importance of Hunter Biden's testimony it's worth just for two seconds remembering how far we have come along here. You go back to the fall of 2020, the *New York Post* says it has this laptop, publishes stories about Hunter's business dealings. Candidate Joe Biden says, 'No, no, no, I've never had anything to do with my son's business. I don't talk to him about it, walled off,' and goes along with this fiction that got promulgated in the media and social media and these fifty-one intel officials that this is somehow disinformation. We now know that laptop's not disinformation. And what was most striking to me about Hunter's testimony was how much of, in fact some of the worst aspects of what was contained on that laptop, he admitted to during this hearing."[6]

Hunter Biden's testimony confirmed much of the evidence uncovered to date in the impeachment inquiry of President Joe Biden. However, parts of his testimony were completely inconsistent with the testimonies of other witnesses in major matters. That is why when I walked out of the deposition to address the media, I announced that the next step in my investigation would be a public hearing with Hunter Biden so we might clarify these inconsistencies.

After seven hours, what was the most important fact we had discovered? That Hunter Biden, despite all his drama and all his drug talk, was basically the family tool. His go-to response was to backpedal his previous, well-known braggadocio—although we got a taste of that ("I literally was on seventeen—like, twelve different boards. I only listed like, you know, ten of them")—and deny, deny, deny.

Hunter was not the family closer.

The closer was Joe Biden.

# Chapter 21

## THE HUR WHITEWASH

Robert K. Hur testified before Jim Jordan's Judiciary Committee on March 12, 2024, about his special counsel report on Joe Biden's mishandling of classified documents. Hur's report was profoundly disappointing and disturbing, a direct blow to the principle that no man, even the president of the United States, is above the law.

Hur concluded that, despite mishandling classified documents for decades, President Joe Biden should not be prosecuted because a jury would see him as an "elderly man with a poor memory," and thus have pity on him.[1] So much for equal justice under the law.

The Hur Report was clear in its conclusion. Joe knew he had in his possession classified documents. He knew full well the legal policy surrounding the possession and sharing of classified documents, yet he still shared the documents with Mark Zwonitzer, his ghostwriter.[2]

Joe Biden received a cool $8 million advance[3] for his 2017 book, *Promise Me, Dad*.[4] Perhaps he felt he needed to use the classified documents because he lacked the ability to write his own book from his failing memory. Whatever the reason, Joe read a portion of his trove of illegal classified documents[5] to a ghostwriter.

Back on the farm, we call that pure greed.

As Jim Jordan said in the hearing, "Joe Biden had eight million reasons to break the rules."[6]

A few weeks before Hur was named special counsel to investigate President Biden's mishandling of classified documents, I launched an Oversight Committee investigation into the subject. I brought in for transcribed interviews former vice president Biden's assistant Kathy Chung[7] as well as two employees of the Penn Biden Center for Diplomacy.

The White House's narrative of President Biden's mishandling of classified documents was that their discovery happened after Trump's classified document subpoena return date. But Dana Remus, a lawyer at the White House Counsel's Office, had tasked Department of Defense employee Chung on May 24, 2022—the same day as the subpoena return date for former president Trump—to go pack up the probable classified documents at the Penn Biden Center. What's more, they had sat around there in an unsecured location for months (as Chung told us, there was no "locked closet," as the administration claimed).[8]

What Oversight discovered was monumental. We proved that President Biden's DOJ ordered an unprecedented raid on their predecessor and likely opponent in the upcoming election for the same crime that their boss had committed . . . and they knew of Biden's actions all along.[9]

The Trump raid was, at least in part, an engineered distraction from another Biden family scandal.

That is similar to the intelligence community (led by the man who would become Biden's secretary of state) providing signatures for a letter declaring that the Hunter Biden laptop was not real when they must have known all along that it was authentic. A corrupt president with a corrupt attorney general and a corrupt secretary of state all conspiring to imprison a political opponent—*not* in a third-world country.

In the USA.

While my concerns had not been taken up by the media, there is no doubt that Hur and his special counsel team knew about them. I'd sent enough letters to government officials requesting further details on the Biden classified hoards to make my concerns well-known within the administration.

The Hur Report determined that there were eight different locations where Biden's classified documents were found, locations spread across the eastern United States. Hur concluded that they were mishandled in the Penn Biden Center as well as the president's private Delaware home.[10] What Hur conveniently *failed* to mention was that the Penn Biden Center is funded with anonymous donations from the government of China[11]—our biggest adversary. Joe Biden's Delaware residence was also the primary residence of his drug-addicted son, who was at that time actively influence-peddling with China, Russia, and Ukraine—and receiving millions of dollars while doing so.

Why is this a big deal? One reason is that there are possible classified government documents related to Hunter Biden's dealings with Ukraine's Burisma and Chinese state-owned enterprises that could be in those boxes Joe Biden was hanging on to.

Why would a special counsel investigating mishandling classified documents fail to mention the astounding discrepancy in the purported dates when those documents were found? Why would he fail to mention the fact that China, our most serious international threat and known for having extensive spy rings, funded the location of most of the documents? Why also would his report fail to mention the fact that the family was under a very high-profile congressional investigation for influence peddling?

Furthermore, there is great concern over the White House counsel sending a known Biden family lackey to rifle through the documents at Penn Biden Center and elsewhere.

As Jordan Boyd of the *Federalist* put it, "Because the DOJ granted Biden's legal team the luxury of sifting through the confidential records without surveillance or oversight, there's no way for the public to know if Biden's legal team vetted, removed, or tampered with the materials before handing them over."[12]

Robert Hur knew that the Oversight Committee was concerned about a specific document on Hunter Biden's laptop. This was a document emailed to a corrupt Ukrainian oligarch at a time when the oligarch was cutting Hunter's excessive pay from the Burisma board in half now that Joe Biden was no longer in office. The document was attached possibly to prove Hunter's value to the oligarch in that he, Hunter, knew classified information.[13]

Was this information culled from the trove in Biden's possession? Was that where Hunter nipped it?

There is little doubt that Hur understood that the Oversight Committee was concerned about this matter.

Yet Hur failed to mention it in his report.

Another glowing omission from the Hur Report was an account of which documents Joe Biden may have mishandled. The report briefly mentioned the countries represented in the mishandled classified documents cache, but not what particular documents they were, or even what they pertained to. Ukraine[14] and Russia were two countries mentioned. Special Counsel Hur knew that Oversight had discovered that Hunter Biden had taken in from corrupt sources roughly $5 million from Ukraine and $3.5 million from Russia *and* that we discovered two specific emails that we believed could have been classified government documents pertaining to those governments. These were documents that Hunter had emailed to his shady benefactors in those countries.

I was criticized by Jake Tapper on CNN days after the appointment of the special counsel when I expressed my opinion that Merrick Garland appointed Hur for the sole purpose of protecting Joe Biden from the Oversight Committee.[15]

Tapper has proved himself a fool, or at least a willing dupe. I am right to have been concerned. One merely has to look at the outcome of the "investigation" and the contents of Hur's report to bear me out.

We found some of the most damaging evidence quickly about the timeline of discovery being incorrect. We found that multiple people had access to the documents and that the White House knew about it *before* Trump's Palm Beach residence was raided for the same type of document retention.

Furthermore, once the special counsel was appointed, my Oversight Committee was legally blocked from obtaining any further evidence or getting any further testimony.

How convenient was that for the Bidens?

Now that the Hur Report is completed, say I were to call Dana Remus, a key witness in the Biden document scandal, or say new evidence in that scandal emerges. You can be certain what the mainstream media would clamor: Hur already exonerated Joe! Case closed!

Robert Hur might be an appealing advocate with his extremely qualified misgivings, but his report is what it was always intended to be.

A whitewash.

Look at Hur's insertion of what he knew would be the focal point of the report: the obvious fact of Joe Biden's declining mental state. Polling showed that most voters were concerned about Biden's mental state because of his age, but also that older voters were upset that Republicans were using his old age as an issue.[16] Rather than a confession of legal disadvantage, Hur's insertion is a play for sympathy.

It's a blatant emotional excuse, not a reason to decline prosecution. It was meant to go over well with older voters.

Hur and his report are a crock, just as I predicted they would be.

Days after the Hur Report was released, Joe Biden delivered his "fiery" State of the Union speech where, in the opinion of most of my Republican colleagues as well as many conservative media commentators, the president appeared to be "jacked up" on some kind of stimulant that made him appear unusually vibrant, one might even say maniacal. In his speech, Biden also owned the fact that he was an older leader but claimed that gave him wisdom and maturity. In politics, taking an opponent's successful issue (which with Trump and the GOP would be Biden's age and feebleness) and turning it into an asset is an old stunt called triangulation.

Hur's report failed to mention the facts that Oversight had already discovered. Joe Biden illegally stored documents in a facility funded by the Chinese Communist Party, and at his house where his influence-peddling and drug-addicted son lived, as well as the fact that the timeline of discovery was off by more than a year, was drowned out by Hur's alleged old-age slur. Within days this was successfully adapted into a political triangulation move by President Biden himself in his prime-time address to the nation. And of course, the media echo chamber complemented everything Joe Biden was pushing to a T—just as cackling court sycophants always do.

And how did the so-called loyal opposition Democrats react? The Hur hearing in Judiciary was effective in demonstrating to America that the Judiciary Democrats (like the Oversight Democrats) were only interested in providing oversight of Donald Trump. They too behaved as an extension of the Biden legal defense team rather than as true investigators after the truth.

Unlike the colluding media, the clueless Judiciary Democrats acted more like marionettes with half their strings cut. They clearly were not in the inner circle of the mysterious people who run the Biden White House and coordinate the administration's false narratives. The pitiful Hank Johnson and hopeless Sheila Jackson Lee tried to attack Hur's report by spinning a kindergarten narrative that Hur had "exonerated" Joe Biden. In this, they were met with a quick correction by Hur himself.

That wasn't the story the administration wanted told.

Hur testified the obvious, that Joe Biden willfully retained and disclosed classified materials. In Hunter Biden's Oversight deposition, the president's son played the drug card whenever he didn't feel like answering a potentially incriminating question. Here in the special counsel's report, Hunter's dad showed his boy how it was done. Joe played the dementia card perfectly. Like father, like son.

I had a couple of fascinating observations about participating in my first-ever Judiciary hearing. Judiciary Committee members at the hearing were much more professional and disciplined than my members. One of my big pet peeves concerning my committee is that my members cannot sit still. They constantly roam in and out of the hearing chamber. It's distracting and a little bit maddening. Perhaps because the Judiciary Committee members are mostly attorneys, used to the decorum of a courtroom where you're expected to sit calmly throughout the trial, they behaved in a different manner than my members.

The other observation of the Judiciary membership was that Jim Jordan dealt with the same kind of petty behind-the-scenes drama as I did. At the Hur hearing, Jim did as I normally do during high-profile hearings when they're being covered live on national TV: he went out of the standard order of questioning by seniority. Jim, like me, wants to put his best questioners first to set a tone for the hearing. This meant that he skipped over more senior members Darrell Issa and Ken Buck and went first to Kelly Armstrong and Matt Gaetz. Since I was an addition to the committee as chair of Oversight, I sat directly between Jordan, Issa, and Buck. They were visibly upset and vocally complaining to Judiciary staff about Jordan's decision.

Soon after the hearing, both Issa and Buck were quick to criticize both the hearing and the overall impeachment inquiry. In fact, Buck got so mad at going nearly dead last that he announced he was leaving Congress that afternoon.[17]

Good riddance!

I did feel some sympathy for Special Counsel Hur. It couldn't have been easy pushing himself to what he knew must be a foreordained conclusion. When I later reread the Hur Report, I could feel Hur's pain in having to deal with Joe Biden. It is very frustrating dealing with any Biden because, by nature, they are totally dishonest people. They have lied about their businesses, broken every ethics law along the way, and likely avoided paying taxes on most of the millions of dollars they received through their influence-peddling endeavors. The government not only turns a blind eye to the Biden family corruption, but they also repeatedly tell anyone investigating their crimes to stand down as well as cover up any traces of evidence. Former associates are imprisoned, potential whistleblowers indicted. When a corrupt regime is in power and the executive branch (the FBI, CIA, DOJ,[18] IRS, and *even* the benighted National Archives and Records Administration[19]) is in cahoots with the regime, then the last two instruments in the service of the United States democratic system of checks and balances are the mainstream media and congressional oversight.

Yeah, right. Not the media. The mainstream media were a gleeful bunch of Biden family colluders almost to a man and woman, and possessed of the unity of a pack of coyotes yowling at the moon.

Hur faced a firestorm from the mainstream media at the time of his hearing for correctly implying that Joe Biden knowingly and willfully broke the law, but he didn't want to prosecute because the president could easily play the "old fool" card. This was the same thing that I dealt with throughout my Biden investigation, a hostile media attacking me for having the audacity to criticize President Biden.

Of course, for Hur this media whine went up at the trivial admission that Joe Biden's mind was obviously in decay. I instead triggered them with the much more dangerous assertion I shouted from every rooftop I could find.

The contention that the Big Guy willfully and repeatedly broke the law for profit.

# CLOSING

At the very beginning of the investigation, I said my two primary objectives were to provide the American people with the truth about any crimes the Biden family may have committed and to pass legislation that would define and prevent influence peddling by anyone from happening in the future. The truth is in this book, and the legislation is making its way through Congress. Hopefully, it will soon become the law of the land.

It is my sincere belief that Joe Biden committed impeachable offenses while he served as vice president and president. Hunter Biden acknowledges collecting millions of dollars from problematic foreign individuals while (or soon after) Joe Biden oversaw policies that benefited those individuals or their countries. Whistleblowers came forward to say their investigations were stalled or blocked. Key witnesses, including Hunter, gave testimony that contradicted bank statements or their previous statements. Many of Hunter Biden's associates have gone to prison while statutes of limitations expired on accusations against Hunter. The Biden family and their allies have denied any wrongdoing every step of the way.

Unfortunately, but predictably, most Americans know much more about the denials than the facts. With no groundswell in the polling, the fear that voters would view a Biden impeachment as a form of political warfare—much like what the Democrats did to Donald Trump twice during the last Congress—impeachment, as was always the case from day one, would never happen. As I stated earlier in the book, no president in history has ever been removed from office as a result of impeachment.

The American people had an opportunity to decide for themselves in November 2024 what the appropriate form of accountability could be for Joe Biden and his allies. Unlike in 2020, the voters had access to the truth about the tens of millions flowing to Hunter and James Biden, as well as the extent to which Deep State bureaucrats at the FBI, CIA, DOJ, IRS, and SEC ignored evidence and slow-walked investigations, leaking to the mainstream media and their "nothing to see here" narratives. The only reason the voters will be armed with the truth is because of the successful Biden Family Influence-Peddling Investigation led by the House Oversight Committee.

IRS whistleblowers Joseph Ziegler and Gary Shapley testified to my committee that the Department of Justice intentionally allowed the statue of limitations to expire on most of the crimes the Bidens committed while Joe Biden served as vice president. But the criminal referrals sent to the DOJ on Hunter and Jim Biden during my investigation have a five-year statute of limitations which gives a potential new attorney general the opportunity to finally hold the family accountable.

Leading any investigation in Congress is hard, especially if it is one against a Democrat, being the constant target of the left and their endless supply of dark money charades, fighting the mainstream media's daily misreporting of the facts, while navigating some of the most difficult personalities in Congress to support my strategy and messaging is the hardest thing I have ever done. But it was a challenge which I will be forever grateful to have had the opportunity to embark.

This was the biggest public corruption scandal of my lifetime. And the reaction of the intelligence agencies has led to a historic lack of confidence in our nation's federal law enforcement agencies.

I have often said that the two most important things Congress can do to fix itself is to pass a balanced budget amendment and term limits. The amendment would ensure that necessary cuts to wasteful spending happen and there are no better examples of wasteful spending than what we see at the FBI (new building about to be constructed as well as secret divisions that monitor conservative social media posts), the IRS (doubling its size to go after select tax cheats whose last name is not Biden), and the DOJ (stocked full of deep state bureaucrats). Term limits would get rid of all the aged politicians, particularly in the Senate who not only have bankrupted our children but have refused to ever hold anyone accountable for wrongdoing, whether it be at the southern border or in the form of influence peddling. I will continue to strongly support and advocate for both the Balanced Budget Amendment and Congressional term limits.

I will also continue to lead the fight in Washington for a more transparent government which holds bad actors accountable for wrongdoing.

# APPENDIX A: THE BIDEN LLCS

Here are the former Biden associates who were primarily involved in the initial receipt of the foreign wires that would then be laundered through a series of LLCs and bank accounts before ultimately going into ten different Biden family members' personal accounts:

Rob Walker
Devon Archer
James Gilliar

The companies that Hunter and James Biden were all or partial owners of and that were involved in the money-laundering schemes:

Robinson Walker LLC
Rosemont Seneca Partners LLC
Rosemont Seneca Thornton LLC
Rosemont Seneca Bohai LLC
Rosemont Seneca Principal Investments LLC
Rosemont Seneca Global Advisors LLC
Rosemont Seneca Global Risk Services LLC
Rosemont Seneca Advisors LLC
Rosemont Seneca Technology Partners LLC
Rosemont Realty LLC
Seneca Global Advisors LLC
Owasco PC
Owasco LLC
Skaneateles LLC
JBBSR Inc.
Lion Hall Group LLC
Paradigm Companies LLC
BHR Partners LLC
RSP Holdings LLC

Hudson West III
Hudson West V
RSTP II Alpha Partners LLC
RSTP II Bravo Partners LLC
CEFC Infrastructure Investment (US) LLC

# APPENDIX B: CRIMINAL REFERRALS

# Congress of the United States
## Washington, DC 20515

June 5, 2024

The Honorable Merrick B. Garland
Attorney General
Department of Justice
950 Pennsylvania Avenue, NW
Washington, D.C. 20530

The Honorable David C. Weiss
Special Counsel & United States Attorney
United States Attorney's Office
District of Delaware
1313 N Market Street
PO Box 2046
Wilmington, DE 19801

Dear Attorney General Garland and Special Counsel Weiss:

The House Committee on Oversight and Accountability, the House Committee on the Judiciary, and the House Committee on Ways and Means (the Committees) are investigating whether sufficient grounds exist to draft articles of impeachment against President Biden for consideration by the full House.[1] Specifically, the Committees are investigating the President's role in and knowledge of his family's international influence peddling schemes that have generated over $18 million for Biden family members and their related companies, and over $27 million when including the payments to their business associates, who often were used to transfer funds to Biden family members.[2] This figure does not include an additional $8 million in loans—most of which has not been repaid—to Robert Hunter Biden (Hunter Biden) and James Brian Biden (James Biden), the President's son and brother, respectively.[3] In total, since 2014, the Committees have accounted for over $35 million received by Biden family members, their companies, and business associates, which includes financial transactions described as loans.[4] Despite much effort, the Committees have not identified legitimate services warranting such lucrative payments. The amount of money the Biden family has received from concerning companies and individuals is alarming.

In furtherance of the impeachment inquiry, the Oversight Committee and the Judiciary Committee have interviewed multiple witnesses regarding President Biden's knowledge of and involvement in his family's business dealings, including Biden family associates and Biden family members themselves, namely Hunter Biden and James Biden. On February 21, 2024, the

---

[1] *See* H. Res. 918, 118th Cong. (2023).
[2] *See generally* attached Criminal Referral.
[3] *Id.*
[4] *Id.*

Oversight Committee and the Judiciary Committee conducted a transcribed interview with James Biden, who was accompanied by counsel. On February 28, 2024, the Oversight Committee and the Judiciary Committee conducted a deposition with Hunter Biden, who testified under oath and also was accompanied by counsel.

The Committees attach to this letter a referral for criminal charges against Hunter Biden and James Biden, under 18 U.S.C. § 1001 (false statements), and, additionally, for Hunter Biden under 18 U.S.C. § 1621 (perjury). As the attached referral shows, Hunter Biden and James Biden made provably false statements to the Oversight Committee and the Judiciary Committee about key aspects of the impeachment inquiry, in what appears to be a conscious effort to hinder the investigation's focus on President Joe Biden.

Specifically, Hunter Biden falsely distanced himself from a corporate entity—Rosemont Seneca Bohai, LLC—and its bank account (Rosemont Seneca Bohai Bank Account) that was the recipient of millions of dollars from foreign individuals and foreign entities who met with then-Vice President Biden before and after transmitting money to the Rosemont Seneca Bohai Bank Account that then transferred funds to Hunter Biden.[5] Hunter Biden made additional false statements as to whether he held positions at Rosemont Seneca Bohai, LLC. After deposing Hunter Biden, the Committees obtained documents showing Hunter Biden represented that he was the corporate secretary.[6] Additionally, Hunter Biden during his testimony relayed an entirely fictitious account about threatening text messages he sent to his Chinese business partner while invoking his father's presence with him as he wrote the messages. Hunter Biden told the Oversight Committee and the Judiciary Committee he had transmitted this threat to an unrelated individual with the same surname.[7] However, documents released by the Committee on Ways and Means demonstrate conclusively that Hunter Biden made this threat to the intended individual, and bank records prove Hunter Biden's Chinese business partners wired millions of dollars to him after his threat.[8] A portion of the proceeds has been traced to Joe Biden's bank account.[9]

With respect to James Biden, he stated unequivocally during his transcribed interview that Joe Biden did not meet with Mr. Tony Bobulinski, a business associate of James and Hunter Biden, in 2017 while pursuing a deal with a Chinese entity, CEFC China Energy. Specifically, James Biden stated he did not attend a meeting with Joe Biden, Hunter Biden, and Tony Bobulinski on May 2, 2017 at the Beverly Hilton Hotel.[10] These statements were contradicted

---

[5] *Id.*
[6] *See* Statement of Joseph Ziegler dated March 12, 2024, Affidavit 9 at ¶ 7.
[7] Transcript of Hunter Biden, H. Comm. on Oversight & Accountability & H. Comm. on the Judiciary at 105-107:1-3 (Hunter Biden Tr.).
[8] *See* Memorandum (Nov. 1, 2023), H. Comm. on Oversight & Accountability. From Maj. Comm. staff to Comm. Members. Re: Fourth Bank Records Memorandum from the Oversight Committee's Investigation into the Biden Family's Influence Peddling and Business Schemes, at 5 (Fourth Bank Memo); Production to H. Comm. on Ways & Means, Exhibit 801, at 533-549.
[9] *See* Fourth Bank Memo, *supra* note 8, at 5-10.
[10] Transcript of James Biden, H. Comm. on Oversight & Accountability & H. Comm. on the Judiciary, at 100: 11-15.

not only by Mr. Bobulinski, but Hunter Biden.[11] Mr. Bobulinski also produced text messages that establish the events leading up to and immediately following his meeting with Joe Biden on May 2, 2017.[12]

Hunter Biden and James Biden made materially false statements to the Oversight Committee and the Judiciary Committee, as demonstrated by the evidence presented in the attached referral. The nature of these false statements is not lost on the Committees: every instance implicates Joe Biden's knowledge of and role in his family's influence peddling. Hunter Biden denying his affiliation with the Rosemont Seneca Bohai Bank Account obfuscates the account to which foreign individuals who met with Joe Biden transmitted funds. Similarly, Hunter Biden creating from whole cloth a fiction in which he transmitted a threat to the wrong individual appears to be an attempt to hide the fact that invoking Joe Biden succeeded in coercing his Chinese partners to send him money. It also calls into doubt Hunter Biden's other testimony about that event, such as his contention that his father was not, in fact, sitting next to him when he transmitted the message.[13] James Biden's denial that Joe Biden's meeting with James Biden, Hunter Biden, and Hunter Biden's business associate for a Chinese transaction, Tony Bobulinski, took place—despite evidence being placed in front of him and being given multiple opportunities to amend his response—appears to be a clumsy attempt to protect Joe Biden from the reality that Joe Biden has indeed met with his family's business associates.

Hunter Biden and James Biden provided false testimony to the Oversight Committee and the Judiciary Committee, in what appears to be a conscious, calculated effort to insulate Joe Biden from the duly authorized impeachment inquiry. The Committees recommend that both Hunter Biden and James Biden be charged under 18 U.S.C. § 1001 (false statements), and, additionally, that Hunter Biden be charged under 18 U.S.C. § 1621 (perjury). The Department of Justice should consider Hunter Biden's prior alleged criminal activity when evaluating whether to charge him for the false statements described in the attached.[14] Because Hunter Biden was federally indicted in two different jurisdictions at the time of his Congressional deposition, he was also subject to two federal court orders stating that he could not commit any crimes while on federal supervised release.[15]

Thank you for your prompt attention to this matter.

---

[11] Hunter Biden Tr., *supra* note 7, at 141: 12-25; 142: 1-3.

[12] *See generally* Transcript of Tony Bobulinski, H. Comm. on Oversight & Accountability & H. Comm. on the Judiciary.

[13] Hunter Biden Tr., *supra* note 7, at 105: 24.

[14] *See* DOJ Manual, 9-27.230, Initiating and Declining Charges—Substantial Federal Interest, The Person's Criminal History ("If a person is known to have a prior conviction **or is reasonably believed to have engaged in criminal activity at an earlier time, this should be considered in determining whether to commence or recommend federal prosecution.**") (emphasis added).

[15] *See United States v. Hunter Biden*, Case no. 1:23-cr-00061-MN, Doc. 47, Order Setting Conditions of Release (Oct. 3, 2023) ("The defendant must not violate federal, state, or local law while on release."); *United States v. Hunter Biden*, Case no. 2:23-cr-00599-MCS (C.D. Cal.) (Jan. 11, 2024), Doc. 14, at 5 (stating, "I will not commit a federal, state, or local crime during the period of release.").

Sincerely,

James Comer
Chairman
Committee on Oversight and Accountability

Jim Jordan
Chairman
Committee on the Judiciary

Jason Smith
Chairman
Committee on Ways and Means

cc: The Honorable Jamie Raskin, Ranking Member
Committee on Oversight and Accountability

The Honorable Jerrold L. Nadler, Ranking Member
Committee on the Judiciary

The Honorable Richard E. Neal, Ranking Member
Committee on Ways and Means

## TABLE OF CONTENTS

## A. THE FINANCIAL INVESTIGATION INTO PRESIDENT BIDEN'S INFLUENCE PEDDLING

1. In January 2023, the House Committee on Oversight and Accountability (Oversight Committee) launched an investigation into President Joseph R. Biden Jr.'s involvement in his family's foreign business dealings and influence peddling. Then, in light of evidence gathered during that investigation, the Oversight Committee, the House Committee on the Judiciary (Judiciary Committee), and the House Committee on Ways and Means (Ways and Means Committee) (collectively, the Committees) in September 2023 began an inquiry into whether sufficient grounds exist to draft articles of impeachment against President Biden for consideration by the full House.[1] On December 13, 2023, the House of Representatives adopted House Resolution 918 directing the Committees to continue the impeachment inquiry.[2] By approving House Resolution 918, the House also adopted House Resolution 917,[3] which affirmed that "[t]he authority provided by clause 2(m) of Rule XI of the Rules of the House of Representatives to the Chairs of the Committees . . . included, from the beginning of the existing House of Representatives impeachment inquiry . . . the authority to issue subpoenas on behalf of such Committees for the purpose of furthering the impeachment inquiry."[4] House Resolution 917 also "ratifie[d] and affirm[ed] any subpoenas previously issued . . . by the Chairs of the Committees . . . as part of the impeachment inquiry."[5]

2. During the Committees' investigation, the Committees interviewed witnesses who were involved in suspicious financial transactions involving certain Biden family members and

---

[1] *See* H. Res. 918, 118th Cong. (2023) (H. Res. 918); Memorandum from Hon. James Comer, Chairman, H. Comm. on Oversight & Accountability, Hon. Jim Jordan, Chairman, H. Comm. on the Judiciary, & Hon. Jason Smith, Chairman, H. Comm. on Ways & Means, to H. Comm. on Oversight & Accountability, H. Comm. on the Judiciary, & H. Comm. on Ways & Means. Re: Impeachment Inquiry (Sept. 27, 2023) (Impeachment Inquiry Memorandum).
[2] H. Res. 918, *supra* note 1.
[3] H. Res. 918, *supra* note 1; H. Res. 917, 118th Cong. (2023) (H. Res. 917).
[4] H. Res. 917, *supra* note 3.
[5] *Id.*

received significant funds into their personal and corporate bank accounts from foreign sources. The investigation included interviews of Robert Hunter Biden (Hunter Biden), James Biden, Eric Schwerin, Devon Archer, John Robinson Walker (Rob Walker), Tony Bobulinski, and other business associates of the Bidens.[6]

3. Prior to conducting witness interviews, the Oversight Committee identified relevant bank accounts by reviewing Suspicious Activity Reports (SARs) at the U.S. Department of the Treasury (Treasury Department). The Bank Secrecy Act (BSA) requires financial institutions to file reports with the Financial Crimes Enforcement Network (FinCEN) to prevent money laundering and other potential violations of the BSA.[7] The Oversight Committee provided a list of individuals and entities to the Treasury Department seeking to review any SARs filed by financial institutions with FinCEN regarding those on that list.[8] In conjunction with identifying pertinent bank account information held at the Treasury Department, the Oversight Committee began issuing targeted subpoenas to banks for specific financial records related to corporate and individual accounts. Once the impeachment inquiry began, the Judiciary Committee also issued bank subpoenas identical to and simultaneous with the Oversight Committee's subsequent rounds of bank subpoenas. The banks have complied with the Oversight and Judiciary Committees' subpoenas and have produced thousands of bank records.

---

[6] *See* Transcript of Hunter Biden, H. Comm. on Oversight & Accountability, Attached as Exhibit 1 (Hunter Biden Tr.); Transcript of James Biden, H. Comm. on Oversight & Accountability, Attached as Exhibit 2 (James Biden Tr.); Transcript of Eric Schwerin, H. Comm. on Oversight & Accountability, Attached as Exhibit 3 (Eric Schwerin Tr.); Transcript of Devon Archer, H. Comm. on Oversight & Accountability, Attached as Exhibit 4 (Devon Archer Tr.); Transcript of Rob Walker, H. Comm. on Oversight & Accountability, Attached as Exhibit 5 (Rob Walker Tr.); Transcript of Tony Bobulinski, H. Comm. on Oversight & Accountability, Attached as Exhibit 6 (Tony Bobulinski Tr.).

[7] 12 C.F.R. § 21.11(a) ("This section ensures that national banks file a Suspicious Activity Report when they detect a known or suspected violation of Federal law or a suspicious transaction related to a money laundering activity or a violation of the Bank Secrecy Act.")

[8] *See* Letter from Hon. James Comer, Chairman, H. Comm. on Oversight & Accountability, to Hon. Janet Yellen, Secretary, Dep't of Treasury (Jan. 11, 2023).

The Oversight and Judiciary Committees continue to receive bank records on a rolling basis from financial institutions and have recently issued additional bank subpoenas for more documents. The charts and financial figures below rely on the subpoenaed bank records, which are a key aspect of this investigation.

4. The subpoenaed bank records revealed that from 2014 to 2023, Hunter Biden, James Biden, their associated companies, and certain other Biden family members received over $18 million from foreign sources.[9] Additionally, the bank records established that when Biden business associates and their companies are included, over $27 million was received from foreign sources during the same time period.[10] The Bidens, their business associates, and their related companies received funds from individuals and entities associated with Russia, Ukraine, Kazakhstan, China, Romania, Panama, and other locations.

5. These figures do not include the approximately $8 million in loans Hunter Biden and James Biden received from Democratic benefactors such as Kevin Morris, Joey Langston, and John Hynansky.[11] The amount of money Hunter Biden, James Biden, and even Joe Biden sourced from foreign and domestic companies and then later described as a "loan," often without documentation to show the terms of the loan and much of which was never repaid, is alarming.

6. In total, since 2014, the Committees have accounted for over $35 million received by Biden family members, their companies, and business associates, which includes financial

---

[9] *See infra* charts at 4-10.
[10] *Id.*
[11] *See* Letter from Kevin Morris's counsel to General Counsel, H. Comm. on Oversight & Accountability (January 25, 2024), attached as Exhibit 7; *see* James Biden Tr., *supra* note 6, at 171; 174-175; This is a conservative estimate as there are additional, significant "loans" James Biden received from Americore and Michael Lewitt.

transactions described as loans.[12] Despite much effort, the Committees have not identified legitimate services warranting such lucrative payments.

7. The charts below summarize subpoenaed bank records of foreign payments to certain Biden family members and their entities:[13]

Russia

| Date | Originator | Biden Affiliated Entity | Biden Affiliated Entity | Amount |
|---|---|---|---|---|
| 2/14/2014 | Yelena Baturina | Rosemont Seneca Thornton | Rosemont Seneca Bohai | $ 3,500,000.00 |
| | | | | **$ 3,500,000.00** |

[REMAINDER OF PAGE INTENTIONALLY BLANK]

[12] *See supra* notes 9-11; *see generally* Memorandum from Majority Staff, H. Comm. on Oversight & Accountability, to Majority Members, H. Comm. on Oversight & Accountability (Mar. 16, 2023) (First Bank Memo); Memorandum from Majority Staff, H. Comm. on Oversight & Accountability, to Majority Members, H. Comm. on Oversight & Accountability (May 10, 2023) (Second Bank Memo); Memorandum from Majority Staff, H. Comm. on Oversight & Accountability, to Majority Members, H. Comm. on Oversight & Accountability (Aug. 9, 2023) (Third Bank Memo); Memorandum from Majority Staff, H. Comm. on Oversight & Accountability, to Majority Members, H. Comm. on Oversight & Accountability (Nov. 1, 2023) (Fourth Bank Memo).

[13] Subpoenaed bank records for the following charts are on file with the Committees.

Ukraine

| Date | Originator | Biden Affiliated Entity | Amount |
|---|---|---|---|
| 5/15/2014 | Burisma Holdings Limited | Rosemont Seneca Bohai | $ 83,333.33 |
| 6/17/2014 | Burisma Holdings Limited | Rosemont Seneca Bohai | $ 83,333.33 |
| 6/18/2014 | Burisma Holdings Limited | Rosemont Seneca Bohai | $ 60,954.54 |
| 7/15/2014 | Burisma Holdings Limited | Rosemont Seneca Bohai | $ 83,333.33 |
| 8/18/2014 | Burisma Holdings Limited | Rosemont Seneca Bohai | $ 83,333.33 |
| 9/16/2014 | Burisma Holdings Limited | Rosemont Seneca Bohai | $ 83,333.33 |
| 10/7/2014 | Burisma Holdings Limited | Rosemont Seneca Bohai | $ 28,913.89 |
| 10/15/2014 | Burisma Holdings Limited | Rosemont Seneca Bohai | $ 83,333.33 |
| 11/18/2014 | Burisma Holdings Limited | Rosemont Seneca Bohai | $ 83,333.33 |
| 12/16/2014 | Burisma Holdings Limited | Rosemont Seneca Bohai | $ 83,333.33 |
| 1/6/2015 | Burisma Holdings Limited | Rosemont Seneca Bohai | $ 47,249.07 |
| 1/15/2015 | Burisma Holdings Limited | Rosemont Seneca Bohai | $ 83,333.33 |
| 2/17/2015 | Burisma Holdings Limited | Rosemont Seneca Bohai | $ 83,333.33 |
| 3/16/2015 | Burisma Holdings Limited | Rosemont Seneca Bohai | $ 83,333.33 |
| 4/15/2015 | Burisma Holdings Limited | Rosemont Seneca Bohai | $ 83,333.33 |
| 5/18/2015 | Burisma Holdings Limited | Rosemont Seneca Bohai | $ 83,333.33 |
| 6/9/2015 | Burisma Holdings Limited | Rosemont Seneca Bohai | $ 3,668.47 |
| 6/18/2015 | Burisma Holdings Limited | Rosemont Seneca Bohai | $ 83,333.33 |
| 7/16/2015 | Burisma Holdings Limited | Rosemont Seneca Bohai | $ 83,333.33 |
| 7/28/2015 | Burisma Holdings Limited | Rosemont Seneca Bohai | $ 60,554.53 |
| 8/19/2015 | Burisma Holdings Limited | Rosemont Seneca Bohai | $ 83,333.33 |
| 9/17/2015 | Burisma Holdings Limited | Rosemont Seneca Bohai | $ 83,333.33 |
| 10/16/2015 | Burisma Holdings Limited | Rosemont Seneca Bohai | $ 83,333.33 |

| Date | Originator | Biden Affiliated Entity | Amount |
|---|---|---|---|
| 1/25/2016 | Burisma Holdings Limited | Owasco P.C. | $ 84,992.33 |
| 2/2/2016 | Burisma Holdings Limited | Owasco P.C. | $ 1,659.00 |
| 2/12/2016 | Burisma Holdings Limited | Owasco P.C. | $ 83,293.33 |
| 3/15/2016 | Burisma Holdings Limited | Owasco P.C. | $ 83,333.33 |
| 4/28/2016 | Burisma Holdings Limited | Owasco P.C. | $ 83,333.33 |
| 5/17/2016 | Burisma Holdings Limited | Owasco P.C. | $ 83,333.33 |
| 6/17/2016 | Burisma Holdings Limited | Owasco P.C. | $ 83,333.33 |
| 7/14/2016 | Burisma Holdings Limited | Owasco P.C. | $ 83,731.02 |
| 7/18/2016 | Burisma Holdings Limited | Owasco P.C. | $ 152.00 |
| 8/19/2016 | Burisma Holdings Limited | Owasco P.C. | $ 83,333.33 |
| 9/21/2016 | Burisma Holdings Limited | Owasco P.C. | $ 83,333.33 |
| 10/18/2016 | Burisma Holdings Limited | Owasco P.C. | $ 83,333.33 |
| 11/16/2016 | Burisma Holdings Limited | Owasco P.C. | $ 83,333.33 |
| 12/16/2016 | Burisma Holdings Limited | Owasco P.C. | $ 83,333.33 |
| 1/19/2017 | Burisma Holdings Limited | Owasco P.C. | $ 83,333.33 |
| 2/27/2017 | Burisma Holdings Limited | Owasco P.C. | $ 81,595.64 |
| 3/20/2017 | Burisma Holdings Limited | Owasco P.C. | $ 82,512.53 |
| 4/18/2017 | Burisma Holdings Limited | Owasco P.C. | $ 40,318.62 |
| 5/19/2017 | Burisma Holdings Limited | Owasco P.C. | $ 45,680.48 |
| 6/19/2017 | Burisma Holdings Limited | Owasco P.C. | $ 40,436.93 |
| 8/4/2017 | Burisma Holdings Limited | Owasco P.C. | $ 43,306.83 |
| 8/25/2017 | Burisma Holdings Limited | Owasco P.C. | $ 41,002.96 |
| 9/21/2017 | Burisma Holdings Limited | Owasco P.C. | $ 41,126.26 |
| 10/19/2017 | Burisma Holdings Limited | Owasco P.C. | $ 40,831.24 |
| 11/3/2017 | Burisma Holdings Limited | Owasco P.C. | $ 8,749.06 |
| 11/20/2017 | Burisma Holdings Limited | Owasco P.C. | $ 41,368.65 |
| 12/19/2017 | Burisma Holdings Limited | Owasco P.C. | $ 40,293.09 |
| 1/22/2018 | Burisma Holdings Limited | Owasco P.C. | $ 42,002.91 |
| 2/22/2018 | Burisma Holdings Limited | Owasco P.C. | $ 42,315.95 |
| 3/27/2018 | Burisma Holdings Limited | Owasco P.C. | $ 42,399.91 |
| 4/19/2018 | Burisma Holdings Limited | Owasco P.C. | $ 42,420.77 |
| 5/18/2018 | Burisma Holdings Limited | Owasco P.C. | $ 40,572.29 |
| 6/26/2018 | Burisma Holdings Limited | Owasco P.C. | $ 38,883.24 |
| 7/24/2018 | Burisma Holdings Limited | Owasco P.C. | $ 39,911.17 |
| 8/17/2018 | Burisma Holdings Limited | Owasco P.C. | $ 39,985.96 |
| 9/25/2018 | Burisma Holdings Limited | Owasco P.C. | $ 41,524.38 |
| 10/19/2018 | Burisma Holdings Limited | Owasco P.C. | $ 40,547.34 |
| 11/3/2018 | Burisma Holdings Limited | Owasco P.C. | $ 40,087.08 |
| 12/21/2018 | Burisma Holdings Limited | Owasco P.C. | $ 40,287.82 |
| 1/22/2019 | Burisma Holdings Limited | Owasco P.C. | $ 40,144.32 |
| 2/26/2019 | Burisma Holdings Limited | Owasco P.C. | $ 39,989.02 |
| 3/21/2019 | Burisma Holdings Limited | Owasco P.C. | $ 40,150.56 |
| 4/24/2019 | Burisma Holdings Limited | Owasco P.C. | $ 39,923.10 |
| | | | **$ 3,986,869.53** |

Kazakhstan

| Date | Originator | Biden Affiliated Entity | Ultimate Beneficiary | Amount |
|---|---|---|---|---|
| 4/23/2014 | Novatus Holding PTE. LTD. | Rosemont Seneca Bohai | Car Dealership | $ 142,300.00 |
| | | | | **$ 142,300.00** |

China

| Date | Originator | Intermediary | Biden Affiliated Entity | Amount |
|---|---|---|---|---|
| 12/30/2014 | Bohai Harvest RST | Rosemont Seneca Bohai | Hunter Biden | $ 23,157.63 |
| 12/30/2014 | Bohai Harvest RST | Rosemont Seneca Bohai | Hunter Biden | $ 7,456.04 |
| 2/9/2015 | Bohai Harvest RST | Rosemont Seneca Bohai | Hunter Biden | $ 1,225.87 |
| 8/21/2015 | Gemini Investments Ltd. | Rosemont Property MGT LLC | Rosemont Seneca Bohai | $ 188,616.56 |
| 11/5/2015 | Bank of China Bohai Harvest RST | Rosemont Seneca Bohai | Hunter Biden | $ 875.00 |
| 2/2/2016 | Harves Investment Group | | Rosemont Seneca Advisors | $ 20,000.00 |
| 2/22/2016 | Hualien Media | | Skaneateles LLC | $ 233,382.00 |
| 2/23/2016 | Harves Investment Group | | Rosemont Seneca Advisors | $ 20,000.00 |
| 3/9/2016 | Harves Investment Group | | Rosemont Seneca Advisors | $ 20,000.00 |
| 4/1/2016 | Harves Investment Group | | Rosemont Seneca Advisors | $ 25,000.00 |
| 7/7/2016 | Harves Investment Group | | Rosemont Seneca Advisors | $ 25,000.00 |
| 9/1/2016 | Wei Wei | Eric Schwerin | Rosemont Seneca Partners | $ 25,000.00 |
| 9/1/2016 | Wei Wei | Eric Schwerin | Rosemont Seneca Partners | $ 25,000.00 |
| 11/1/2016 | Harves Investment Group | | Rosemont Seneca Advisors | $ 35,000.00 |
| 11/29/2016 | Bohai Harvest RST | | Rosemont Seneca Advisors | $ 2,000.00 |
| 12/20/2016 | Bohai Harvest RST | | Rosemont Seneca Advisors | $ 1,000.00 |
| 1/2/2017 | Bohai Harvest RST | | Rosemont Seneca Advisors | $ 3,000.00 |
| 3/6/2017 | State Energy HK Limited | Robinson Walker, LLC | "Biden" | $ 5,000.00 |
| 3/13/2017 | State Energy HK Limited | Robinson Walker, LLC | "Biden" | $ 25,000.00 |
| 3/20/2017 | State Energy HK Limited | Robinson Walker, LLC | Hallie Biden | $ 25,000.00 |
| 3/27/2017 | State Energy HK Limited | Robinson Walker, LLC | Owasco P.C. | $ 50,000.00 |
| 3/29/2017 | State Energy HK Limited | Robinson Walker, LLC | First Clearing, LLC | $ 100,000.00 |
| 3/31/2017 | State Energy HK Limited | Robinson Walker, LLC | Owasco P.C. | $ 50,000.00 |
| 3/31/2017 | State Energy HK Limited | Robinson Walker, LLC | Owasco P.C. | $ 100,000.00 |
| 4/3/2017 | State Energy HK Limited | Robinson Walker, LLC | JBBSR INC | $ 50,000.00 |
| 4/3/2017 | State Energy HK Limited | Robinson Walker, LLC | JBBSR INC | $ 50,000.00 |
| 4/14/2017 | State Energy HK Limited | Robinson Walker, LLC | RSTP II, LLC | $ 10,962.00 |
| 4/18/2017 | State Energy HK Limited | Robinson Walker, LLC | Owasco P.C. | $ 300,000.00 |
| 4/20/2017 | State Energy HK Limited | Robinson Walker, LLC | JBBSR INC | $ 120,000.00 |
| 4/21/2017 | State Energy HK Limited | Robinson Walker, LLC | "Biden" | $ 25,000.00 |
| 4/24/2017 | State Energy HK Limited | Robinson Walker, LLC | JBBSR INC | $ 125,000.00 |
| 5/17/2017 | State Energy HK Limited | Robinson Walker, LLC | "Biden" | $ 15,000.00 |
| 5/18/2017 | State Energy HK Limited | Robinson Walker, LLC | JBBSR INC | $ 15,000.00 |

| Date | Originator | Biden Affiliated Entity | Amount |
|---|---|---|---|
| 8/4/2017 | CEFC Infrastructure Investment | Owasco P.C. | $ 100,000.00 |
| 8/8/2017 | Hudson West III | Owasco P.C. | $ 400,000.00 |
| 8/17/2017 | Bank of China Bohai Harvest RST | Skaneateles LLC | $ 11,442.26 |
| 8/31/2017 | Hudson West III | Owasco P.C. | $ 165,000.00 |
| 9/25/2017 | Hudson West III | Owasco P.C. | $ 220,386.87 |
| 9/27/2017 | Hudson West III | Owasco P.C. | $ 165,000.00 |
| 9/27/2017 | Hudson West III | Owasco P.C. | $ 165,000.00 |
| 11/1/2017 | Hudson West III | Owasco P.C. | $ 165,000.00 |
| 12/1/2017 | Hong Kong (BHR) Jonathan Li | Skaneateles LLC | $ 119,975.00 |
| 12/4/2017 | Hudson West III | Owasco P.C. | $ 165,000.00 |
| 12/4/2017 | Wang Xin (BHR) | Skaneateles LLC | $ 37,975.00 |
| 1/2/2018 | Hudson West III | Owasco P.C. | $ 165,000.00 |
| 1/10/2018 | Hudson West III | Owasco P.C. | $ 165,000.00 |
| 1/17/2018 | Hudson West III | Lion Hall Group | $ 17,992.99 |
| 2/5/2018 | Hudson West III | Owasco P.C. | $ 165,000.00 |
| 2/6/2018 | Hudson West III | Owasco P.C. | $ 165,000.00 |
| 2/28/2018 | Hudson West III | Owasco P.C. | $ 165,000.00 |
| 3/15/2018 | Hudson West III | Owasco P.C. | $ 157,494.19 |
| 3/16/2018 | Hudson West III | Owasco P.C. | $ 157,494.19 |
| 3/22/2018 | Patrick Ho | Owasco LLC | $ 1,000,000.00 |
| 4/3/2018 | Hudson West III | Lion Hall Group | $ 33,941.11 |
| 4/4/2018 | Hudson West III | Owasco P.C. | $ 165,000.00 |
| 5/23/2018 | Hudson West III | Owasco P.C. | $ 165,000.00 |
| 6/1/2018 | Hudson West III | Lion Hall Group | $ 7,612.41 |
| 6/1/2018 | Hudson West III | Owasco P.C. | $ 165,000.00 |
| 7/2/2018 | Hudson West III | Owasco P.C. | $ 165,000.00 |
| 7/25/2018 | Hudson West III | Owasco P.C. | $ 50,000.00 |
| 8/1/2018 | Hudson West III | Lion Hall Group | $ 4,762.41 |
| 8/1/2018 | Hudson West III | Owasco P.C. | $ 165,000.00 |
| 9/4/2018 | Hudson West III | Owasco P.C. | $ 165,000.00 |
| 9/14/2018 | Hudson West III | Owasco P.C. | $ 10,000.00 |
| 9/18/2018 | Hudson West III | Lion Hall Group | $ 8,324.82 |
| 9/20/2018 | Hudson West III | Owasco P.C. | $ 25,000.00 |
| 9/25/2018 | Hudson West III | Owasco P.C. | $ 295,000.00 |
| 10/5/2018 | Hudson West III | Lion Hall Group | $ 4,112.41 |
| 7/26/2019 | Wang Xin (BHR) | Robert H. Biden | $ 10,000.00 |
| 8/2/2019 | Jonathan Li (BHR) | Robert H. Biden | $ 250,000.00 |
| | | | **$ 7,283,188.76** |

Romania

| Date | Originator | Intermediary | Biden Affiliated Entity | Amount |
|---|---|---|---|---|
| 11/9/2015 | Bladon Enterprises Limited | Robinson Walker, LLC | Robert Biden | $ 59,900.00 |
| 12/7/2015 | Bladon Enterprises Limited | Robinson Walker, LLC | Robert Biden | $ 59,725.00 |
| 12/23/2015 | Bladon Enterprises Limited | Robinson Walker, LLC | Robert Biden | $ 60,091.24 |
| 2/12/2016 | Bladon Enterprises Limited | Robinson Walker, LLC | Owasco P.C. | $ 60,220.28 |
| 2/24/2016 | Bladon Enterprises Limited | Robinson Walker, LLC | Owasco P.C. | $ 61,126.24 |
| 3/24/2016 | Bladon Enterprises Limited | Robinson Walker, LLC | Owasco P.C. | $ 61,816.05 |
| 5/23/2016 | Bladon Enterprises Limited | Robinson Walker, LLC | Owasco P.C. | $ 123,830.80 |
| 7/11/2016 | Bladon Enterprises Limited | Robinson Walker, LLC | Owasco P.C. | $ 116,860.93 |
| 8/15/2016 | Bladon Enterprises Limited | Robinson Walker, LLC | Owasco P.C. | $ 53,419.74 |
| 8/31/2016 | Bladon Enterprises Limited | Robinson Walker, LLC | Robert Biden | $ 20,000.00 |
| 9/22/2016 | Bladon Enterprises Limited | Robinson Walker, LLC | Owasco P.C. | $ 32,092.81 |
| 9/29/2016 | Bladon Enterprises Limited | Robinson Walker, LLC | "Biden" | $ 20,000.00 |
| 10/11/2016 | Bladon Enterprises Limited | Robinson Walker, LLC | Owasco P.C. | $ 41,638.12 |
| 11/15/2016 | Bladon Enterprises Limited | Robinson Walker, LLC | Robert Biden | $ 122,179.00 |
| 2/2/2017 | Bladon Enterprises Limited | Robinson Walker, LLC | "Biden" | $ 20,000.00 |
| 2/10/2017 | Bladon Enterprises Limited | Robinson Walker, LLC | "Biden" | $ 20,000.00 |
| 2/13/2017 | Bladon Enterprises Limited | Robinson Walker, LLC | Hallie Biden | $ 10,000.00 |
| 2/16/2017 | Bladon Enterprises Limited | Robinson Walker, LLC | "Biden" | $ 20,000.00 |
| 2/27/2017 | Bladon Enterprises Limited | Robinson Walker, LLC | Robert Biden | $ 14,000.00 |
| 6/2/2017 | Bladon Enterprises Limited | Robinson Walker, LLC | Owasco P.C. | $ 61,726.87 |
| | | | | **$ 1,038,627.08** |

Panama

| Date | Originator | Biden Affiliated Entity | Amount |
|---|---|---|---|
| 12/27/2016 | Stanhope Worldwide Services | James Biden | $ 50,000.00 |
| 1/26/2017 | Stanhope Worldwide Services | James Biden | $ 50,000.00 |
| 2/2/2017 | Stanhope Worldwide Services | James Biden | $ 50,000.00 |
| 3/20/2017 | Stanhope Worldwide Services | James Biden | $ 50,000.00 |
| 11/30/2022 | Briest Trading International Company | James Biden | $ 200,000.00 |
| 12/31/2022 | Briest Trading International Company | James Biden | $ 290,000.00 |
| 2/28/2023 | Briest Trading International Company | James Biden | $ 200,000.00 |
| 7/31/2023 | Briest Trading International Company | James Biden | $ 150,000.00 |
| | | | **$ 1,040,000.00** |

Other Global Investments[14]

| Date | Originator | Biden Affiliated Entity | Amount |
|---|---|---|---|
| 3/3/2015 | ePlata | Minor Biden Child | $ 50,000.00 |
| 3/30/2015 | ePlata | Minor Biden Child | $ 20,000.00 |
| 4/15/2015 | ePlata | Minor Biden Child | $ 20,000.00 |
| 9/10/2015 | Mbloom BDC Advisors | Rosemont Seneca Bohai | $ 275,000.00 |
| 9/21/2017 | Eudora | Skaneateles LLC | $ 666,572.16 |
| | | | **$ 1,031,572.16** |

8. The Oversight Committee's investigation revealed a pattern in which Hunter Biden would use a business associate's corporate bank account (an intermediary account) to receive millions of dollars in foreign funds. For instance, Hunter Biden used Devon Archer's limited liability company (LLC), Rosemont Seneca Bohai, LLC (Rosemont Seneca Bohai), and Rob Walker's LLC, Robinson Walker, LLC, to receive money from foreign companies and individuals.[15] Devon Archer and Rob Walker were business associates of Hunter Biden. After the business associates' LLCs received the foreign wires, the business associates would transfer Hunter Biden, his companies, and other Biden family members significant payments.[16]

9. Based upon a review of the bank records, the Committees sought to interview witnesses who were involved in particular financial transactions and could explain why Hunter Biden used his business associates' corporate bank accounts to receive millions of dollars from foreign parties, despite having his companies in Delaware and Washington, D.C.[17] In April 2024, after the interviews of these business associates, Devon Archer's counsel produced millions of documents to the Committees, and the Ways and Means Committee publicly released

[14] These entities either engaged in international activities or obtained international investments.
[15] *See* First Bank Memo; Second Bank Memo; Third Bank Memo; *see also supra* note 9.
[16] *See* Second Bank Memo, *supra* note 12, at 31-32.
[17] *See id.* at 7 (listing some of Hunter Biden's limited liability companies during this time).

lawful disclosures from IRS whistleblowers. Prior to receiving these documents, on February 21, 2024, James Biden appeared before the Committees for a transcribed interview. One week later, on February 28, 2024, the Committees deposed Hunter Biden who testified under oath. Based upon a review of recently obtained evidence, the Committees can demonstrate that Hunter Biden and James Biden made false and misleading statements during their interviews. The basis and evidence supporting this criminal referral are laid out in detail below.

## B. MAKING FALSE STATEMENTS TO CONGRESS IS A FEDERAL CRIME

10. It is a federal crime to make false statements to Committee staff and Members of Congress during a Congressional investigation so long as that investigation is "conducted pursuant to the authority of any committee, subcommittee, commission or office of the Congress, consistent with applicable rules of the House or Senate."[18] The Committees set forth overwhelming evidence below establishing that Hunter Biden and James Biden made false statements to the Committees during a Congressional investigation, in violation of 18 U.S.C. § 1001(a).

11. In order to establish a violation of 18 U.S.C. § 1001, the Department of Justice (DOJ) must prove the following elements of the crime beyond a reasonable doubt:

(1) the defendant made the statement charged;

(2) the statement was false, fictitious, or fraudulent;

(3) the statement was material;

(4) the defendant acted knowingly and willfully; and

(5) the false statement pertained to a matter within the jurisdiction of the legislative branch of the government of the United States.[19]

---

[18] *See* 18 U.S.C. § 1001(c)(2).
[19] *See United States v. Bowser*, 318 F. Supp. 3d 154, 171 (D.D.C. July 17, 2018) (setting forth the elements of the statute).

12. DOJ has prosecuted witnesses for making false statements to congressional committees. For instance, in 2019, DOJ Special Counsel Robert Mueller prosecuted Roger Stone for obstruction of a proceeding and making false statements to the United States House of Representatives Permanent Select Committee on Intelligence.[20] Prior to trial, DOJ filed its proposed jury instructions describing the purpose of the statute and addressed the importance of protecting the authorized functions of Congressional committees from "deceptive practices."[21] DOJ submitted the following to the Court:

> The purpose of § 1001 is to protect the authorized functions of the various governmental departments from any type of misleading or deceptive practice and from the adverse consequences that might result from such deceptive practices.
>
> To establish a violation of § 1001, it is necessary for the government to prove certain essential elements . . . beyond a reasonable doubt. However, I want to point out now that it is not necessary for the government to prove that the House committee was, in fact, misled as a result of the defendant's actions. It does not matter whether the House committee was in fact misled, or even whether it knew of the misleading or deceptive act, should you find that the act occurred. These circumstances would not excuse or justify a concealment undertaken, or a false, fictitious or fraudulent statement made, or a false writing or document submitted, willfully and knowingly about a matter within the jurisdiction of the government of the United States.[22]

13. DOJ must follow the same reasoning and rationale when evaluating this criminal referral. As discussed below, Hunter Biden's responses to questions from the Committees about his involvement with and knowledge of Rosemont Seneca Bohai and its bank account (Rosemont Seneca Bohai Bank Account),[23] as well as communications with officials working for CEFC China were false and warrant criminal prosecution. Furthermore, James Biden told the Committee that Joe Biden did not attend a meeting with Hunter Biden and his business associate,

---

[20] *See United States v. Roger Stone, Jr.*, 1:19-cr-00018-ABJ (D.D.C. Jan. 24, 2019), Doc. 1.
[21] *See* Proposed Jury Instructions, *United States v. Roger Stone, Jr.*, 1:19-cr-00018-ABJ (D.D.C. Sept. 6, 2019), Doc. No. 199-2.
[22] *Id.* at 11.
[23] Financial records show there are multiple Rosemont Seneca Bohai bank account numbers at the same financial institution where Rosemont Seneca Bohai banked. The Committees will refer to those account numbers collectively as the Rosemont Seneca Bohai Bank Account.

Tony Bobulinski, at the Beverly Hilton Hotel on May 2, 2017, a false statement that also merits prosecution.

14. Additionally, the Committees deposed Hunter Biden under oath pursuant to a subpoena.[24] Under 18 U.S.C. § 1621, a witness commits perjury if after taking "an oath" the witness "willfully and contrary to such oath states . . . any material matter which he does not believe to be true . . . ."[25] As such, the Committees are also referring Hunter Biden to DOJ for perjury in violation of 18 U.S.C. § 1621.

### C. THE COMMITTEES WARNED HUNTER BIDEN AND JAMES BIDEN THAT MAKING FALSE STATEMENTS TO CONGRESS WAS A CRIME

15. On February 28, 2024, Hunter Biden testified under oath before the Committees during a deposition in Washington, D.C.[26] Counsel accompanied Hunter Biden during the deposition. Prior to testifying, Committee counsel warned Hunter Biden that he was "required to answer questions from Congress truthfully"[27] and that if he knowingly made false statements during the deposition, he could be criminally prosecuted.[28] Hunter Biden acknowledged he had to tell the truth and raised no reasons why he could not be truthful.[29] Hunter Biden also swore under the penalty of perjury to tell the truth during his testimony.[30] The deposition transcript establishes Hunter Biden knew he was required to tell the truth to Congress and that knowingly making false statements constituted a crime.

16. Indeed, prior to testifying before the Committees, Hunter Biden, an attorney, was already a criminal defendant in a federal prosecution for making false statements to purchase a

---

[24] Hunter Biden Tr., *supra* note 6, at 16: 4-8.
[25] *See* 18 U.S.C. § 1621.
[26] *See* Hunter Biden Tr., *supra* note 6.
[27] *Id.* at 10: 5-7.
[28] *Id.* at 10: 5-19.
[29] *Id.* at 10: 5-22.
[30] *Id.* at 16: 4-8.

firearm.[31] On September 14, 2023, DOJ indicted Hunter Biden in the U.S. District Court for the District of Delaware with three felony counts.[32] Two of the federal charges revolved around Hunter Biden's alleged false statement when buying a firearm.[33] On December 7, 2023, DOJ charged Hunter Biden with other federal crimes alleging dishonest acts and omissions covering various tax offenses in the U.S. District Court for the Central District of California.[34] According to the Justice Manual, DOJ should consider Hunter Biden's prior alleged criminal activity when evaluating whether to charge him for the false statements described below.[35] Because Hunter Biden was federally indicted in two different jurisdictions at the time of his Congressional deposition, he was also subject to two federal court orders stating that he could not commit any crimes while on supervised release.[36] As set forth below, Hunter Biden's false statements to the Committees are also a potential violation of the conditions of his supervised release.

17. On February 21, 2024, James Biden participated in a voluntary transcribed interview with the Committees.[37] James Biden was accompanied by counsel during the transcribed interview.[38] The Committees also warned James Biden that he was "required to answer questions from Congress truthfully."[39] James Biden responded he understood that

---

[31] *See United States v. Robert Hunter Biden*, 1:23-cr-00061-MN (D. Del. Sept. 14, 2023), Doc. 40.
[32] *See id.*, Counts I and II.
[33] *See id.*
[34] *See United States v. Robert Hunter Biden*, 2:23-cr-00599-MCS (C.D. Cal. Dec. 7, 2023), Doc. 1.
[35] *See* DOJ Manual, 9-27.230, Initiating and Declining Charges—Substantial Federal Interest, The Person's Criminal History ("If a person is known to have a prior conviction **or is reasonably believed to have engaged in criminal activity at an earlier time, this should be considered in determining whether to commence or recommend federal prosecution.**") (emphasis added).
[36] *See* Order Setting Conditions of Release, *United States v. Hunter Biden*, 1:23-cr-00061-MN, Doc. 47 (D. Del. Oct. 3, 2023) ("The defendant must not violate federal, state, or local law while on release."); *United States v. Hunter Biden*, 2:23-cr-00599-MCS (C.D. Cal.) (Jan. 11, 2024), Doc. 14, at 5 (stating, "I will not commit a federal, state, or local crime during the period of release.").
[37] James Biden Tr., *supra* note 6.
[38] *Id.* at 6: 19-25.
[39] *Id.* at 7: 15-18.

knowingly providing false testimony could subject him to criminal prosecution.[40] James Biden provided no reason why he could not be truthful during the interview.[41]

18. Based upon the Committees warnings to Hunter Biden and James Biden, they knew making false statements to Congress was a crime.

### D. HUNTER BIDEN MADE FALSE STATEMENTS ABOUT ROSEMONT SENECA BOHAI

19. According to DOJ, Rosemont Seneca Bohai "was a Delaware limited liability company, established on February 13, 2014, with its principal place of business in New York, New York."[42] Further, "[o]n September 23, 2014, a law firm in Florida . . . acting as registered agent for Rosemont [Seneca Bohai], filed with the Florida Secretary of State an application for authorization for Rosemont [Seneca Bohai] to transact business in Florida."[43] According to bank records subpoenaed by the Oversight Committee, Devon Archer opened a bank account for Rosemont Seneca Bohai (Rosemont Seneca Bohai Bank Account), and the bank records listed Sebastian Momtazi as a managing member or general partner.[44] Rosemont Seneca Bohai also had a credit card (Rosemont Seneca Bohai Credit Card) through a different financial institution.[45] The Oversight Committee subpoenaed financial records for the Rosemont Seneca Bohai Bank Account and Rosemont Seneca Bohai Credit Card.

20. The subpoenaed bank records for the Rosemont Seneca Bohai Bank Account and Rosemont Seneca Bohai Credit Card did not list Hunter Biden as a client or contact. However, despite not being named on the Rosemont Seneca Bohai Bank Account or Rosemont Seneca

[40] *Id.* at 7: 22-25.
[41] *Id.* at 8: 6-8.
[42] Complaint, *United States of America v. Jason Galanis*, 1:16-cr-00371-RA Doc. 1 (S.D.N.Y. May 9, 2016), at 8-9.
[43] *Id.* at 9.
[44] Financial Institution 1, Records on file with the Oversight Committee.
[45] Financial Institution 2, Records on file with the Oversight Committee.

Bohai Credit Card, bank records established that foreign companies wired millions of dollars into the Rosemont Seneca Bohai Bank Account intended for Hunter Biden, and that payments were made on Hunter Biden's behalf using the Rosemont Seneca Bohai Credit Card.[46]

21. Because Joe Biden met with and talked to some of the foreign nationals responsible for wiring money into the Rosemont Seneca Bohai Bank Account while he was Vice President,[47] the Committees were concerned that Hunter Biden used this account to hide his involvement in particular financial transactions. Similarly, the Rosemont Seneca Bohai Credit Card was used to make significant purchases on behalf of Hunter Biden, but he was not listed on the account. It is material to the Committees' investigation to understand why Hunter Biden received foreign payments into the Rosemont Seneca Bohai Bank Account and benefited from the Rosemont Seneca Bohai Credit Card when he had his own companies and credit cards.

22. The Committees questioned Hunter Biden about Rosemont Seneca Bohai and the Rosemont Seneca Bohai Bank Account. During the deposition, Hunter Biden testified that the Rosemont Seneca Bohai Bank Account was "not for my benefit, and not in – I had no control or understanding of."[48] Hunter Biden testified to the following:

> Q: Well, Rosemont Seneca Bohai, let's just go through the name real quickly, the Rosemont deals with Devon, correct?
>
> A: Well –
>
> Q: Pertains to Devon?
>
> A: -- originally Devon's firm was Rosemont Capital. Originally my firm was Seneca Global Advisors. I changed the name of my firm to Rosemont Seneca Partners, which is not Rosemont Seneca Thornton, and it's not Rosemont Seneca Bohai. **If**

---

[46] *See* Second Bank Memo, *supra* note 12, at 16-17; *see* Third Bank Memo, *supra* note 12, at 15-16; *See infra* Charts 34-39.
[47] *See* Devon Archer Tr., *supra* note 6, at 45-47; 63-66.
[48] Hunter Biden Tr., *supra* note 6, at 25: 10-14.

**Devon set up accounts on his own under those names, they were not at my behest, not for my benefit, and not in – I had no control or understanding of**.[49]

23. Upon further questioning, Hunter Biden continued to disassociate himself from the Rosemont Seneca Bohai Bank Account and stated it was not under his control or "affiliated with" him:

Q: And then I want to also discuss a second portion of – another 10 percent that was purchased out of the Rosemont Seneca Bohai account to purchase another 10 percent equity into BHR Partners. Were you aware that, in December of 2014, that there was another 10 percent purchase out of the Rosemont Seneca Bohai account for 10 percent of BHR Partners?

A: No, not directly aware, no. Again, I would like to state for the – **for everybody here is that neither of these accounts were under my control nor affiliated with me. Any of this is outside of my knowledge**.[50]

24. The Committees continued questioning Hunter Biden regarding foreign payments into the Rosemont Seneca Bohai Bank Account and asked:

Q: . . .

Did you receive payments from other foreign sources into the Rosemont Seneca Bohai account?

A: Again, you say "foreign sources." The people that I did business with that were from other countries other than the United States, the answer is, yes; I have received – but not – **I don't know whether they went into Rosemont Seneca Bohai or that they went into Rosemont Seneca Thornton. I had no control. I have no authority over those accounts, and I have no view inside of it. There was no transparency to me that I know of.**[51]

25. During the deposition, Hunter Biden made false statements about his involvement with the Rosemont Seneca Bohai Account, including:

a. Hunter Biden did not know if foreign payments were made into the Rosemont Seneca Bohai Bank Account;

---

[49] *Id.* at 25: 6-14 (emphasis added).
[50] *Id.* at 24: 23-25; 25: 1-5 (emphasis added).
[51] *Id.* at 26: 12-25 (emphasis added).

b. The Rosemont Seneca Bohai Bank Account was not for his benefit;

c. He had no understanding of or affiliation with the Rosemont Seneca Bohai Bank Account; and

d. Hunter Biden had no control or authority over the Rosemont Seneca Bohai Bank Account.

26. As shown below, Hunter Biden directed wires into the Rosemont Seneca Bohai Bank Account, received over $2 million in foreign proceeds into this account, understood the purpose of the account, and exerted control and authority over the account.

*Hunter Biden directed foreign payments to the Rosemont Seneca Bohai Bank Account*

27. On May 22, 2024, the Ways and Means Committee lawfully disclosed documents from IRS whistleblowers Supervisory Special Agent (SSA) Gary Shapley and Special Agent (SA) Joseph Ziegler.[52] These documents were submitted to the Ways and Means Committee after the Hunter Biden deposition.[53] In particular, SA Ziegler provided the Committee with a document obtained during the investigation of Hunter Biden via an electronic search warrant.[54] The document shows a string of emails among Hunter Biden, Devon Archer, Sebastian Momtazi (an employee of Devon Archer), and Vadym Pozharskyi, the corporate secretary for the Ukrainian energy company Burisma.

28. The emails show that in 2014, after Hunter Biden became a board member of Burisma, Vadym Pozharskyi, requested a letter setting forth information regarding the bank account where Hunter Biden wanted to receive his monthly payments.[55] Hunter Biden asked Sebastian Momtazi, Devon Archer's assistant, to edit the banking letter for Burisma for Hunter

---

[52] *See* Ways and Means Committee Releases Evidence Showing Hunter Biden Lied Under Oath During Recent Congressional Testimony, May 22, 2024.

[53] *See* Statement of Joseph Ziegler dated March 12, 2024, Affidavits 8 and 9.

[54] *See* Statement of Joseph Ziegler dated March 12, 2024, Affidavit 9, at ¶ 6.

[55] Emails from Vadym Pozharskyi to Sebastian Momtazi, Hunter Biden & Devon Archer (May 14, 2014) (Ways & Means Exhibit 901).

Biden to sign and return to Burisma.[56] Mr. Momtazi appears to have finalized the letter from Hunter Biden that was attached to the email, which directed the Burisma payments to the Rosemont Seneca Bohai Bank Account and referred to Hunter Biden as a "beneficial owner" of the account.[57] The Burisma payments were then wired to the Rosemont Seneca Bohai Bank Account on the same day.[58]

29. Specifically, on May 15, 2014, Hunter Biden wrote an email to Vadym Pozharskyi, copying Sebastian Momtazi and Devon Archer, with the subject line "Re: Monthly Fees invoices[.]"[59] Hunter Biden wrote:

> Seb-
>
> Can you pls edit doc for my signature and ill sign and return.
>
> RHB

30. Attached to the email was a document from Rosemont Seneca Partners. Hunter Biden was the president of Rosemont Seneca Partners.[60] The document—a letter—was dated May 14, 2014 and stated, "Please let this letter act as confirmation that Hunter Biden is the beneficial owner of Rosemont Seneca Partners, and of the bank account in the name of Rosemont Seneca Bohai, LLC."[61] Furthermore, the document stated that Hunter Biden "requests the company Burisma to pay his monthly fees (salary) to the Rosemont Seneca Bohai, LLC bank account[,]" the details of which (such as the account number) were provided in the letter.[62]

---

[56] Email from Hunter Biden to Vadym Pozharskyi, Sebastian Momtazi & Devon Archer (May 15, 2014, 11:51 AM) (Ways & Means Exhibit 901); Joseph Ziegler Affidavit 9, *supra* note 54.
[57] *See* Letter from Hunter Biden (May 14, 2014) (Ways & Means Exhibit 901) (Notes 55-57 attached as Exhibit 8).
[58] *See infra* at ¶ 31.
[59] *See* Exhibit 8.
[60] *See* Hunter Biden Tr., *supra* note 6, at 23:14-16.
[61] *See* Exhibit 8.
[62] *Id.*

Hunter Biden further asked to have "reasonable expenses" paid to the Rosemont Seneca Bohai Bank Account.[63]

**Exhibit 901**

**From:** Sebastian Momtazi <[redacted]
**To:** Hunter Biden
**CC:** Devon Archer
**Sent:** 5/15/2014 1:17:09 PM
**Subject:** RE: Monthly Fees invoices
**Attachments:** Hunter burisma fees expenses.docx

Here you go.

NB wires received today--

S

---

**From:** Hunter Biden [redacted]
**Sent:** Thursday, May 15, 2014 11:51 AM
**To:** Vadim Pozharskyi
**Cc:** Sebastian Momtazi; Devon Archer
**Subject:** Re: Monthly Fees invoices

Seb-
Can you pls edit doc for my signature and ill sign and return.

RHB

On May 15, 2014, at 3:41 AM, Vadim Pozharskyi <[redacted]> wrote:

Dear Sebastian, please find the example of the letter that I asked for attached.

Thank you, vadym

2014-05-14 13:04 GMT+03:00 Vadim Pozharskyi <[redacted]>:
Dear Sebastian, as we earlier spoke on 15th we plan to make our monthly fees to the directors.
Could you please send me invoices today for Hunter and Devon.
Thanks, look forward

Vadym

Отправлено с iPad

<Archer Burisma fees and expenses.pdf>

---

[63] *Id.*

14th May 2014

To whom it may concern:

**Please let this letter act as confirmation that Hunter Biden is the beneficial owner of Rosemont Seneca Partners, and of the bank account in the name of Rosemont Seneca Bohai, LLC.**

**Mr. Biden has executed the Service Agreement with Burisma Holdings Limited dated 18th April, 2014, and according to sub-clause 5.1 of the Agreement serves Burisma Holdings Limited as Member of the Board of Directors; and he has the will and requests the company Burisma to pay his monthly fees (salary) to the Rosemont Seneca Bohai, LLC bank account detailed here:**

| | |
|---|---|
| Bank Name: | Citibank, NY |
| ABA: | [redacted] |
| Account Name: | Morgan Stanley Smith Barney LLC |
| Account #: | [redacted]1172 |
| FFC Account Name: | Rosemont Seneca Bohai LLC |
| FFC Account #: | [redacted]18483 |

**Furthermore, pursuant to sub-clause 8.1 of the Agreement Burisma Holdings shall cover all his reasonable expenses, and in this respect and I kindly request that these be paid to the same bank account.**

Thank you

Kind regards,

R. Hunter Biden

31. The Oversight Committee subpoenaed the Rosemont Seneca Bohai Bank Account. The subpoenaed bank records show that on the same day Hunter Biden sent the email described above—May 15, 2014—Burisma wired him $83,333.33 into the Rosemont Seneca Bohai Bank Account.[64] Burisma then continued to make Hunter Biden's monthly payments into the Rosemont Seneca Bohai Bank Account until approximately October 2015.[65] This evidence proves Hunter Biden directed foreign payments into the Rosemont Seneca Bohai Bank Account, he knowingly benefited from the bank account, and he exerted control and authority over it.

32. The Committees believe that Hunter Biden lied about the Rosemont Seneca Bohai Bank Account for several reasons. First, Hunter Biden has previously responded to federal inquiries related to Rosemont Seneca Bohai and was seeking to avoid any connection to the company. In 2016, Devon Archer and others were arrested on federal charges filed in the U.S. District Court for the Southern District of New York for their role in an alleged tribal bond fraud scheme.[66] The United States Securities and Exchange Commission (SEC) filed fraud charges in a parallel investigation.[67] As part of their investigations, federal authorities investigated Rosemont Seneca Bohai and its financial transactions, including Hunter Biden's involvement with Rosemont Seneca Bohai.

33. After Hunter Biden's deposition, on April 19, 2024, Devon Archer's counsel produced over 3 million documents to the Oversight and Judiciary Committees' subpoenas

---

[64] Financial Institution 1, Record on file with the Oversight Committee.
[65] *Id.*
[66] *See* DOJ Press Release, *Seven Defendants Charged in Manhattan Federal Court with Defrauding a Native American Tribe and Investors of Over $60 Million* (May 11, 2016), available at https://www.justice.gov/usao-sdny/pr/seven-defendants-charged-manhattan-federal-court-defrauding-native-american-tribe-and.
[67] *See* SEC Litigation Release No. 23535 (May 11, 2016), available at https://www.sec.gov/litigation/litreleases/lr-23535.

(Archer Documents).[68] Despite prior requests, these documents were not disclosed until after Hunter Biden's testimony, and the Committees' concerns with the delay in producing the documents are discussed in more detail below. The Archer Documents provide insight as to why Hunter Biden misled the Committees about his knowledge and involvement with Rosemont Seneca Bohai and the Rosemont Seneca Bohai Bank Account.

34. The Archer Documents reveal that on March 16, 2016, the SEC subpoenaed Hunter Biden for a production of materials regarding his involvement with Rosemont Seneca Bohai (and other companies involved in the tribal bond scheme).[69] An image of the SEC's letter and subpoena directed to Hunter Biden and his attorneys is provided below:

[REMAINDER OF PAGE INTENTIONALLY BLANK]

[68] The Oversight Committee first requested certain documents in the custody of Mr. Archer, including Rosemont Seneca Bohai materials, on August 25, 2023.

[69] *See* Letter and Subpoena from U.S. Sec. and Exch. Comm'n Counsel to Hunter Biden (Mar. 16, 2016), attached as Exhibit 9.

UNITED STATES
**SECURITIES AND EXCHANGE COMMISSION**
NEW YORK REGIONAL OFFICE
BROOKFIELD PLACE, 200 VESEY STREET, SUITE 400
NEW YORK, NEW YORK 10281-1022

March 16, 2016

**Via UPS**

Robert Hunter Biden
Washington, DC

**Re: In the Matter of Hughes Capital Management (NY-**

Dear Mr. Biden:

The staff of the United States Securities and Exchange Commission (the "Commission") is conducting a non-public investigation in the matter identified above. The enclosed subpoena has been issued to you pursuant to a formal order entered by the United States Securities and Exchange Commission ("Commission"). The subpoena requires you to produce documents specified in the subpoena attachment to the Commission by **Wednesday, March 30, 2016**.

Unless otherwise indicated, the subpoena requires the production of original materials. For your convenience and at your expense, however, you may for now satisfy this requirement by producing complete, clear and legible copies of the documents specified. If you do produce copies, you must maintain the originals in a safe and secure manner and make the originals available to the staff on request. I will notify you if and when they are required.

Please produce all documents in an electronic format consistent with the enclosed SEC Data Delivery Standards. All electronic documents responsive to the document subpoena, including all metadata, should be produced in their native software format. For smaller electronic productions under 10MB in size, the materials may be emailed to the following email address: @sec.gov. Passwords for documents, files, compressed archives, and encrypted media should be provided separately either via email addressed to @sec.gov, or in a separate cover letter mailed separately from the data. If you have any questions concerning the production of documents in an electronic format, please contact me as soon as possible and, in any event, before producing

Robert Hunter Biden
March 16, 2016

documents.

This inquiry is non-public and should not be construed as an indication by the Commission or its staff that any violation of law has occurred, nor as a reflection upon any person, entity, or security. Information provided is subject to the Commission's routine uses. A description of those uses is contained in the enclosed copy of SEC Form 1662, which also contains other important information. Please review SEC Form 1662 prior to providing any information responsive to this subpoena.

Please note that, in any matter in which enforcement action is ultimately deemed to be warranted, the Division of Enforcement will not recommend any settlement to the Commission unless the party wishing to settle certifies, under penalty of perjury, that all documents responsive to Commission subpoenas and formal and informal document requests in this matter have been produced.

Please send all documents to [redacted] **U.S. Securities & Exchange Commission,** [redacted] **Washington, DC** [redacted] along with a copy of the subpoena.

If you have any questions concerning this matter, you may call me at [redacted] or [redacted] at [redacted]

Very truly yours,

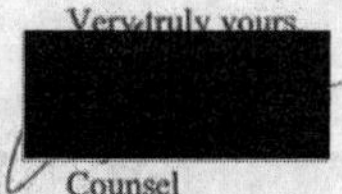

Counsel

Enclosures:

SEC Form 1662
Subpoena with Attachment
SEC Data Delivery Standards

## SUBPOENA

# UNITED STATES OF AMERICA

### SECURITIES AND EXCHANGE COMMISSION

**In the Matter of Hughes Capital Management (NY-[redacted]**

To: Robert Hunter Biden
Washington, DC [redacted]

**YOU MUST PRODUCE** everything specified in the Attachment to this subpoena to officers of the Securities and Exchange Commission at the place, date and time specified below:

[redacted] U.S. Securities and Exchange Commission, [redacted] [redacted] Washington, DC [redacted], on **Wednesday, March 30, 2016** at 10:00 a.m.

**FEDERAL LAW REQUIRES YOU TO COMPLY WITH THIS SUBPOENA.**
Failure to comply may subject you to a fine and/or imprisonment.

By: [redacted] Date: March 16, 2016
Counsel
Division of Enforcement

I am an officer of the Securities and Exchange Commission authorized to issue subpoenas in this matter. The Securities and Exchange Commission has issued a formal order authorizing this investigation under Section 20(a) of the Securities Act of 1933 and Section 21(a) of the Securities Exchange Act of 1934.

35. In the Subpoena Attachment, the SEC sought "[a]ll Documents, including Communications, concerning Rosemont Seneca Bohai, LLC ("RSB"), including but not limited to:

a. All Documents concerning payments that you made to or received from RSB;

b. Documents sufficient to identify any ownership interest that you have in RSB;

c. Documents sufficient to identify any positions that you hold with respect to RSB;

d. All Documents concerning RSB's purchase of a $15 million bond issued by the Wakpamni Lake Community Corporation in October 2014; and

e. All Documents concerning RSB's purchase of shares of Valor Group Limited in April 2015."[70]

36. On April 20, 2016, Hunter Biden's counsel responded to the SEC and appears to have produced approximately 1,700 pages of documents.[71] Hunter Biden's counsel's response to the SEC invoked Vice President Joe Biden and stated:

> As a threshold matter, we request that you treat this matter with the highest degree of confidentiality, consistent with Commission policy and applicable law. The confidential nature of this investigation is very important to our client and it would be unfair, not just to our client, **but also to his father, the Vice President of the United States, if his involvement in an SEC investigation and parallel criminal probe were to become the subject of any media attention.**[72]

37. An image of Hunter Biden's counsel's response to the SEC is provided below:

[REMAINDER OF PAGE INTENTIONALLY BLANK]

[70] *See* Exhibit 9.
[71] Letter from Hunter Biden's Counsel to U.S. Sec. and Exch. Comm'n Counsel (April 20, 2016), attached as Exhibit 10.
[72] *Id.*

*Confidential Treatment Requested Pursuant to 17 C.F.R. § 200.83*

April 20, 2016 **VIA EMAIL**

U.S. Securities and Exchange Commission
New York Regional Office

New York, NY

Re: Hughes Capital Management (NY-

Dear Ms.

On behalf of our client, R. Hunter Biden, enclosed please find documents Bates-stamped RHB0000001-RHB00001749, which are responsive to your subpoena issued in the above-captioned investiation.

As a threshold matter, we request that you treat this matter with the highest degree of confidentiality, consitent with Commission policy and applicable law. The confidential nature of this investigation is very important to our client and it would be unfair, not just to our client, but also to his father, the Vice President of the United States, if his involvement in an SEC investigation and parallel criminal probe were to become the subject of any media attention.

Please be advised that notwithstanding the subpoena's definition of Rosemont Seneca Bohai LLC ("RSB") as including its "affilliates," "officers," "directors," and "employees," Mr. Biden's production of communications "concerning" RSB is limited to emails that he sent or received, or on which he was copied, given the fact that the subpoena was issued to him personally. The production does not include all communications with Devon Archer, the purported sole member of RSB.

Please also be advised that we are continuing to review two potentially privileged documents. In the near future, we anticipate either producing these documents or withholding them subject to a privilege log.

In response to Instructions Nos. 14 and 15, at Mr. Biden's instruction, Joan Mayer and Eric Schwerin of Rosemont Seneca Advisors, LLC ("RSA"), searched RSA's offices for hard copy documents, and searched Mr. Biden's RSA email account, using search terms derived from the portion

Counsel
Page 2
April 20, 2016

of the subpoena describing what documents should be produced. These documents were reviewed for responsiveness and privilege by Mr. Biden's outside counsel. Original documents are maintained at RSA's offices located at Washington, DC Mr. Biden believes he has met his obligations under the subpoena.

All letters and documents produced to the staff are being provided to the SEC solely for its use in its investigation. In accordance with 17 C.F.R. § 200.83 pertaining to the Freedom of Information Act ("FOIA"), we hereby request confidential treatment of such material to the extent allowed by law. We further request that these materials be kept in a non-public file and that access to it by any third party inconsistent with the SEC's routine uses be denied. Moreover, we request that any materials provided be returned to the undersigned when the investigation is completed.

We understand that upon receipt of any FOIA requests, if the SEC determines that there is no ground to withhold the information, the SEC will seek substantiation from the firm (through undersigned counsel) to afford continued confidential treatment and for withholding the information.

If you need any additional information, please call me at

Sincerely,

Enclosures: (as stated above)

cc: FOIA Office
AUSA Esq.

38. Hunter Biden's counsel claimed that Joan Mayer and Eric Schwerin performed searches at Rosemont Seneca Advisors for responsive documents.[73] The letter referenced a "parallel criminal probe" and copied a federal prosecutor who worked at the U.S. Attorney's Office for the Southern District of New York.[74] Notably, the letter was sent to the SEC and copied DOJ while Joe Biden was Vice President, but the Committees are aware of no special counsel being appointed by either agency to handle this investigation.

39. Given the government's prior subpoena and federal investigation involving Hunter Biden's connections to Rosemont Seneca Bohai, Hunter Biden distanced himself from the company during the Committees' deposition by denying any involvement, knowledge, or understanding of the Rosemont Seneca Bohai Bank Account. The most recent IRS whistleblower disclosures show that he directed his Burisma payments into the Rosemont Seneca Bohai Bank Account.

40. In addition to the federal investigation of Rosemont Seneca Bohai, the Committees believe Hunter Biden lied about his involvement with the company to protect Joe Biden—the target of the Committees' impeachment inquiry. Some of the foreign transactions in the Rosemont Seneca Bohai Bank Account raise red flags because those payments were made around the same time Joe Biden met with the relevant foreign business associates, and there is no compelling evidence showing Hunter Biden provided legitimate services for such large sums of money. For instance, neither Devon Archer nor Hunter Biden could explain why on April 22, 2014, Novatus Holding Pte., Ltd., a company associated with Kenes Rakishev who was from Kazakhstan, deposited $142,300 in the Rosemont Seneca Bahai Bank Account to purchase a

[73] *Id.*
[74] *Id.*

sports car in the United States for Hunter Biden.[75] According to Devon Archer and subpoenaed bank records, this payment occurred soon after Vice President Biden met with Kenes Rakishev at Café Milano in Washington, D.C.[76] This payment appears to have been made as part of the Bidens' influence peddling, and Hunter Biden received additional money into this account from other foreign sources. Indeed, the Committees can prove that Hunter Biden received $2 million into the Rosemont Seneca Bohai Bank Account from foreign sources.

*Hunter Biden benefited financially from the Rosemont Seneca Bohai Bank Account*

41. Hunter Biden's claim that the Rosemont Seneca Bohai Bank Account was not for his benefit is completely false. On July 31, 2023, the Oversight Committee conducted a transcribed interview of Devon Archer—the named client for the Rosemont Seneca Bohai Bank Account and Rosemont Seneca Bohai Credit Card.[77] Devon Archer told the Oversight Committee that Hunter Biden received foreign payments through the Rosemont Seneca Bohai Bank Account and held equity in Rosemont Seneca Bohai.[78]

42. According to Mr. Archer, the Rosemont Seneca Bohai Bank Account was opened to hold the equity of a Chinese investment fund, BHR, where Jonathan Li was the CEO.[79] In 2013, Vice President Joe Biden met with Jonathan Li during a foreign trip to China where Hunter Biden accompanied his father on Air Force Two.[80] In addition to holding equity for BHR, Mr. Archer confirmed that the Rosemont Seneca Bohai Bank Account received Hunter Biden's payments from Burisma (and other foreign companies) and that the money was then disbursed to Hunter Biden or reinvested into other companies.[81] Devon Archer explained that "we were

---

[75] Devon Archer Tr., *supra* note 6, at 65-66; Hunter Biden Tr., *supra* note 6, at 39-40.
[76] Devon Archer Tr., *supra* note 6 at 46: 1-23; 57: 11-19; 61-64.
[77] *Id.* at 1.
[78] *Id.* at 64; 24: 3-5.
[79] *Id.* at 14; 15: 1-9; 68.
[80] *See Beautiful Things*, A Memoir, Hunter Biden (2021), at 122-123.
[81] Devon Archer Tr., *supra* note 6, at 15: 11-13; 24.

running it [Rosemont Seneca Bohai] as a business, so it was – it was to Rosemont Seneca Bohai for – there were other investments that were made. There were, you know, investments on behalf of the business. So, you know, as the business was capitalized, we did other things with it."[82]

43. Subpoenaed bank records corroborated Devon Archer's testimony and prove that Hunter Biden significantly benefited from the Rosemont Seneca Bohai Bank Account and Rosemont Seneca Bohai Credit Card Account. Devon Archer informed the Oversight Committee that when the bank records for Rosemont Seneca Bohai Bank Account show two Burisma payments in the same month for the same amount ($83,333.33), one of the payments was for Devon Archer and the other was for Hunter Biden.[83]

44. An image from the subpoenaed bank records showing an example of two simultaneous $83,333.33 payments on the same day into the Rosemont Seneca Bohai Bank Account is shown below:

[REMAINDER OF PAGE INTENTIONALLY BLANK]

[82] *Id.* at 24: 7-10.
[83] *Id.* at 24: 3-5.

Account Detail

Active Assets Account
ROSEMONT SENECA BOHAI, LLC
C/O DEVON ARCHER

ACTIVITY

CASH FLOW ACTIVITY BY DATE

| Transaction Date | Settlement Date | Activity Type | Description | Comments | Quantity | Price | Credits/(Debits) |
|---|---|---|---|---|---|---|---|
| 7/8 | 7/8 | Automated Payment | | AUTOMATIC BILL PAYMENT | | | $(1,339.48) |
| 7/10 | 7/10 | Funds Transferred | WIRED FUNDS SENT | BENE: ROSEMONT SELECT OPPORTUN ACCT: XXXXX | | | (83,500.00) |
| 7/11 | 7/11 | Funds Transferred | WIRED FUNDS SENT | BENE: ACCT: XXXXX | | | (6,000.00) |
| 7/11 | 7/11 | Funds Transferred | WIRED FUNDS SENT | BENE: ROBERT BIDEN ACCT: XXXX | | | (5,000.00) |
| 7/11 | 7/11 | Funds Transferred | WIRED FUNDS SENT | BENE: ACCT: XXXXX | | | (4,500.00) |
| 7/14 | 7/14 | Funds Transferred | WIRED FUNDS SENT | BENE: ACCT: XXXXX | | | (17,710.36) |
| 7/15 | 7/15 | Funds Received | WIRED FUNDS RECEIVED | AS PRIVATBANK BURISMA HOLDINGS LIMITED | | | 83,333.33 |
| 7/15 | 7/15 | Funds Received | WIRED FUNDS RECEIVED | AS PRIVATBANK BURISMA HOLDINGS LIMITED | | | 83,333.33 |
| 7/18 | 7/18 | Funds Transferred | WIRED FUNDS SENT | BENE: ROBERT BIDEN ACCT: XXXX | | | (20,000.00) |
| 7/21 | 7/21 | Automated Payment | AMEX EPayment ACH PMT | AUTOMATIC BILL PAYMENT | | | (49,481.26) |
| 7/23 | 7/23 | Funds Received | | ACCT CNFRM | | | 0.27 |
| 7/23 | 7/23 | Funds Received | | ACCT CNFRM | | | 0.14 |
| 7/23 | 7/23 | Automated Payment | | AUTOMATIC BILL PAYMENT | | | (0.41) |
| 7/24 | 7/24 | Automated Payment | | AUTOMATIC BILL PAYMENT | | | (5,588.74) |
| 7/29 | 7/29 | Funds Transferred | WIRED FUNDS SENT | BENE: ROBERT BIDEN ACCT: XXXX | | | (20,000.00) |
| 7/30 | 7/30 | Interest Income | (Period 06/28-07/30) | | | | 6.05 |
| 7/30 | 7/30 | Interest Income | (Period 06/28-07/30) | | | | 2.22 |
| NET CREDITS/(DEBITS) | | | | | | | $(46,443.91) |

45. Between April 2014 and October 2015, Hunter Biden and Devon Archer collectively received over $3.3 million from Burisma Holdings Ltd. into the Rosemont Seneca Bohai Bank Account:[84]

[REMAINDER OF PAGE INTENTIONALLY BLANK]

[84] This is not the total amount of money Hunter Biden received from Burisma as he also received wires from Burisma into another corporate account, Owasco, P.C.

| DATE | ORIGINATOR | BIDEN AFFILIATED ENTITY | AMOUNT |
|---|---|---|---|
| 4/15/2014 | Burisma Holdings Limited | Rosemont Seneca Bohai | $ 83,333.33 |
| 4/15/2014 | Burisma Holdings Limited | Rosemont Seneca Bohai | $ 29,424.82 |
| 5/15/2014 | Burisma Holdings Limited | Rosemont Seneca Bohai | $ 83,333.33 |
| 5/15/2014 | Burisma Holdings Limited | Rosemont Seneca Bohai | $ 83,333.33 |
| 6/17/2014 | Burisma Holdings Limited | Rosemont Seneca Bohai | $ 83,333.33 |
| 6/17/2014 | Burisma Holdings Limited | Rosemont Seneca Bohai | $ 83,333.33 |
| 6/18/2014 | Burisma Holdings Limited | Rosemont Seneca Bohai | $ 60,954.54 |
| 7/15/2014 | Burisma Holdings Limited | Rosemont Seneca Bohai | $ 83,333.33 |
| 7/15/2014 | Burisma Holdings Limited | Rosemont Seneca Bohai | $ 83,333.33 |
| 8/18/2014 | Burisma Holdings Limited | Rosemont Seneca Bohai | $ 83,333.33 |
| 8/18/2014 | Burisma Holdings Limited | Rosemont Seneca Bohai | $ 83,333.33 |
| 9/16/2014 | Burisma Holdings Limited | Rosemont Seneca Bohai | $ 83,333.33 |
| 9/16/2014 | Burisma Holdings Limited | Rosemont Seneca Bohai | $ 83,333.33 |
| 10/7/2014 | Burisma Holdings Limited | Rosemont Seneca Bohai | $ 28,913.89 |
| 10/7/2014 | Burisma Holdings Limited | Rosemont Seneca Bohai | $ 2,543.38 |
| 10/15/2014 | Burisma Holdings Limited | Rosemont Seneca Bohai | $ 83,333.33 |
| 10/15/2014 | Burisma Holdings Limited | Rosemont Seneca Bohai | $ 83,333.33 |
| 11/18/2014 | Burisma Holdings Limited | Rosemont Seneca Bohai | $ 83,333.33 |
| 11/18/2014 | Burisma Holdings Limited | Rosemont Seneca Bohai | $ 83,333.33 |
| 12/16/2014 | Burisma Holdings Limited | Rosemont Seneca Bohai | $ 83,333.33 |
| 12/16/2014 | Burisma Holdings Limited | Rosemont Seneca Bohai | $ 83,333.33 |
| 1/6/2015 | Burisma Holdings Limited | Rosemont Seneca Bohai | $ 47,249.07 |
| 1/15/2015 | Burisma Holdings Limited | Rosemont Seneca Bohai | $ 83,333.33 |
| 1/15/2015 | Burisma Holdings Limited | Rosemont Seneca Bohai | $ 83,333.33 |
| 2/17/2015 | Burisma Holdings Limited | Rosemont Seneca Bohai | $ 83,333.33 |
| 2/17/2015 | Burisma Holdings Limited | Rosemont Seneca Bohai | $ 83,333.33 |
| 3/16/2015 | Burisma Holdings Limited | Rosemont Seneca Bohai | $ 83,333.33 |
| 3/16/2015 | Burisma Holdings Limited | Rosemont Seneca Bohai | $ 83,333.33 |
| 4/15/2015 | Burisma Holdings Limited | Rosemont Seneca Bohai | $ 83,333.33 |
| 4/15/2015 | Burisma Holdings Limited | Rosemont Seneca Bohai | $ 83,333.33 |
| 5/18/2015 | Burisma Holdings Limited | Rosemont Seneca Bohai | $ 83,333.33 |
| 5/18/2015 | Burisma Holdings Limited | Rosemont Seneca Bohai | $ 83,333.33 |
| 6/9/2015 | Burisma Holdings Limited | Rosemont Seneca Bohai | $ 3,668.47 |
| 6/18/2015 | Burisma Holdings Limited | Rosemont Seneca Bohai | $ 83,333.33 |
| 6/18/2015 | Burisma Holdings Limited | Rosemont Seneca Bohai | $ 83,333.33 |
| 7/16/2015 | Burisma Holdings Limited | Rosemont Seneca Bohai | $ 83,333.33 |
| 7/16/2015 | Burisma Holdings Limited | Rosemont Seneca Bohai | $ 83,333.33 |
| 7/28/2015 | Burisma Holdings Limited | Rosemont Seneca Bohai | $ 60,554.53 |
| 8/19/2015 | Burisma Holdings Limited | Rosemont Seneca Bohai | $ 83,333.33 |

| | | | |
|---|---|---|---|
| 8/19/2015 | Burisma Holdings Limited | Rosemont Seneca Bohai | $ 83,333.33 |
| 9/17/2015 | Burisma Holdings Limited | Rosemont Seneca Bohai | $ 83,333.33 |
| 9/17/2015 | Burisma Holdings Limited | Rosemont Seneca Bohai | $ 83,333.33 |
| 10/16/2015 | Burisma Holdings Limited | Rosemont Seneca Bohai | $ 83,333.33 |
| 10/16/2015 | Burisma Holdings Limited | Rosemont Seneca Bohai | $ 83,333.33 |
| 10/16/2015 | Burisma Holdings Limited | Rosemont Seneca Bohai | $ 4,737.58 |
| | | | **$ 3,321,379.49** |

46. Approximately half of the monthly wires from Burisma in the chart above were designated for Hunter Biden, totaling approximately $1.7 million in payments from April 2014 to October 2015.[85] After October 2015, Hunter Biden began receiving his Burisma payments into his professional corporation bank account, Owasco, P.C., which was around the time federal agencies began investigating Devon Archer.[86] Burisma paid Hunter Biden approximately $2.3 million into the Owasco, P.C. bank account, bringing Hunter Biden's total amount of Burisma payments calculated by the Committees to approximately $4 million.[87] IRS whistleblower testimony reported Hunter Biden and Devon Archer earned a combined $6.5 million from Burisma, and this finding is consistent with the Committee's investigation.[88]

47. In addition to using foreign payments as equity for investments, Hunter Biden received wires into his personal and corporate accounts from the Rosemont Seneca Bohai Bank Account.[89] Hunter Biden received approximately $1 million dollars in payments to his personal and corporate bank accounts from Rosemont Seneca Bohai Bank Account while Joe Biden was a public official, including the following transactions:[90]

---

[85] Records on file with the Oversight Committee.
[86] *See* Eric Schwerin Tr., *supra* note 6, at 31: 1-5.
[87] Records on file with the Oversight Committee.
[88] *See* Transcript of Special Agent Joseph Ziegler, Internal Revenue Service, H. Comm. on Ways and Means, at 99.
[89] *See* Chart 36-38.
[90] Records on file with the Oversight Committee.

| DATE | COMPANY ACCOUNT | BENEFICIARY | AMOUNT |
|---|---|---|---|
| 6/5/2014 | RSB Bank Account | Robert Biden | $15,000 |
| 6/13/2014 | RSB Bank Account | Robert Biden | $10,000 |
| 6/23/2014 | RSB Bank Account | Robert Biden | $25,000 |
| 7/11/2014 | RSB Bank Account | Robert Biden | $5,000 |
| 7/18/2014 | RSB Bank Account | Robert Biden | $20,000 |
| 7/29/2014 | RSB Bank Account | Robert Biden | $20,000 |
| 8/6/2014 | RSB Bank Account | Robert Biden | $15,000 |
| 8/13/2014 | RSB Bank Account | Robert Biden | $20,000 |
| 8/25/2014 | RSB Bank Account | Robert Biden | $20,000 |
| 9/4/2014 | RSB Bank Account | Robert Biden | $20,000 |
| 9/12/2014 | RSB Bank Account | Robert Biden | $15,000 |
| 10/7/2014 | RSB Bank Account | Robert Biden | $20,000 |
| 10/10/2014 | RSB Bank Account | Robert Biden | $20,000 |
| 10/22/2014 | RSB Bank Account | Robert Biden | $10,000 |
| 10/27/2014 | RSB Bank Account | Robert Biden | $20,000 |
| 11/10/2014 | RSB Bank Account | Robert Biden | $20,000 |
| 11/25/2014 | RSB Bank Account | Robert Biden | $25,000 |
| 12/10/2014 | RSB Bank Account | RSTP Capital | $100,000 |
| 12/19/2014 | RSB Bank Account | Robert Biden | $15,000 |
| 1/8/2015 | RSB Bank Account | Robert Biden | $10,000 |
| 1/21/2015 | RSB Bank Account | RSTP Capital | $25,000 |

| | | | |
|---|---|---|---|
| 1/22/2015 | RSB Bank Account | Robert Biden | $15,000 |
| 1/30/2015 | RSB Bank Account | Robert Biden | $15,000 |
| 2/6/2015 | RSB Bank Account | Robert Biden | $15,000 |
| 2/23/2015 | RSB Bank Account | Robert Biden | $15,000 |
| 3/2/2015 | RSB Bank Account | Robert Biden | $10,000 |
| 4/6/2015 | RSB Bank Account | Robert Biden | $20,000 |
| 5/13/2015 | RSB Bank Account | Robert Biden | $15,000 |
| 5/18/2015 | RSB Bank Account | Owasco PC | $5,000 |
| 6/8/2015 | RSB Bank Account | Robert Biden | $15,000 |
| 6/15/2015 | RSB Bank Account | First Clearing LLC | $3,668.47 |
| 6/23/2015 | RSB Bank Account | Robert Biden | $15,000 |
| 7/9/2015 | RSB Bank Account | Robert Biden | $20,000 |
| 7/17/2015 | RSB Bank Account | Robert Biden | $19,000 |
| 7/24/2015 | RSB Bank Account | Robert Biden | $97,979 |
| 7/30/2015 | RSB Bank Account | Robert Biden | $14,000 |
| 8/3/2015 | RSB Bank Account | Owasco PC | $5,000 |
| 8/13/2015 | RSB Bank Account | Robert Biden | $19,000 |
| 8/26/2015 | RSB Bank Account | MFTCG Holdings LLC Biden | $150,000 |
| 8/31/2015 | RSB Bank Account | Robert Biden | $14,000 |
| 9/1/2015 | RSB Bank Account | Owasco, P.C. | $5,000 |
| 9/3/2015 | RSB Bank Account | Robert Biden | $5,000 |
| 9/16/2015 | RSB Bank Account | Robert Biden | $19,000 |
| 9/30/2015 | RSB Bank Account | Robert Biden | $19,000 |

| 10/5/2015 | RSB Bank Account | Robert Biden | $15,000 |
|---|---|---|---|
| 10/19/2015 | RSB Bank Account | Robert Biden | $6,333.40 |
| | | | **$1,001,980.87** |

48. Subpoenaed bank records revealed that Hunter Biden's then-minor child also received a wire from Rosemont Seneca Bohai for $97,979 on July 24, 2015.[91]

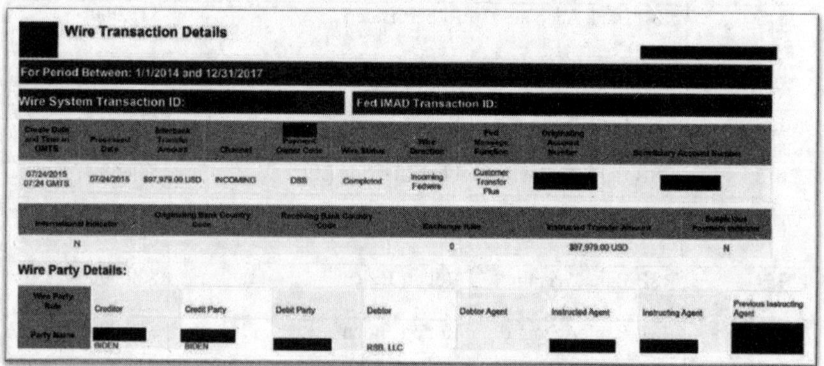

**Wire Transaction Details**

For Period Between: 1/1/2014 and 12/31/2017

Wire System Transaction ID: Fed IMAD Transaction ID:

| Create Date and Time in GMTS | Processed Date | Interbank Transfer Amount | Channel | Payment Owner Code | Wire Status | Wire Direction | Fed Message Function | Originating Account Number | Beneficiary Account Number |
|---|---|---|---|---|---|---|---|---|---|
| 07/24/2015 07:24 GMTS | 07/24/2015 | $97,979.00 USD | INCOMING | DSS | Completed | Incoming Fedwire | Customer Transfer Plus | | |

| International Indicator | Originating Bank Country Code | Receiving Bank Country Code | Exchange Rate | Instructed Transfer Amount | [illegible] Payment Indicator |
|---|---|---|---|---|---|
| N | | | 0 | $97,979.00 USD | N |

**Wire Party Details:**

| Wire Party Role | Creditor | Credit Party | Debit Party | Debtor | Debtor Agent | Instructed Agent | Instructing Agent | Previous Instructing Agent |
|---|---|---|---|---|---|---|---|---|
| Party Name | BIDEN | BIDEN | | RSB, LLC | | | | |

49. Hunter Biden also benefited from the Rosemont Seneca Bohai Credit Card Account. Subpoenaed documents from a credit card company show purchases for Hunter Biden's expenses, including his travel, totaling approximately $40,878 from the corporate credit card. The purchases for Hunter Biden are provided below:

[REMAINDER OF PAGE INTENTIONALLY BLANK]

[91] Financial Institution 3, Record on file with the Oversight Committee.

| DATE | COMPANY ACCOUNT | BENEFICIARY | AMOUNT |
|---|---|---|---|
| 5/21/2014 | RSB Credit Card | Hunter Biden | $100 |
| 5/21/2014 | RSB Credit Card | Hunter Biden | $7,392.50 |
| 5/23/2014 | RSB Credit Card | Hunter Biden | $7,267.50 |
| 5/25/2014 | RSB Credit Card | Hunter Biden | $6,255.00 |
| 6/8/2014 | RSB Credit Card | Hunter Biden | $6,901.20 |
| 1/22/2015 | RSB Credit Card | Hunter Biden | $1,832.50 |
| 3/2/2015 | RSB Credit Card | Hunter Biden | $100.00 |
| 3/2/2015 | RSB Credit Card | Hunter Biden | $9,142.10 |
| 3/3/2015 | RSB Credit Card | Hunter Biden | $946.70 |
| 3/10/2015 | RSB Credit Card | Hunter Biden | $941.20 |
| | | | **$40,878.70** |

50. There is no conceivable reason for the Rosemont Seneca Bohai Credit Card to pay approximately $40,000 in expenses for Hunter Biden, in less than one year, if he had no affiliation with the company, knowledge of its bank accounts, or position with Rosemont Seneca Bohai. Hunter Biden's claim of ignorance about these accounts is absurd given the amount of money he received from Rosemont Seneca Bohai.

51. The evidence overwhelmingly demonstrates that Hunter Biden benefited from the Rosemont Seneca Bohai Bank Account, exerted a level of control and authority over the account, and knew foreign payments were made into the account on his behalf. Indeed, he directed that Burisma send his monthly fees to the account. As discussed below, evidence also shows Hunter Biden represented to others that he held a position with Rosemont Seneca Bohai.

*Hunter Biden falsely testified about his position with Rosemont Seneca Bohai*

52. During Hunter Biden's deposition, Committee Democrats asked Hunter Biden, "[s]o it seems to me that Devon Archer's testimony and your testimony are the same: You had no position with Rosemont Seneca Bohai. Is that correct?"[92] Hunter Biden responded, "That is correct."[93] However, the Committees received documents after Hunter Biden's deposition showing he and his business associates, including Eric Schwerin, represented to investors that Hunter Biden did hold a position with Rosemont Seneca Bohai.

53. Subpoenaed bank records show that on April 22, 2014, the Rosemont Seneca Bohai Bank Account received a $142,300 payment from Novatus Holding Pte., Ltd., a Singaporean company associated with Kenes Rakishev, who was a Kazakhstani oligarch.[94] On the following day, that exact amount was wired from the Rosemont Seneca Bohai Bank Account to a domestic car dealership for Hunter Biden's sports car in the amount of $142,300.[95] This wire was sent after Vice President Joe Biden met with Kenes Rakishev and Hunter Biden at a dinner at Café Milano in Washington, D.C.[96] An image of the wire transaction is below:

[REMAINDER OF PAGE INTENTIONALLY BLANK]

---

[92] Hunter Biden Tr., *supra* note 6, at 61: 19-23.
[93] *Id.* at 61: 19-24.
[94] Records on file with the Oversight Committee.
[95] Records on file with the Oversight Committee.
[96] Devon Archer Tr., *supra* note 6 at 46: 1-23; 57: 11-19; 61-64.

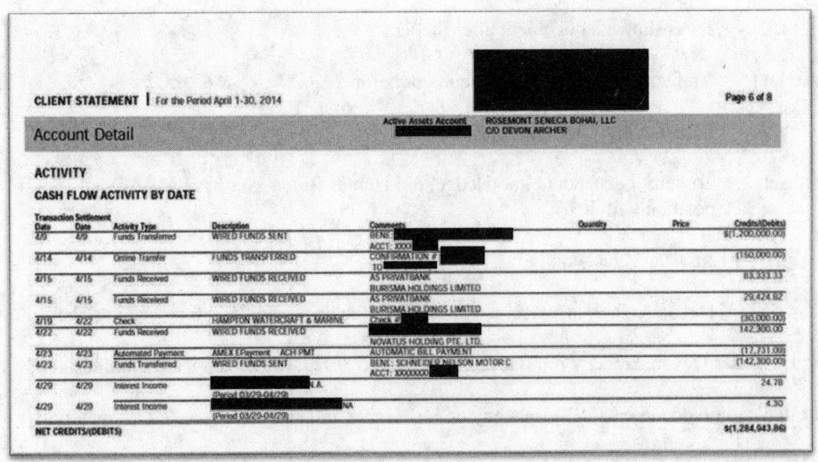

**CLIENT STATEMENT** | For the Period April 1-30, 2014

Page 6 of 8

Account Detail

Active Assets Account — ROSEMONT SENECA BOHAI, LLC C/O DEVON ARCHER

**ACTIVITY**

**CASH FLOW ACTIVITY BY DATE**

| Transaction Date | Settlement Date | Activity Type | Description | Comments | Quantity | Price | Credits/(Debits) |
|---|---|---|---|---|---|---|---|
| 4/9 | 4/9 | Funds Transferred | WIRED FUNDS SENT | BENE: ACCT: XXXX | | | $(1,200,000.00) |
| 4/14 | 4/14 | Online Transfer | FUNDS TRANSFERRED | CONFIRMATION # TO | | | (150,000.00) |
| 4/15 | 4/15 | Funds Received | WIRED FUNDS RECEIVED | AS PRIVATBANK BURISMA HOLDINGS LIMITED | | | 83,333.33 |
| 4/16 | 4/15 | Funds Received | WIRED FUNDS RECEIVED | AS PRIVATBANK BURISMA HOLDINGS LIMITED | | | 29,424.82 |
| 4/19 | 4/22 | Check | HAMPTON WATERCRAFT & MARINE | Check # | | | (30,000.00) |
| 4/22 | 4/22 | Funds Received | WIRED FUNDS RECEIVED | NOVATUS HOLDING PTE. LTD. | | | 142,300.00 |
| 4/23 | 4/23 | Automated Payment | AMEX EPayment ACH PMT | AUTOMATIC BILL PAYMENT | | | (17,731.00) |
| 4/23 | 4/23 | Funds Transferred | WIRED FUNDS SENT | BENE: SCHNEIDER NELSON MOTOR C ACCT: XXXXXXX | | | (142,300.00) |
| 4/29 | 4/29 | Interest Income | N.A. (Period 03/29-04/29) | | | | 24.78 |
| 4/29 | 4/29 | Interest Income | NA (Period 03/29-04/29) | | | | 4.30 |
| **NET CREDITS/(DEBITS)** | | | | | | | $(1,284,943.86) |

54. The Oversight Committee questioned Devon Archer as to why Novatus Holding, Pte. Ltd.—a foreign company—wired the exact same amount to Rosemont Seneca Bohai to purchase Hunter Biden's sports car. Mr. Archer did not know the details regarding the financial transaction and stated, "I wasn't, like, doing this banking. Hunter was a corporate secretary of RSB. We had a handshake 50-50 ownership. And he conducted, you know, banking business with the COO."[97] Mr. Archer's counsel interjected with the following:

Counsel: Yeah. Let's just clean that up.

A: Okay.

Counsel: I think you said it a second ago, that Hunter Biden was the corporate secretary of RSB. Do you know that to be true, or are you recalling a document you have been shown after the fact?

[97] Devon Archer Tr., *supra* note 6, at 64: 22-24.

A: I was shown a document after the fact.

Counsel : And you hadn't seen that document before?

A: I had not seen that document before.

Counsel : To your independent knowledge, did Hunter Biden ever have any official position with RSB?

A: Just – no. Just equity.[98]

55. Devon Archer's counsel did not submit the document he referenced into the record.[99] After Devon Archer's interview, on August 25, 2023, the Oversight Committee requested certain documents in the custody of Mr. Archer and specifically asked for materials involving Rosemont Seneca Bohai (hereinafter August 2023 Request).[100] Mr. Archer's counsel did not produce the documents pursuant to the Oversight Committee's request.

56. On February 28, 2024, when the Committees interviewed Hunter Biden, Devon Archer's counsel still had not produced documents responsive to the Oversight Committee's August 2023 Request. The Committees asked Hunter Biden why the $142,300 was wired to Rosemont Seneca Bohai and if he was corporate secretary of Rosemont Seneca Bohai. Hunter Biden responded with the following:

Q: He [Devon Archer] also said that you were the corporate secretary of Rosemont Seneca Bohai. Is that incorrect?

A: The corporate secretary?

Q: Yes, sir.

A: ***I didn't even know that there was such a thing.*** [101]

---

[98] *Id.* at 66: 20-25; 67: 1-5.
[99] After Devon Archer said Hunter Biden was the corporate secretary of Rosemont Seneca Bohai and his attorney interjected, Devon Archer told the Committee that Hunter Biden "had no position with RSB[.]" *Id.* at 67: 9-10.
[100] Letter from Hon. James Comer, Chairman, Comm. on Oversight & Accountability, to Devon Archer's Counsel (Aug. 25, 2023).
[101] Hunter Biden Tr., *supra* note 6, at 27: 6-25.

57. Similar to Devon Archer's counsel, Hunter Biden's counsel then interjected and raised a question about "the document" indicating Hunter Biden was the corporate secretary, despite the Committees not referencing a document in the questioning:

Counsel: Do you have the document that indicates that company [Rosemont Seneca Bohai] as having a company so that there would be a secretary? Do you have that too?

Q: We provided you the Rosemont Seneca Bohai bank accounts, so –

A: No, I'm saying –

Q: – in advance we provided these to you.

A: – is there a registration that says –

Q: I'm not going to answer questions, sir. We provided the documents to you. In addition –

Counsel: I will state for the record that there's no document that you sent out of the hundred and – 200-plus documents and thousands of pages that indicates what you just said.

A: Yes.

Q: I referred to Devon Archer making the statement. I didn't refer to a document from a bank record.[102]

58. After the Hunter Biden interview, the Committees were concerned Hunter Biden's counsel was aware of documents regarding Hunter Biden's position with Rosemont Seneca Bohai that were unavailable to the Committees. The Committees' concerns were well-founded.

59. On May 22, 2024, the Ways and Means Committee lawfully disclosed documents from IRS whistleblower SA Joseph Ziegler.[103] These documents were submitted to the Ways and Means Committee after the Hunter Biden deposition. SA Ziegler provided an email to the Ways and Means Committee that the investigation team obtained via an electronic search warrant.[104]

---

[102] *Id.* at 27: 11-25.
[103] *See supra* footnotes 53-54.
[104] *See* Statement of Joseph Ziegler dated March 12, 2024, Affidavit 9, at ¶ 7.

60. The email shows that on April 29, 2014, Katie Dodge, an employee of Hunter Biden, emailed an employee of Grand Prix Motors (a car dealership) and attached a signed document from Hunter Biden to the dealership.[105] The title of the document is "CORPORATE RESOLUTION" and shows that Robert Hunter Biden certified he was the Secretary of Rosemont Seneca Bohai LLC.[106] The document stated, "Robert Hunter Biden is hereby authorized and empowered to enter into a contractual obligation with Grand Prix Motors . . . ."[107] In addition, the document provided, "I have hereunto set my hand as Secretary of this corporation and affixed the corporate seal of this corporation this 29th day of April, 2014."[108] Hunter Biden signed the document as the "Secretary of Corporation[.]"[109]

[REMAINDER OF PAGE INTENTIONALLY BLANK]

[105] Ways & Means Exhibit 902 document, attached as Exhibit 11.
[106] *See* Exhibit 11. A portion of this document was handwritten.
[107] *Id.*
[108] *Id.*
[109] *Id.*
[109] *Id.*

## CORPORATE RESOLUTION

I, Robert Hunter Biden, hereby certify that I am the duly elected, qualified and acting Secretary of Rosemont Seneca Bohai LLC, a Corporation organized and existing under the Laws of the State of DE, and that at a meeting of the Board of Directors of said corporation, held on the 29th day of April (Month), 2014 (Year), at which a quorum was present, the following Resolution was duly introduced and adopted:

RESOLVED, that Robert Hunter Biden (Name of individual executing contract) is hereby authorized and empowered to enter into a contractual obligation with Grand Prix Motors (Name of Dealership), which will be or has been assigned to Porsche Financial Services, Inc. or an assignee designated by Porsche Financial Services, Inc., in the form presented to the Board of Directors.

IN WITNESS WHEREOF, I have hereunto set my hand as Secretary of this corporation and affixed the corporate seal of this corporation this 29th day of April (Month), 2014 (Year).

[signature]
Signature of Secretary of Corporation

[signature]
(Seal)

PFS 1011 (3/01)

61. According to this document, Hunter Biden certified that he was the Corporate Secretary of Rosemont Seneca Bohai as of April 29, 2014. This document contradicts Hunter Biden's testimony that he "didn't even know that there was such a thing" as a corporate secretary and that he had no position with Rosemont Seneca Bohai.[110] It appears Hunter Biden not only knew of the corporate secretary position but that he held that title at Rosemont Seneca Bohai.

62. In reality, Hunter Biden received over $1 million from Rosemont Seneca Bohai, was a 50-50 equity owner in the company,[111] directed foreign payments from Burisma into its bank account, and certified he was the corporate secretary of the company. Hunter Biden's statements during his deposition were false beyond a reasonable doubt and should be prosecuted accordingly. Hunter Biden knew his statements were false because this was a corporate position he held at a company through which he received millions of dollars. His answer to the Committees' questions regarding his position did not indicate he could not remember whether he had a position; rather, he affirmatively denied ever knowing about the position of corporate secretary despite documents showing otherwise. Furthermore, Hunter Biden easily recalled other positions he held with companies that pre-dated the 2014 to 2015 timeframe.[112] Despite providing an extensive professional background to the Committees, he omitted any involvement with Rosemont Seneca Bohai and serving on the board of Burisma.[113] And as discussed above, Hunter Biden had a motive to conceal his involvement with Rosemont Seneca Bohai.

63. Rosemont Seneca Bohai and the Rosemont Seneca Bohai Bank Account are material to this Congressional investigation. This company and its bank accounts were

---

[110] Hunter Biden Tr., *supra* note 6, at 27: 6-25.
[111] *See* Devon Archer Tr., *supra* note 6, at 64:22-24 ("That's why I clarified the point, like, I wasn't, like, doing this banking. Hunter was a corporate secretary of RSB. We had handshake 50-50 ownership. And he conducted, you know, banking business with the COO."); 65:15-17 (Q: "And Rosemont Seneca Bohai, like you just said, was a 50-50 handshake between you and Hunter Biden, right?" A: Correct.")
[112] Hunter Biden Tr., *supra* note 6, at 16:19-25;17:1-25.
[113] *Id.*

purposely used to receive suspicious wires from foreign companies and individuals who met with Vice President Biden. Indeed, the Rosemont Seneca Bohai Bank Account was specifically referenced in the Committees' Impeachment Inquiry Memorandum.[114] The scoping memorandum discussed how, "Money wired by Burisma to the Rosemont Seneca Bohai account was often later transferred to Hunter Biden directly and his professional corporation, Owasco, P.C., in small increments."[115] Additionally, the Impeachment Inquiry Memorandum expressed concerns as to why money from Russia and Kazakhstan was sent to the Rosemont Seneca Bohai bank account.[116] The Oversight Committee subpoenaed its financial accounts and credit card account and questioned witnesses about financial transactions involving Rosemont Seneca Bohai. This company and its bank accounts undoubtedly played a central role in the influence peddling operation that the Committees are investigating and are relevant to whether Joe Biden abused his federal office to enrich his family.

64. Additionally, because of Hunter Biden's false testimony, certain avenues of questioning were curtailed during his deposition. If Hunter Biden would have answered questions regarding Rosemont Seneca Bohai truthfully, the Committees' line of questioning would have been different and additional evidence would have been elicited. For instance, if Hunter Biden told the truth that he held a position at Rosemont Seneca Bohai and directed money into the bank account, the Committees would have further inquired as to why the Burisma money was not sent to Owasco, P.C.; when and why he stepped down as the corporate secretary of the company; why he selected that company to accept money from Kenes Rakishev; and why Yelena Baturina's money was funneled into that bank account from Rosemont Seneca Thornton.

---

[114] Impeachment Inquiry Memorandum, *supra* note 1, at 7.
[115] *Id.*
[116] *Id.* at 11-12.

Instead, Hunter Biden's false testimony impeded the investigation and required the Committees to take additional investigative steps and hold another hearing to correct his false statements.

### E. HUNTER BIDEN FALSELY TESTIFIED ABOUT HIS COMMUNICATION WITH CHINESE BUSINESS PARTNERS

65. On March 1, 2017—less than two months after Vice President Joe Biden left public office—State Energy HK Ltd. (State Energy HK), a company associated with Ye Jianming, the Chairman of the Chinese energy company CEFC, wired $3 million to Robinson Walker, LLC.[117] Rob Walker, a business associate of Hunter Biden, owned Robinson Walker, LLC. On January 26, 2024, the Committees interviewed Rob Walker.[118] During the interview, Mr. Walker stated that he, Hunter Biden, and James Gilliar, began performing work for CEFC "probably in the 2015-2016 timeframe[.]"[119] According to Rob Walker, the $3 million payment from State Energy HK was payment for services that Hunter Biden, James Gilliar, and Rob Walker provided prior to being paid by the Chinese company in March 2017.[120]

66. A document produced by Rob Walker corroborated that he, James Gilliar, and Hunter Biden were engaged in business dealings with CEFC while Vice President Joe Biden was in office.[121] Although Rob Walker could not state the exact timing of the meeting,[122] he confirmed that Joe Biden, after leaving public office, met with Ye Jianming.[123] Financial records show that on March 1, 2017, State Energy HK wired the $3 million to Robinson Walker, LLC.[124]

---

[117] *See* First Bank Memo, *supra* note 12.
[118] *See* Rob Walker Tr., *supra* note 6.
[119] *Id.* at 22: 5-8.
[120] *Id.* at 80: 6-21.
[121] Document attached as Exhibit 12.
[122] Rob Walker Tr., *supra* note 6, at 42-43 (Q: Did this meeting occur before or after your company received a $3 million payment from State Energy HK? A: I don't know for sure. I believe—I believe—I don't know.")
[123] *Id.* at 41: 14-16.
[124] *See* First Bank Memo, *supra* note 12.

67. The next day, Rob Walker wired one-third of the amount, $1,065,000, to James Gilliar's company, European Energy and Infrastructure Group (EEIG), in Abu Dhabi.[125] Rob Walker retained approximately one-third of the money for himself.[126] Rob Walker did not immediately send one-third to Hunter Biden or his companies. Instead, from March 6, 2017 to May 18, 2017, Hunter Biden, James Biden, Hallie Biden, and their companies received 16 separate payments to personal and corporate accounts totaling $1,065,692.[127] Hunter Biden instructed Rob Walker to make incremental payments to various bank accounts over a period of months.[128] These transactions reduced the size of the wires and concealed the source of the money: State Energy HK, a Chinese company associated with CEFC. Despite receiving millions of dollars from the company, Rob Walker could not confirm whether the company that paid them was state owned by China or not.[129]

68. The chart below shows the complicated financial transactions after Robinson Walker, LLC received the $3 million wire from the Chinese company, State Energy HK, and then sent 16 subsequent wire transfers to Hunter Biden, his companies, James Biden's company (JBBSR, INC), and Hallie Biden:[130]

[REMAINDER OF PAGE INTENTIONALLY BLANK]

---

[125] *See* Second Bank Memo, *supra* note 12, at 31-32.
[126] *Id.*
[127] *Id.*
[128] Rob Walker Tr., *supra* note 6, at 83: 2-5.
[129] *Id.* at 78: 17-19.
[130] Records on file with the Oversight Committee.

| Date | Originating Account | Beneficiary Account | Amount |
|---|---|---|---|
| 3/6/2017 | Robinson Walker, LLC | "Biden" | $5,000 |
| 3/13/2017 | Robinson Walker, LLC | "Biden" | $25,000 |
| 3/20/2017 | Robinson Walker, LLC | Hallie Biden | $25,000 |
| 3/27/2017 | Robinson Walker, LLC | Owasco P.C. | $50,000 |
| 3/29/2017 | Robinson Walker, LLC | First Clearing, LLC | $100,000 |
| 3/31/2017 | Robinson Walker, LLC | Owasco P.C. | $50,000 |
| 3/31/2017 | Robinson Walker, LLC | Owasco P.C. | $100,000 |
| 4/3/2017 | Robinson Walker, LLC | JBBSR INC | $50,000 |
| 4/3/2017 | Robinson Walker, LLC | JBBSR INC | $50,000 |
| 4/14/2017 | Robinson Walker, LLC | RSTP II, LLC | $10,692 |
| 4/18/2017 | Robinson Walker, LLC | Owasco P.C. | $300,000 |
| 4/20/2017 | Robinson Walker, LLC | JBBSR INC | $120,000 |
| 4/21/2017 | Robinson Walker, LLC | "Biden" | $25,000 |
| 4/24/2017 | Robinson Walker, LLC | JBBSR INC | $125,000 |
| 5/17/2017 | Robinson Walker, LLC | "Biden" | $15,000 |
| 5/18/2017 | Robinson Walker, LLC | JBBSR INC | $15,000 |
| Total | | | $1,065,692 |

69. After receiving the $3 million payment from State Energy HK, Hunter Biden, James Biden, Rob Walker, James Gilliar, and Tony Bobulinski formed a joint venture with CEFC known as SinoHawk Holdings.[131] However, Hunter Biden and James Biden then sought to circumvent their business partners and create Hudson West III, LLC (Hudson West III), a different joint venture between Hunter Biden's company, Owasco, P.C. and Hudson West V, LLC, a company owned by a CEFC official, Gongwen Dong.[132]

70. As of July 2017, CEFC had not funded the joint venture with Hunter Biden, so Hunter Biden leveraged Joe Biden to obtain the money from his Chinese business partners. The

[131] Tony Bobulinski Tr., *supra* note 6, at 14: 23-25.
[132] *Id.* at 15: 5-10 (". . . Hunter [Biden] demanded CEFC circumvent SinoHawk Holdings. The Biden family violated their fiduciary duties to SinoHawk and Oneida as they enriched themselves at the CEFC trough.").

IRS whistleblowers provided Apple iCloud backup messages related to Hunter Biden.[133] The chart showed an exchange between Hunter Biden and a person named "Zhao," where Hunter Biden told Zhao on July 30, 2017, "I am sitting here with my father and we would like to understand why the commitment made has not been fulfilled."[134] Hunter Biden continued, "And Z if I get a call or text from anyone involved in this other than you, Zhang or the Chairman I will make certain that between the man sitting next to me and every person he knows and my ability to forever hold a grudge that you will regret not following my direction."[135]

71. On July 31, 2017, Zhao responded to Hunter Biden, "CEFC is willing to cooperate with the family."[136] The Oversight Committee subpoenaed bank records related to CEFC and Hunter Biden's businesses. The bank records establish that on August 8, 2017—within approximately a week of the WhatsApp message above—Northern International Capital, a Chinese company, wired $5 million to Hudson West III.[137] An image of the that wire is below:

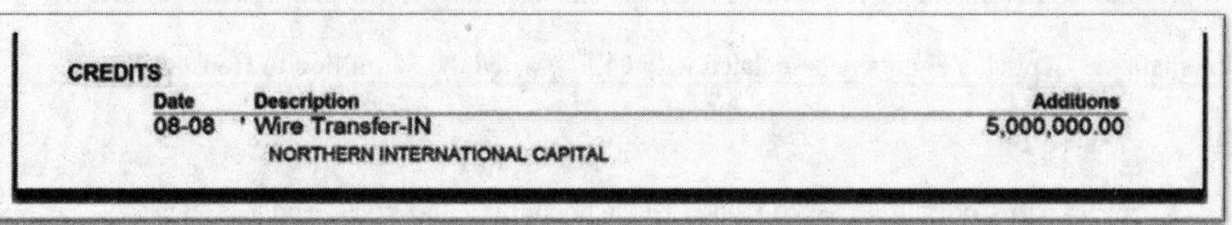
CREDITS

| Date | Description | Additions |
|---|---|---|
| 08-08 | ' Wire Transfer-IN<br>NORTHERN INTERNATIONAL CAPITAL | 5,000,000.00 |

72. On the same day, Hunter Biden transferred $400,000 to his professional corporation, Owasco, P.C.[138] Through a series of financial transactions, the Oversight Committee traced $40,000 of the proceeds to Joe Biden's bank account.[139] These

---

[133] *See* H. Comm. on Ways and Means, Release of IRS Whistleblower Disclosure, Exhibit 300, at 4 (Sept. 27, 2023).
[134] *Id.*
[135] *Id.*
[136] *Id.*
[137] Records on file with the Oversight Committee
[138] *See* Fourth Bank Memo, *supra* note 12, at 4-9.
[139] *Id.*

communications and the identities of the individuals with whom Hunter Biden communicated about these financial transactions were material to the Congressional investigation because they directly implicate Joe Biden in his family's foreign entanglements.

73. During Hunter Biden's testimony, there were two different individuals referenced with the last name "Zhao." Henry Zhao was "the principal for Harvest[.]"[140] Harvest was a Chinese investment fund with ties to the BHR fund and was unrelated to CEFC.[141] Raymond Zhao, on the other hand, worked for CEFC, the Chinese energy conglomerate that used Northern International Capital to wire $5 million to Hudson West III on August 8, 2017.[142] Hunter Biden confirmed during his testimony that the $5 million deposit into Hudson West III was for the "capitalization" of his joint venture with Ye Jianming, the Chairman of CEFC.[143]

74. Because the threatening WhatsApp chats concern business deals with CEFC, the Committees understood that "Zhao" in the message was Raymond Zhao. After Hunter Biden sent the messages referencing his father, Joe Biden, and his family to Raymond Zhao, Northern International Capital, a company associated with CEFC, wired the $5 million to Hudson West III.[144]

75. The Committees asked Hunter Biden about the Zhao WhatsApp messages:

Q: Do you have any recollection of sending these?

A: No, but I've seen this and –

Counsel: Is there a question?

Q: Yes. Does he have a recollection of sending the message?

---

[140] Hunter Biden Tr., *supra* note 6, at 20: 15-16.
[141] *Id.* at 20:8-16.
[142] Tony Bobulinski Tr., *supra* note 6, at 35: 25; 36: 1-6.
[143] Hunter Biden Tr., *supra* note 6, at 54:25; 55:1-7.
[144] Records on file with the Oversight Committee.

A: And I do not, but I do know this. I have now seen it, which it's been presented. I would say two things about this message.

Mr. Nadler: Can you speak up?

A: I would say two things about this message. The first thing is this. ***<u>Is that the Zhao that this is sent to is not the Zhao that was connected to CEFC.</u>***

Q: Okay.

A: Which I think is the best indication of how out of my mind I was at this moment in time.

Again, I don't – my addiction is not an excuse, but I can tell you this: I am more embarrassed of this text message, if it actually did come from me, than any text message I've ever sent.

The fact of the matter is, is that there's no other text message that you have in which I say anything remotely to this. And I was out of my mind.

I can also tell you this: My father was not sitting next to me. My father had no awareness. My father had no awareness of the business that I was doing. My father never benefited from any of the business that I was doing.

And so, I take full responsibility for being an absolute ass and idiot when I sent this message, if I did send this message.

Q: Okay

Q: When you say it wasn't Zhao from CEFC, who –

Mr. Nadler: Would you speak up, please?

Q: Which Zhao are you referring to if it wasn't from CEFC?

A: ***<u>The number that I believe it went to was to Henry Zhao.</u>*** Zhao is a very common—it's not a surname—surname in China. I mean, obviously, very common surname.

And I, like an idiot, directed it towards Henry Zhao who had no involvement, who had no understanding or even remotely knew what the hell I was even Goddamn talking about.

Excuse my language.

Q: And he seems to –

A: No, no, no, no, no, the Zhao—it's a different—you're conflating now.

Q: Okay.

A: And this [sic] why this report from the IRS is absolutely wrong. They're two different messages.

The Zhao that calls me is not related to the message that was sent. I speak to him the next day. They're two completely different sets of messages. One goes a number because, I made the Goddamn—excuse my language again—because I made like an idiot, and I was drunk and probably high, **sent a—this ridiculous message to a Zhao, to a Henry Zhao.**

**But then the next day, I speak to a Raymond Zhao, who has never received the message that Henry Zhao got**. And so that's why this report is very misleading in many ways.[145]

76. Hunter Biden's counsel also lodged the following unfounded accusation against the IRS whistleblowers, "The IRS agents—[interjection by witness omitted]—took two different times and two different messages and conflated them. That's what he's explaining."[146]

77. The documents released by the Ways and Means Committee show Hunter Biden had a continuous conversation using WhatsApp with the same person referenced as Zhao. There is no indication in the phone records that Hunter Biden sent the WhatsApp messages to Henry Zhao of Harvest. The Committees know that the "Zhao" referenced in the WhatsApp messages is Raymond Zhao based on the context of the communications. Indeed, the records show Raymond Zhao responded in the WhatsApp conversation referencing CEFC and stating, "CEFC is willing to cooperate with the family. He thinks now the priority is to solve the problem mentioned last night."[147] Henry Zhao does not work for CEFC and would not have any reason to speak on CEFC's behalf. In short, the evidence released by the Ways and Means Committee completely refutes Hunter Biden's testimony.

---

[145] Hunter Biden Tr., *supra* note 6, at 105-107 (emphasis added).
[146] *Id.* at 107: 4-8.
[147] *See* Ways and Means, Exhibit 801, at 533-549, attached as Exhibit 13.

78. Hunter Biden falsely testified that his threatening message was sent to Henry Zhao of Harvest, not Raymond Zhao of CEFC. This is relevant because CEFC wired the $5 million soon after Hunter Biden leveraged his father and made the threat in his message. The evidence shows that he knowingly made this false statement because he fabricated the story out of whole cloth. Indeed, it strains credulity to think that he could not remember sending the threatening message, but at the same time recall that he "like an idiot" sent this message to a different Zhao. Rather, Hunter Biden concocted the fictious story that he sent the message to Henry Zhao, instead of a CEFC official, to undercut that the $5 million payment was sent by CEFC in response to Hunter Biden's threats invoking Joe Biden. Based upon the newly disclosed evidence, the Committees can demonstrate that Hunter Biden made false statements that he was communicating with Henry Zhao, not Raymond Zhao in the threatening WhatsApp message.

### F. JAMES BIDEN FALSELY TESTIFIED HE WAS NOT PRESENT DURING A MEETING WITH JOE BIDEN, HUNTER BIDEN, AND TONY BOBULINSKI

79. On May 2, 2017, Joe Biden, James Biden, Hunter Biden, and Tony Bobulinski met at the Beverly Hilton Hotel. During his interview, James Biden denied the meeting occurred despite Hunter Biden's and Tony Bobulinski's testimony that it did take place. Text messages provided to the Oversight Committee also corroborate that Joe Biden attended the meeting at the Beverly Hilton Hotel.

80. This meeting was material to the Congressional investigation because Joe Biden has publicly denied discussing business with Hunter Biden and James Biden.[148] Furthermore, Joe Biden has claimed he never met with any of Hunter Biden's business associates.[149] This

---

[148] *See* Oversight Committee's website, *Joe Biden Lied at Least 16 Times about his Family's Business Schemes*, (Aug. 24, 23).
[149] *Id.*

meeting proved Joe Biden made misleading statements regarding his knowledge of and involvement in his family's foreign business endeavors.

81. The Committees asked James Biden about the meeting, and he denied being present:

> Q: When you were at the [Beverly Hilton H]otel, do you recall having a meeting with Hunter Biden and Tony Bobulinski and Joe Biden?
>
> A: Absolutely not.
>
> Q: It's your testimony here today that meeting never took place?
>
> A: Yes, sir.
>
> Counsel: That he was present for.
>
> A: That I was present for. [150]

82. The Committee sought to clarify if James Biden could not remember the meeting or was denying the meeting occurred. James Biden's counsel clarified "You asked him if he had a meeting with Bobulinski and Hunter. He said no to that, a meeting."[151]

83. In complete contrast to James Biden's testimony, Hunter Biden testified Tony Bobulinski met with Joe Biden at the lobby bar in the Beverly Hilton Hotel in the presence of James Biden. Hunter Biden stated:

> Q: And did Mr. Bobulinski meet with your father during that trip?
>
> A: He met with him in the lobby of the hotel of the – I believe it was the – the –
>
> Q: Beverly Hilton?
>
> A: Beverly Hilton. My dad's flight arrived I think at 11 a.m. We –
>
> Counsel: 11 p.m.

---

[150] James Biden Tr., *supra* note 6, at 100: 11-17.
[151] *Id.* at 101: 10-11.

A: Excuse me, 11 p.m. We were in the lobby bar with Mr. Bobulinski having coffee.

Q: And your uncle as well?

A: What?

Q: Was your uncle there too?

A: My uncle and myself. I think my uncle was also staying at that hotel. And so yeah. I know that, if you go further, it says – but I think that the reality is that he didn't – anyway, my dad went and shook hands with Tony.

They talked about – I believe at that time, I don't know whether it was Tony's father was suffering from cancer, and his sister was suffering from cancer, and he invited him to the speech at the Milken Conference.[152]

84. On February 13, 2024, Tony Bobulinski testified under oath before the Committees. Mr. Bobulinski also testified in great detail regarding the meeting at the Beverly Hilton Hotel. He stated:

Q: And can you tell the committee about that meeting and how that developed, the meeting with Joe Biden?

A: . . .
So I show up at the Beverly Hilton early. And, obviously, next to Davos, the Milken Conference is probably the largest, you know, private conference of billionaires and successful people in all kinds of walks of life that show up for that conference every year. So the Beverly Hilton's busy.

But we go into the bar there – I forget its name—and it's sort of cleared out. The only people in that bar—I think there was literally one individual—or two individuals, Steve Wynn and it appeared to be a woman that was working for him. And they had cleared out the bar. And Hunter, Jim, and I were sitting in the back, sort of behind a column for privacy and –

Q: When you say Jim – because there's James Gilliar –

A: Yeah, yeah.

Q: --and there's James Biden. Which is it?

A: Yeah, yeah. So James Biden went by Jim Biden.[153]

[152] Hunter Biden Tr., *supra* note 6, at 141: 12-25; 142: 1-3.
[153] Tony Bobulinski Tr., *supra* note 6, at 47-48.

85. Tony Bobulinski continued, "So it was Jim Biden, Hunter Biden, and myself sitting there, and his dad was running a little bit late. And so what I thought was sort of slightly odd at the time is Hunter and Jim started coaching me about the meeting."[154] Mr. Bobulinski stated that the meeting occurred for "45 minutes to an hour."[155] He also explained how prior to meeting Joe Biden, Hunter Biden and James Biden "coached" him not to go into a lot of detail.[156]

86. Later that night, at 11:40pm, Tony Bobulinski texted James Biden, "Great to meet u and spend some time together, please thank Joe for his time, was great to talk thx Tony b[.]"[157]

87. The Oversight Committee received evidence from Tony Bobulinski that included text messages between Mr. Bobulinski and other business associates, including James Biden. The text messages corroborate Hunter Biden's and Mr. Bobulinski's testimony that there was a meeting on May 2, 2017 with Joe Biden, Hunter Biden, James Biden, and Tony Bobulinski. In one message, on May 2, 2017, Hunter Biden texted Tony Bobulinski at 3:56pm, "Dad not in now until 11 – lets me I and Jim meet at 10 at Beverly Hilton where he's staying[.]"[158]

88. During the interview, the Committees showed James Biden a text message from James Biden to Tony Bobulinski stating, "I'll get back to you 15 min! Let's meet at same place as last night! Jim[.]"[159] The Committees again asked James Biden whether Joe Biden was at the meeting:

Q: And then the first text, which appears to be from you, says, "I'll get back to you 15 min! Let's meet at same place as last night! Jim."

---

[154] *Id.* at 61: 1-4.
[155] *Id.* at 50: 22-24.
[156] *Id.* at 49:14-15.
[157] *See* Text from Tony Bobulinski to James Biden (May 2, 2017, 11:40 PM), attached as Exhibit 14.
[158] *See* Text from Hunter Biden to Tony Bobulinski (May 2, 2017, 3:56 PM), attached as Exhibit 15.
[159] *See* Text from James Biden to Tony Bobulinski (May 3, 2017, 7:36 AM), attached as Exhibit 16.

Do you remember what you're referring to when you say that?

A: It could have been the bar. I don't know.

Q: Well, did you go to the Beverly Hotel bar the night before the Milken Conference?

A: I don't recall.

Q: Do you recall whether you were at the bar with Hunter Biden, Tony Bobulinski, and Joe Biden?

A: That I know did not happen.

Q: Who were you at the bar with?

A: I could have been there just with Tony Bobulinski. I could have been there with Hunter as well. But my brother was never there.[160]

89. The Committees provided another opportunity for James Biden to correct himself with additional questioning about whether Tony Bobulinski ever met with Joe Biden:

Q: But it's your testimony here today that Tony Bobulinski never met Joe Biden in your presence? Is that correct?

A: That's correct.

Q: And it's your testimony here today that Tony Bobulinski, you're not aware of him meeting with Joe Biden while you were not in the room.

A: Correct. He never, to my knowledge, met with my brother.[161]

90. Given the testimony from Hunter Biden and Tony Bobulinski and the text messages, the evidence shows that a meeting occurred on May 2, 2017 at the Beverly Hilton Hotel and that Joe Biden, Hunter Biden, Tony Bobulinski, and James Biden were present for the meeting. James Biden knowingly made a false statement to the Committees because he completely denied any meeting between Joe Biden and Tony Bobulinski occurred, despite the

---

[160] James Biden Tr. *supra* note 6, at 103: 3-15.
[161] *Id.* at 134: 24-25; 135: 1-4.

Committees requesting clarification if he could not remember and showing him text messages that disproved his testimony. James Biden lied about this meeting for at least two reasons. First, Joe Biden has denied publicly that his family received money from China and that he ever met with his family's business associates. If James Biden admitted that Tony Bobulinski, a business associate who was leading a Chinese business deal, met with his Joe Biden and Hunter Biden, then Joe Biden's lies would be exposed because of his testimony. Second, the Oversight Committee has traced money from James and Sara Biden's bank accounts to Joe Biden that was funded by a CEFC related company, and Jim Biden therefore wanted to distance Joe Biden from any involvement in his family's Chinese-related business ventures.[162]

91. The Committees gave James Biden several opportunities to correct his claim that Joe Biden did not attend the meeting, but the evidence proves his statements regarding this meeting were knowingly false.

92. For these reasons, the Committees make this referral to the Department of Justice for further action.

---

[162] *See generally* Fourth Bank Memo, *supra* note 12.

# ACKNOWLEDGMENTS

In order to write a book that shines a light on the biggest public corruption scandal from the highest levels of the U.S. government in our nation's great history, it required a lot of assistance that came in many forms from many people.

I would like to first express my deepest gratitude to the majority of American voters who turned out in the 2022 midterm elections and voted for a Republican majority in the U.S. House of Representatives. That historical election flipped control of the House from Democratic to Republican and gave me the chairmanship of the most high-profile investigative committee and along with it essential subpoena power. Without subpoena authority, I never would have obtained Biden bank records, which allowed me to determine the amount of money the Bidens took from shady characters around the globe and how it was laundered through numerous shell companies in an organized series of complex financial transactions.

In order to lead any controversial congressional investigation, especially one that exposes a major coordinated cover-up at the hands of our own government, it was essential to have the support of House leadership and my committee colleagues. I am very thankful to most of my Republican colleagues on the House Oversight Committee for their constant support of my chairmanship throughout the rocky Biden Influence-Peddling Investigation. I also appreciate both Speakers Kevin McCarthy and Mike Johnson as well as House Whip Steve Scalise and Conference Chair Elise Stefanik for always issuing supportive statements to the corrupt mainstream media who constantly coordinated with the Biden White House, Democratic National Committee, Democratic dark money groups, and the high-priced Biden legal defense team to manufacture hundreds of negative stories about the investigation.

A few years prior to my ascension to the Oversight chairmanship, Senators Charles Grassley and Ron Johnson did groundbreaking investigative work from the Senate minority on Biden family corruption. Notably, their discovery of 150 Suspicious Activity Reports (SARs) paved the way for me to lead an investigation and use my subpoena authority to discover an additional twenty primary SARs as well as another fifty SARs where the Biden family were subjects. These major violations that the banks flagged against the Bidens led to the discovery of dozens of previously unknown bank accounts and LLCs that helped trace tens of millions of dollars from our adversaries around the world into the back pockets of ten different Biden family members, including Joe Biden.

The current state of journalism in America is bleak. However, there were a few journalists and television personalities who did tremendous work accurately covering the facts about the investigation. Catherine Herridge, Maria Bartiromo, Miranda Devine, John Solomon, Ben Schreckinger, Rob Schmitt, Jesse Waters, Lou Dobbs, Elizabeth McDonald, and Sean Hannity all played crucial roles in utilizing their platforms to get the truth about the Bidens to the American people.

Whistleblowers are a necessity in order for any congressional investigation to be successful. Gary Shapley and Joseph Ziegler will go down in history as two of the best and most consequential. Their IRS notes from their years of investigative work against the countless Biden crimes was the difference maker in proving the full extent of Biden corruption as well as exposing the clear cover-up by our government. And Tony Bobulinski was the one decent guy in the Biden orbit whose testimony exposed the fact that the millions of dollars of Chinese money the Bidens raked in was really payments (or as he testified: bribes) from the Chinese Communist Party.

Tracing complex financial transactions through dozens of bank accounts and twenty plus LLCs, reading millions of pages of subpoenaed documents, spending hundreds of hours preparing for depositions and interviews, compiling dozens of successful subpoenas that would win in court whenever anyone would try to defy, and writing thousands of pages of guidance for some of the most unruly and demanding members of Congress required the best committee staff ever assembled. Thank you to all of the great staffers on the House Oversight Committee who worked tirelessly to expose both the Biden crimes and the government cover-ups. Their thorough work, which was always made public, gave citizens ample material to see for themselves the extent of all the crimes committed even though most fell victim to the statute of limitations as a result of previous government investigations being ordered to stand down on the Bidens.

I want to express appreciation also to the Broadside Books team at HarperCollins: to Eric Nelson, for understanding what this book needed to be; to James Neidhardt, for helping the project stay on schedule; and to Frieda Duggan and the production team for graciously and rigorously working within a crazy timeline.

And finally, I want to thank my family (TJ, Reagan, Harlan, and Aniston) for their loving support of me through some very dark days at the hands of the disgraceful mainstream media and their partners in crime affiliated with all the Biden henchmen. I must also acknowledge my late grandparents Harlin and Pauline Comer and Kenneth and Maitred Witcher for planting a seed in my early development that led to my passion for public service.

# NOTES

## Introduction

1. Colin Kalmbacher, "Hunter Biden Sues Laptop Repairman on 6 Counts of Invasion of Privacy over Leaked Data," Law & Crime, March 17, 2023, https://lawandcrime.com/high-profile/hunter-biden-sues-laptop-repairman-on-multiple-counts-of-invasion-of-privacy-over-leaked-data/.
2. The full exchange can be found here: "Hunter Biden Transcript," House Oversight Committee, February 28, 2024, 146–47, https://oversight.house.gov/wp-content/uploads/2024/02/Hunter-Biden-Transcript_Redacted.pdf.
3. For an in-depth discussion of Jared Kushner's ethics-skirting financial doings, see Peter Schweizer, *Secret Empires: How the American Political Class Hides Corruption and Enriches Family and Friends* (New York: HarperCollins, 2018), Kindle, chap. 12, "The Trump Princelings."
4. Schweizer, 204.
5. "The Unusual Journey of China's Newest Oil Baron," *Fortune*, September 28, 2016, https://fortune.com/2016/09/28/cefc-ye-jianming-40-under-40/.
6. "Meet CEFC China, a Private Company Run Like a State Organisation," *South China Morning Post*, December 17, 2023, https://www.scmp.com/business/companies/article/2106498/meet-cefc-china-private-company-thats-managed-state-organisation.
7. Grant Newsham, *When China Attacks: A Warning to America* (Washington, DC: Regnery, 2023), 347, Kindle. Newsham's highly readable book provides a crash course in how the U.S. should understand and respond to the Chinese government's threat to America.
8. Desmond Shum, *Red Roulette: An Insider's Story of Wealth, Power, Corruption, and Vengeance in Today's China* (New York: Scribner, 2021), 271, Kindle. Shum's highly readable memoir tells the story of his imprisoned (or dead) wife's rise and fall as a behind-the-scenes consiglieri and bagman for the PRC's second-most-powerful family.
9. "The Unusual Journey of China's Newest Oil Baron," *Fortune*, September 28, 2016, https://fortune.com/2016/09/28/cefc-ye-jianming-40-under-40/.
10. Jenni Marsh, "The Rise and Fall of a Belt and Road Billionaire," CNN, February 3, 2024, https://www.cnn.com/interactive/2018/12/asia/patrick-ho-ye-jianming-cefc-trial-intl/.
11. WeChatscope Team, "Censored on WeChat: The Disappearance of Ye Jianming, Former Chairman of CEFC China Energy," Global Voices, March 15, 2019, https://advox.globalvoices.org/2019/03/15/censored-on-wechat-the-disappearance-of-ye-jianming-former-chairman-of-cefc-china-energy/.
12. Adam Entous, "Will Hunter Biden Jeopardize His Father's Campaign?" *New Yorker*, July 1, 2019, https://www.newyorker.com/magazine/2019/07/08/will-hunter-biden-jeopardize-his-fathers-campaign.

13. "China's CEFC Adds to Czech Buying Spree with Airline, Brewery Deals," Reuters, September 5, 2015, https://www.reuters.com/article/czech-china-cefc/update-1-chinas-cefc-adds-to-czech-buying-spree-with-airline-brewery-deals-idUSL5N11B05120150905/.
14. Alexandra Stevenson, "Hard-Charging Chinese Energy Tycoon Falls from Xi Government's Graces," *New York Times*, March 14, 2018, https://www.nytimes.com/2018/03/14/business/china-cefc-investigation.html.
15. Maximilian Hess, "China Has Decided Russia Is Too Risky an Investment," *Foreign Policy*, May 16, 2018, https://foreignpolicy.com/2018/05/16/china-has-decided-russia-is-too-risky-an-investment/.
16. Miranda Devine, *The Big Guy: Inside the Biden Family Scandal Machine* (New York: Broadside, 2024), chap. 14, "Busted."
17. Jeff Mordock, "Biden Denies Meeting with Hunter's Business Partners: 'A Bunch of Lies,'" *Washington Times*, December 6, 2023, https://www.washingtontimes.com/news/2023/dec/6/joe-biden-denies-meeting-hunter-bidens-business-pa/.

**Chapter 1: Show Me the Money**

1. "Donald Trump & Joe Biden Final Presidential Debate Transcript 2020," Rev.com, accessed March 18, 2024, https://www.rev.com/blog/transcripts/donald-trump-joe-biden-final-presidential-debate-transcript-2020.
2. House Committee on Oversight and Reform, "Tony Bobulinski Interview Transcript," October 23, 2020, p. 12, https://oversight.house.gov/wp-content/uploads/2024/02/Bobulinski-Transcript.pdf.
3. Devine, *The Big Guy*, chap. 11, "The Big Guy."
4. Steven Nelson, "Bank Watchdog Warned Hunter Biden Got China Cash for 'No Services Rendered': 2018 Email," *New York Post*, November 30, 2023, https://nypost.com/2023/11/29/news/banks-money-laundering-expert-warned-bidens-got-china-cash-without-any-services-rendered/.
5. Victor Nava, "Where the Money Went: The Bidens and Biden Associates Who Received Chinese Cash," *New York Post*, March 17, 2023, https://nypost.com/2023/03/17/where-the-money-went-the-bidens-and-biden-associates-that-received-chinese-cash/.
6. "Transcript of Walker Testimony," House Oversight Committee, January 26, 2024, 80, https://oversight.house.gov/wp-content/uploads/2024/02/Walker-Transcript.pdf.
7. Ben Schreckinger, "Biden's Brother Used His Name to Promote a Hospital Chain. Then . . ." *Politico*, February 18, 2024, https://www.politico.com/news/2024/02/18/the-biden-name-how-the-presidents-brother-became-embroiled-in-a-hospital-fiasco-00141868.
8. Ben Schreckinger, "James Biden's Health Care Ventures Face a Growing Legal Morass," *Politico*, March 9, 2020, https://www.politico.com/news/2020/03/09/james-biden-health-care-ventures-123159.
9. Margot Cleveland, "Biden's $200k Shows He Profited from Family Biz, Innocent Creditors Be Damned," *Federalist*, October 23, 2023, https://

thefederalist.com/2023/10/23/joe-bidens-200k-check-shows-he-profited-from-the-family-biz-to-the-detriment-of-innocent-creditors/.

10. Becky Yerak, "James Biden Settles Loan Lawsuit Tied to Rural Hospitals," *Wall Street Journal*, September 26, 2022, https://www.wsj.com/articles/james-biden-settles-loan-lawsuit-tied-to-rural-hospitals-bank ruptcy-11664236240.
11. Oversight Staff, "Comer Releases Evidence of Direct Payment to Joe Biden," United States House Committee on Oversight and Accountability, November 7, 2023, https://oversight.house.gov/release/comer-releases-evid ence-of-direct-payment-to-joe-biden/.
12. Ben Schreckinger, "Fund Manager Indicates Jim Biden Was in Business with Qatari Officials," *Politico*, April 28, 2024, https://www.politico.com/news/2024/04/28/jim-biden-qatar-testimony-00154704.
13. Steven Nelson, "James Biden Listed His Job as 'Brother' of Joe in 'Flawless' Presentation for Qatar: Emails," *New York Post*, April 29, 2024, https://nypost.com/2024/04/29/us-news/james-biden-listed-his-job-as-brother-of-joe-in-presentation-to-qataris-emails/.
14. "James Biden Transcript," House Oversight Committee, February 21, 2024, 78, https://oversight.house.gov/wp-content/uploads/2024/03/James-Biden-Transcript.pdf. Jim Biden did claim to have brought CEFC an investment opportunity of his own, a potential LNP project on Monkey Island in Louisiana. This, of course, never amounted to anything. An account of the Monkey Island fiasco can be found in Miranda Devine, *Laptop from Hell: Hunter Biden, Big Tech, and the Dirty Secrets the President Tried to Hide* (New York: Post Hill Press, 2021), 163, Kindle.
15. United States House Committee on Oversight and Accountability, "ICYMI: Comer & Oversight Committee Members Present Evidence of Influence Peddling by Biden Family," May 10, 2023, https://oversight.house.gov/release/icymi-comer-oversight-committee-members-present-evidence-of-influence-peddling-by-biden-family%ef%bf%bc/. Also fully discussed in Devine, *The Big Guy*, chap. 17, "No One F★cks with a Biden."
16. Steven Nelson, "Hunter Biden's Staggering $20m Haul from Kazhaks, Chinese, Russians, Romanians and Ukrainians Revealed in New Bank Records: Comer," *New York Post*, August 9, 2023, https://nypost.com/2023/08/09/hunter-biden-linked-foreign-haul-at-20m-with-russia-ukraine-kazak-transfers-comer/.
17. A full account can be found in Mollie Ziegler Hemingway, *Rigged: How the Media, Big Tech, and the Democrats Seized Our Elections* (New York: Regnery, 2021), 225–26, Kindle.
18. Steven Nelson, "Biden Family Moneyman Eric Schwerin Testifies He Gave Joe Free Services While Working with Hunter," *New York Post*, January 31, 2024, https://nypost.com/2024/01/30/news/biden-family-moneyman-eric-schwerin-testifies-in-impeachment-inquiry/.
19. Oversight Committee Staff, "Oversight and Judiciary Committees Release Eric Schwerin Transcript," United States House Committee on Oversight and Accountability, January 30, 2024, https://oversight.house

.gov/release/oversight-and-judiciary-committees-release-eric-schwerin-transcript%EF%BF%BC/.

20. Steven Richards, "James Biden Denied Brother Met with Business Associates, Said Loans from Joe Biden Are Undocumented," Just The News, February 21, 2024, https://justthenews.com/accountability/political-ethics/james-biden-denied-brother-met-business-associates-said-loans-joe.
21. Joseph R. Biden, "Remarks by Vice President Joe Biden to Romanian Civil Society Groups and Students," National Archives and Records Administration, May 21, 2014, https://obamawhitehouse.archives.gov/the-press-office/2014/05/21/remarks-vice-president-joe-biden-romanian-civil-society-groups-and-stude.
22. Biden, "Remarks."
23. Catherine Herridge, "Copy of What's Believed to Be Hunter Biden's Laptop Data Turned Over by Repair Shop to FBI Showed No Tampering, Analysis Says," CBS News, November 21, 2022, https://www.cbsnews.com/news/hunter-biden-laptop-data-analysis/.
24. The details of Hunter Biden's dissipation and its effects on the Biden family business can be found in many sources, including Devine, *Laptop from Hell*; Hunter Biden's own memoir, *Beautiful Things: A Memoir* (New York: Gallery Books, 2021); and the heart-wrenching memoir of Hunter Biden's first wife (and the mother of three of his children), Kathleen Buhle, whom he dumped for his brother's widow, Hallie Biden. See Kathleen Buhle, *If We Break: A Memoir of Marriage, Addiction, and Healing* (New York: Random House, 2022).
25. Khaleda Rahman, "Who Is James Biden? President's Brother Comes under Scrutiny," *Newsweek*, October 18, 2022, https://www.newsweek.com/james-biden-president-brother-under-scrutiny-1752641.
26. Daniel Golden, Chuck Neubauer, and Matthew Malone, "The Benefits of Being Joe Biden's Brother," ProPublica, February 14, 2020, https://www.propublica.org/article/the-profitable-business-of-being-joe-bidens-brother.

**Chapter 2: Unlocking the SARs**

1. Miranda Devine, "Hunter Biden's Legal Team Still Trying to Claim 'Laptop from Hell' Isn't His," *New York Post*, February 15, 2024, https://nypost.com/2024/02/15/us-news/hunter-bidens-legal-team-still-trying-to-claim-lap-top-from-hell-isnt-his/.
2. Emma Green, "The Massive Progressive Dark-Money Group You've Never Heard Of," *Atlantic*, November 2, 2021, https://www.theatlantic.com/politics/archive/2021/11/arabella-advisors-money-democrats/620553/.
3. J. C. Adams and H. Ludwig, "Fight 'Zuckbucks' with Laws, Not Lawsuits," *Federalist*, December 15, 2022, https://thefederalist.com/2022/12/16/fight-zuckbucks-with-laws-not-lawsuits/.
4. Hayden Ludwig, "Meet the Swiss Billionaire behind Arabella Advisors'

'Dark Money' Empire," Capital Research Center, April 22, 2021, https://capitalresearch.org/article/meet-the-swiss-billionaire-behind-arabella-advisors-dark-money-empire/.

**Chapter 3: A Biden Hall of Mirrors**

1. Oversight Staff, "Bank Records Memo," House Oversight Committee, March 16, 2023, https://oversight.house.gov/wp-content/uploads/2023/03/Bank-Records-Memo-3.16.23.pdf.
2. Victor Nava, "Where the Money Went: The Bidens and Biden Associates Who Received Chinese Cash," *New York Post*, March 17, 2023, https://nypost.com/2023/03/17/where-the-money-went-the-bidens-and-biden-associates-that-received-chinese-cash/.
3. Cameron Cawthorne and Jessica Chasmar, "Hunter's Business Partner Who Paid Biden Family $1M Was Frequent WH Visitor During Biden Vice Presidency," Fox News, March 28, 2023, https://www.foxnews.com/politics/hunters-business-partner-who-paid-biden-family-1m-was-frequent-wh-visitor-bid-vice-presidency.
4. John McCormack, "Biden at Last Presidential Debate: 'My Son Has Not Made Money' from China," *National Review*, December 10, 2020, https://www.nationalreview.com/corner/biden-at-last-presidential-debate-my-son-has-not-made-money-from-china/.
5. "Romanian Court Scraps 7-Year Jail Sentence for Fugitive Real Estate Tycoon Popoviciu," Romania Insider, May 29, 2023, https://www.romania-insider.com/court-sraps-popoviciu-jail-sentence-may-2023.
6. A detailed account can be found in Devine, *The Big Guy*, chap. 17, "No One F★cks with a Biden."
7. Brian Burns, "Bombshell House Oversight Report: Biden Famiily Received Millions from Foreign Nationals, China," *Tampa Free Press*, May 10, 2023, https://www.tampafp.com/bombshell-house-oversight-finds-biden-family/.
8. Kenneth P. Vogel, "Giuliani Is Drawing Attention to Hunter Biden's Work in Romania. But There's a Problem," *New York Times*, October 25, 2019, https://www.nytimes.com/2019/10/25/us/politics/giuliani-hunter-biden-romania.html?.
9. *National Review*, March 9, 2020, https://www.nationalreview.com/2020/03/joe-biden-owes-clarence-thomas-apology/.

**Chapter 4: The Deep State Strikes Back**

1. "Mary Doocy—Assistant General Counsel—Federal Bureau of Investigation (FBI)," LinkedIn, accessed April 3, 2024, https://www.linkedin.com/in/mary-doocy-5b0333234/.
2. Isabel Vincent, "Biden, DOJ Scrapping FBI China Initiative Led to More Spying, Experts Say," *New York Post*, February 24, 2023, https://nypost.com/2023/02/24/doj-cutting-fbi-china-initiative-led-to-more-spying-experts/.
3. J. Michael Waller, *Big Intel: How the CIA and FBI Went from Cold War Heroes to Deep State Villains* (Washington, DC: Regnery, 2024), 369.

**Chapter 5: A Game of Chinese Checkers**

1. Oversight Staff, "Second Bank Records Memorandum," House Oversight Committee, May 10, 2023, https://oversight.house.gov/wp-content/uploads/2023/05/Bank-Memorandum-5.10.23.pdf.
2. Michael Raska, "China and the 'Three Warfares,'" The Diplomat, December 18, 2015, https://thediplomat.com/2015/12/hybrid-warfare-with-chinese-characteristics-2/.
3. Jenni Marsh, "The Rise and Fall of a Belt and Road Billionaire," CNN, December 2018, accessed March 27, 2024, https://www.cnn.com/interactive/2018/12/asia/patrick-ho-ye-jianming-cefc-trial-intl/.
4. Matt Viser, Tom Hamburger, and Craig Timberg, "Inside Hunter Biden's Multimillion-Dollar Deals with a Chinese Energy Company," *Washington Post*, March 30, 2023, https://www.washingtonpost.com/politics/2022/03/30/hunter-biden-china-laptop/.
5. "US Business Elite Welcomes Xi Jinping with Standing Ovation," *Financial Times*, November 16, 2023, https://www.ft.com/content/a8633d7f-f785-4195-b0b2-0ea9506968c9.
6. "Patrick Ho, Former Head of Organization Backed by Chinese Energy Conglomerate, Convicted of International Bribery, Money Laundering Offenses," U.S. Attorney's Office, Southern District of New York, December 5, 2018, https://www.justice.gov/usao-sdny/pr/patrick-ho-former-head-organization-backed-chinese-energy-conglomerate-sentenced-3.
7. "Inside Hunter Biden's Multimillion-Dollar Deals with a Chinese," *Washington Post*.
8. Adam Entous, "Will Hunter Biden Jeopardize His Father's Campaign?" *New Yorker*, July 1, 2019, https://www.newyorker.com/magazine/2019/07/08/will-hunter-biden-jeopardize-his-fathers-campaign.
9. John Solomon, "House Probe Unveils Fresh Evidence Contradicting Joe Biden Claims about Family's Foreign Deals," Just The News, May 10, 2023, https://justthenews.com/accountability/political-ethics/house-probe-unveils-fresh-evidence-contradicting-joe-bidens-claim.

**Chapter 6: Oligarchs for Biden**

1. Majority Staff, "Third Bank Records Memorandum from the Oversight Committee's Investigation into the Biden Family's Influence Peddling and Business Schemes," October 9, 2023, https://oversight.house.gov/wp-content/uploads/2023/08/Third-Bank-Records-Memorandum_Redacted.pdf.
2. Tucker Carlson, "The Devon Archer Interview," Tucker Carlson Network, August 2, 2023, https://twitter.com/TuckerCarlson/status/1686799149109256192.
3. A textbook example of how it works: Cameron Cawthorne and Jessica Chasmar, "2011 Emails Reveal Hunter Biden Helped Business Associates Get Access to VP Biden, Top Aide," Fox News, May 2, 2023, https://www.foxnews.com/politics/2011-emails-reveal-hunter-biden-helped-business-associates-get-access-vp-biden-top-aide-ill-do-mtg.

4. Ryan King, "Hunter Boasted 'Bidens Are the Best' at Doing What Chinese Firm Boss Wants," *New York Post*, June 28, 2023, https://nypost.com/2023/06/28/hunter-boasted-bidens-are-the-best-at-doing-what-chinese-firm-boss-wants/.
5. "Elena Baturina," *Forbes*, February 23, 2024, https://www.forbes.com/profile/elena-baturina/?sh=2de824363c29.
6. Miranda Devine, "Hunter Biden's Ukraine Salary Was Cut Two Months after Joe Biden Left Office," *New York Post*, May 26, 2021, https://nypost.com/2021/05/26/hunter-bidens-ukraine-salary-was-cut-after-joe-biden-left-office/.
7. Nadine Shubailat and Victoria Thompson, "Hunter Biden Sits Down for Exclusive Interview with ABC News," *Good Morning America*, October 15, 2019, https://www.goodmorningamerica.com/news/story/hunter-biden-sits-exclusive-interview-abc-news-66252777.
8. Mark Hemingway, "Hunter Biden's Burisma Post Had a Troubling Conflict, Watchdog Says," RealClearInvestigations, November 19, 2019, https://www.realclearinvestigations.com/articles/2019/11/19/hunter_bidens_burisma_post_had_a_troubling_conflict_watchdog_says_121260.html#!.
9. Devine, *Laptop from Hell,* 96, Kindle.
10. Hunter Biden, *Beautiful Things,* 138, Kindle.
11. Miranda Devine, Marjorie Hernandez, and Patrick Reilly, "Hollywood Lawyer Paid Off over $2m of Hunter Biden's Delinquent Taxes," *New York Post*, May 9, 2022, https://nypost.com/2022/05/08/hollywood-lawyer-kevin-morris-paid-off-over-2m-of-hunter-bidens-taxes/.
12. Joseph Simonson, "Hunter Biden Spotted in Beverly Hills Driving $129K Porsche," *Washington Examiner,* January 27, 2020, https://www.washingtonexaminer.com/news/1915812/hunter-biden-spotted-in-beverly-hills-driving-129k-porsche/.
13. Morgan Phillips, "Joe DINED with Oligarchs Who Paid Hunter: New Bank Records Detail Part of the $20 MILLION in Foreign Cash to Biden Family—Including $142,000 from Kazakh Oligarch to President's Son That He Used to Buy Porsche after DC Dinner," *Daily Mail,* August 10, 2023, https://www.dailymail.co.uk/news/article-12387113/The-20-MILLION-foreign-cash-Biden-family-Russian-oligarchs-3-5-million-Hunters-shell-company-142-000-Kazakh-oligarch-Joes-son-used-buy-Porsche-revealed-new-bank-records.html.
14. Devine, *Laptop from Hell*, 96, Kindle.
15. Catherine Putz, "Karim Massimov, Former Kazakh Intelligence Chief, Sentenced to 18 Years on Treason, Coup Charges," The Diplomat, April 25, 2023, https://thediplomat.com/2023/04/karim-massimov-former-kazakh-intelligence-chief-sentenced-to-18-years-on-treason-coup-charges/.
16. Majority Staff, "Comer: Oversight Committee Has Uncovered Mounting Evidence Tying Joe Biden to Family Business Schemes," United States House Committee on Oversight and Accountability, October 2, 2023, https://oversight.house.gov/release/comer-oversight-committee-has-uncovered-mounting-evidence-tying-joe-biden-to-family-business-schemes/.

17. Oversight Staff, "Devon Archer Transcribed Interview," House Oversight Committee, July 31, 2023, https://oversight.house.gov/wp-content/uploads/2023/08/Devon-Archer-Transcript.pdf.

**Chapter 7: Guilt and Corroboration**

1. Oversight Staff, "Fourth Bank Records Memorandum," House Oversight Committee, November 1, 2023, 4, https://oversight.house.gov/wp-content/uploads/2023/10/Fourth-Bank-Records-Memo.pdf.
2. Oversight Staff, "Comer: Oversight Committee Has Uncovered Mounting Evidence Tying Joe Biden to Family Business Schemes," United States House Committee on Oversight and Accountability, October 2, 2023, https://oversight.house.gov/release/comer-oversight-committee-has-uncovered-mounting-evidence-tying-joe-biden-to-family-business-schemes/.
3. Josh Christenson, "Hunter Biden Used Dad Joe as Leverage in China Business Dispute: Text Message," *New York Post,* June 26, 2023, https://nypost.com/2023/06/22/hunter-biden-used-joe-as-leverage-in-china-biz-deal-text/.
4. For a full account of this debacle, see Grant Newsham, *When China Attacks: A Warning to America* (Washington, DC: Regnery Books, 2023), chap. 16, "Objective: Taiwan."
5. Schweizer, *Secret Empires,* 30, Kindle.
6. The story of Hunter Biden's abortive 2013 attempt to serve in the U.S. Navy is simply pathetic. Details can be found in Devine, *Laptop from Hell,* 25–26, Kindle.
7. An even deeper dive into these details can be found in "Fourth Bank Records Memorandum," 4.

**Chapter 8: Forward Motion**

1. Susan Ferrechio, Kerry Picket, and Mica Soellner, "Kevin McCarthy Elected House Speaker on 15th Vote as Matt Gaetz Gives In," *Washington Times,* January 6, 2023, https://www.washingtontimes.com/news/2023/jan/6/kevin-mccarthy-elected-house-speaker-15th-vote-mat/.
2. "House Speaker Kevin McCarthy Joins 'Hannity' for First Interview as Speaker," Fox News, January 11, 2023, https://www.youtube.com/watch?v=ct1nqt0Mx0c.
3. You don't have to take my word for it. The Pulitzer Prize–winning left-wing flack Molly Ball confessed it all shortly after the election in her preening article in *Time*: "The Secret History of the Shadow Campaign That Saved the 2020 Election," *Time,* February 4, 2021, https://time.com/5936036/secret-2020-election-campaign/.

**Chapter 9: Blueprint for a Debacle**

1. Oversight Staff, "Written Statement Jonathan Turley," House Oversight Committee, September 28, 2023, https://oversight.house.gov/wp-content/uploads/2023/09/Turley.Testimony.Biden-Inquiry.pdf.

### Chapter 10: Ten Percent for the Big Guy


1. Josh Christenson, "Here Are the Nine GOP Candidates Who Want to Be House Speaker," *New York Post*, October 23, 2023, https://nypost.com/2023/10/23/news/here-are-the-nine-gop-candidates-who-want-to-be-house-speaker/.
2. Josh Christenson, "Republicans Unanimously Elect Rep. Mike Johnson as House Speaker," *New York Post*, October 25, 2023, https://nypost.com/2023/10/25/news/republicans-unanimously-elect-rep-mike-johnson-as-house-speaker/.
3. James Comer and Jim Jordan, "November 8, 2023, Letter to Abbe D. Lowell Winston & Strawn LLP Re Robert Hunter Biden," November 8, 2023, https://oversight.house.gov/wp-content/uploads/2023/11/Letter-to-HB-Abbe-Lowell-11.8.23-1.pdf.
4. James Comer and Jim Jordan, "Letter of November 8 to Paul J. Fishman Arnold & Porter Kaye Scholer LLP Re: James Biden," November 8, 2023, https://oversight.house.gov/wp-content/uploads/2023/11/Letter-to-James Biden-11.8.23-1.pdf.


### Chapter 11: Revelations and Receipts


1. Steven Nelson, "Bank Watchdog Warned Hunter Biden Got China Cash for 'No Services Rendered': 2018 Email," *New York Post*, November 30, 2023, https://nypost.com/2023/11/29/news/banks-money-laundering-expert-warned-bidens-got-china-cash-without-any-services-rendered/.
2. Evita Duffy-Alfonso, "Oversight Committee Releases Email from Bank Investigator Who Flagged Chinese Money Laundered into Joe Biden's Pocket," *Federalist*, November 29, 2023, https://thefederalist.com/2023/11/29/oversight-committee-releases-email-from-bank-investigator-who-flagged-chinese-money-laundered-into-joe-bidens-pocket/" contains the "Cathay Bank Email," *Federalist*, https://www.scribd.com/document/688427333/Bank-Email#from_embed.
3. Roger Sollenberger, "James Comer, like Joe Biden, Also Paid His Brother $200k," *Daily Beast*, November 9, 2023, https://www.thedailybeast.com/james-comer-like-joe-biden-also-paid-his-brother-dollar200k.
4. Ryan King, "'You Look like a Smurf': Comer Rips Dem Who Targeted Family's Finances," *New York Post*, November 14, 2023, https://nypost.com/2023/11/14/news/you-look-like-a-smurf-comer-explodes-at-dem-who-targeted-his-family-finances/.


### Chapter 12: The Hit Piece That Wasn't


1. Brian Slodysko, "The Republican Leading the Probe of Hunter Biden Has His Own Shell Company and Complicated Friends," AP News, December 15, 2023, https://apnews.com/article/comer-shell-company-biden-hunter-impeachment-6fde28673d5dced307b95cab8425c7ba.
2. Jonathan Swan and Luke Broadwater, "Comer, Republicans' Investigative Chief, Embraces Role of Biden Antagonist," *New York Times*, March 21,

2023, https://www.nytimes.com/2023/03/21/us/politics/james-comer-republican-oversight-biden.html.

3. Heidi Przbyla and Jordain Carney, "Investigating the Investigators: Dem Strategists to Launch Counterpunch to House GOP," *Politico*, November 16, 2022, https://www.politico.com/news/2022/11/16/democratic-strategists-launch-war-room-00065498.
4. "Congressional Integrity Project," Influence Watch, January 4, 2024, https://www.influencewatch.org/organization/congressional-integrity-project/.
5. Rich Calder and Carl Campanile, "Levi Strauss Heir Dan Goldman Uses $2M of Own Fortune for NY Congressional Race," *New York Post*, August 14, 2022, https://nypost.com/2022/08/13/levi-strauss-heir-dan-goldman-spends-2m-of-own-fortune-in-congress-race/.
6. Daniel Chaitin, "Journalist Calls Out Democrat over Hunter Biden Laptop 'Conspiracy Theory' during Hearing," Daily Wire, November 30, 2023, https://www.dailywire.com/news/journalist-calls-out-democrat-over-hunter-biden-laptop-conspiracy-during-hearing.
7. Thomas Catenacci and Joe Schoffstall, "Dem Congressman's Charity Has More than $30 Million Tied Up in Cayman Islands Funds," Fox News, March 15, 2023, https://www.foxnews.com/politics/dem-congressmans-charity-more-30-million-cayman-islands-funds.
8. "Political Lawfare May Get 'Hobbesian,'" editorial, *Wall Street Journal*, September 25, 2023, https://www.wsj.com/articles/brian-schwalb-gop-attorneys-general-arabella-crc-advisors-bh-group-e3cb9875.
9. Joe Schoffstall, "Oversight Dem Linked to Consultants Managing Group Funneling Millions into Torpedoing Biden Investigations," Fox News, March 10, 2023, https://www.foxnews.com/politics/oversight-dem-linked-consultants-managing-group-funneling-millions-torpedoing-biden-investigations.
10. "Congressional Integrity Project," Influence Watch.
11. "Congressional Integrity Project."
12. Complete with insane allegations of rape from a "witness" who never even met Kavanaugh, much less had unpleasant interactions with him. For a detailed report on the sordid operation, see Mollie Ziegler Hemingway and Carrie Severino, *Justice on Trial: The Kavanaugh Confirmation and the Future of the Supreme Court* (Washington, DC: Regnery, 2019).

**Chapter 13: Gearing Up for the Impeachment Vote**

1. James Comer, House Oversight Committee, "Hunter Biden's Business Entity, Owasco PC, Made Direct Monthly Payments to Joe Biden. the Bank Records Don't LIE.OWASCO PC Received Payments from Chinese-State Linked Companies & Other Shady Entities. Joe Biden Knew & Benefitted from His Family's Business Schemes. Pic.Twitter.Com/Mfvta4yezu," Twitter, December 4, 2023, https://twitter.com/RepJamesComer/status/1731719879210770771?s=20.
2. Ryan King, "Comer Rips 'Financially Illiterate' NBC Reporter during

Hunter Biden Exchange," *New York Post*, December 6, 2023, https://nypost.com/2023/12/06/news/comer-rips-financially-illiterate-nbc-reporter-during-hunter-biden-exchange/.

### Chapter 14: The Bagman Doesn't Cometh

1. Miranda Devine, "Hunter Biden's Legal Team Still Trying to Claim 'Laptop from Hell' Isn't His," *New York Post*, February 15, 2024, https://nypost.com/2024/02/15/us-news/hunter-bidens-legal-team-still-trying-to-claim-lap-top-from-hell-isnt-his/.

### Chapter 15: The Sugar Brother

1. Oversight Staff, "Transcribed Kevin Morris Interview, January 18, 2024," House Oversight Committee, January 18, 2024, https://oversight.house.gov/wp-content/uploads/2024/01/Morris_Redacted.pdf.
2. Miranda Devine, "Hunter Biden, Baby Mama Lunden Roberts Settle Child Support Dispute," *New York Post*, June 21, 2023, https://nypost.com/2023/06/20/hunter-biden-baby-mama-luden-roberts-settle-child-support-dispute-with-first-sons-payments-slashed/.
3. Hemingway, *Rigged,* 229–30, Kindle.
4. Devine, *The Big Guy*, chap. 17, "No One F*cks with a Biden."
5. Devine, *Laptop from Hell,* 127–28, Kindle.
6. Dana Kennedy, "Hunter Biden's 'Sugar Brother' Kevin Morris Could Be Prosecuted for 'Lies' as Calif. State Bar Opens Ethics Probe: 'Mutually Destructive Spiral,'" *New York Post*, August 11, 2023, https://nypost.com/2023/08/10/hunter-bidens-sugar-brother-kevin-morris-could-be-prosecuted-for-lies/.
7. Devine, *Laptop from Hell*, 127–28, Kindle.
8. Kennedy, "Hunter Biden's 'Sugar Brother.'"
9. "Schwerin Transcript," Oversight Committee, January 30, 2024, https://oversight.house.gov/wp-content/uploads/2024/03/Schwerin-Transcript.pdf.
10. "Schwerin Transcript," 156.
11. Victor Nava, "Contents of Biden's Pseudonym Emails Tops Comer's List of Material Impeachment Inquiry Needs to Obtain," *New York Post*, December 27, 2023, https://nypost.com/2023/12/27/news/contents-of-bidens-pseudonym-emails-tops-comers-list-of-material-impeachment-inquiry-hopes-to-obtain/.
12. "Biden's Secret Emails: President ROBINWARE456," editorial, *Wall Street Journal*, August 30, 2023, https://www.wsj.com/articles/joe-biden-email-accounts-vice-president-hunter-biden-566bd720.
13. "Schwerin Transcript," 54.
14. Cameron Cawthorne and Jessica Chasmar, "Hunter Biden's Business Partners, Assistants Visited White House Over 80 Times When Biden Was VP," Fox News, April 11, 2023, https://www.foxnews.com/politics/hunter-bidens-business-partners-assistants-visited-white-house-80-times-when-biden-vp.
15. Devine, *The Big Guy*, chap. 3, "Crisis Team."

**Chapter 16: The Bobulinski Blockbuster**


1. Devine, *Laptop from Hell*, 167, Kindle.
2. U.S. Attorney's Office, Southern District of New York, "Patrick Ho, Former Head of Organization Backed by Chinese Energy Conglomerate, Sentenced to 3 Years in Prison for International Bribery and Money Laundering Offenses," March 25, 2019, https://www.justice.gov/usao-sdny/pr/patrick-ho-former-head-organization-backed-chinese-energy-conglomerate-sentenced-3.
3. Devine, *Laptop from Hell*, 172, Kindle.
4. Devine, *Laptop from Hell*, 173, Kindle.
5. Mark Moore, "Court Upholds Bribery Conviction of Chinese Exec Patrick Ho Linked to Hunter Biden," *New York Post*, December 30, 2020, https://nypost.com/2020/12/30/bribery-conviction-of-chinese-exec-linked-to-hunter-biden-upheld/.
6. Devine, *Laptop from Hell*, 167, Kindle.
7. Matt Viser, Tom Hamburger, and Craig Timberg, "Inside Hunter Biden's Multimillion-Dollar Deals with a Chinese Energy Company," *Washington Post,* March 30, 2022, https://www.washingtonpost.com/politics/2022/03/30/hunter-biden-china-laptop/.
8. "Chairmen Jordan and Comer Seek DOJ Documents about Hunter Biden Associate's Bribery Conviction," House Judiciary Committee Republicans, February 20, 2024, https://judiciary.house.gov/media/press-releases/chairmen-jordan-and-comer-seek-doj-documents-about-hunter-biden-associates.
9. Miranda Devine, "Hunter Biden's Chinese Legal 'Client' Threatens to Sue Unless First Son Pays Back $1 Million," *New York Post*, March 4, 2024, https://nypost.com/2024/03/03/opinion/hunter-bidens-chinese-legal-client-threatens-to-sue-unless-first-son-pays-back-1-million/.
10. Miranda Devine, "'Missing' Biden Family Corruption Probe Witness Gal Luft Speaks Out, Living as Fugitive in Undisclosed Location," *New York Post*, June 1, 2023, https://nypost.com/2023/05/31/missing-biden-family-corruption-probe-witness-gal-luft-speaks-out-living-as-fugitive-in-undisclosed-location/.
11. Annie Grayer and Marshall Cohen, "Former Biden Family Business Associate Recycles Unproven Allegations to House Panels," CNN, February 13, 2024, https://edition.cnn.com/2024/02/13/politics/tony-bobulinski-impeachment-investigation/index.html.
12. Corbin Bolies, "Jake Tapper's Ratings-Deficient CNN Primetime Show to End After Midterms," *Daily Beast*, November 2, 2022, https://www.yahoo.com/news/jake-tapper-ratings-deficient-cnn-212932414.html.
13. Daniel Villarreal, "Twitter Caves to New York Post in Awkward Moment for CNN's Jake Tapper," *Newsweek*, October 30, 2020, https://www.newsweek.com/twitter-caves-new-york-post-awkward-moment-cnns-jake-tapper-1543725.
14. "Annie Grayer," *Forbes*, https://www.forbes.com/profile/annie-grayer/?sh=5702540e74e4.

**Chapter 17: The Smirnov Distraction**

1. Josh Christenson and Ryan King, "Republicans Plow Ahead with Biden Impeachment Inquiry Hearing as Dems Rage," *New York Post*, September 29, 2023, https://nypost.com/2023/09/28/house-gop-swat-aside-democratic-attempts-to-derail-first-impeachment-inquiry/.
2. "Jonathan Turley Says Biden Inquiry Is Warranted But Current Evidence Doesn," C-Span, September 28, 2023, https://www.c-span.org/video/?c5085936/jonathan-turley-biden-inquiry-warranted-current-evidence-doesn.
3. Jordan Boyd, "Media Do Biden's Bidding by Blocking GOP Impeachment Inquiry," *Federalist*, September 28, 2023, https://thefederalist.com/2023/09/28/trump-impeachment-cheerleaders-in-media-do-bidens-bidding-with-blackout-on-republicans-impeachment-inquiry/.
4. Melanie Zanona, "New: Frustration in the GOP over 1st impeachment hearing, as the GOP witnesses undercut their narrative &say no evidence of crimes. 'Picking witnesses that refute House Republicans arguments for impeachment is mind blowing. This is an unmitigated disaster,' said senior R aide," Twitter, September 28, 2023, https://twitter.com/MZanona/status/1707434463674671558.
5. Alexandra Steigrad, "CBS Seizes Confidential Files of Fired Reporter Pursuing Hunter Biden Laptop Story in 'Unprecedented' Move: Sources," *New York Post*, February 23, 2024, https://nypost.com/2024/02/22/business/cbs-seizes-confidential-files-of-fired-reporter-pursuing-hunter-biden-laptop-story-in-unprecedented/.
6. Ben Whedon, "Jordan Launches Probe into CBS News's Alleged Seizure of Reporter's Personal Files," Just The News, February 23, 2024, https://justthenews.com/politics-policy/jordan-launches-probe-cbs-newss-alleged-seizure-reporters-personal-files.
7. Ben Whedon, "CBS News Returns Hundreds of Docs to Terminated Reporter," Just The News, February 27, 2024, https://justthenews.com/accountability/media/cbs-news-returns-hundreds-docs-terminated-reporter.
8. Steve Benen, "GOP Suffers 'Most Spectacular Embarrassment Imaginable' in Anti-Biden Case," MSNBC, February 16, 2024, https://www.msnbc.com/rachel-maddow-show/maddowblog/gop-suffers-spectacular-embarrassment-imaginable-anti-biden-case-rcna139159.
9. Susan Ferrechio, "Special Counsel Charges Former FBI Informant with Falsely Claiming Burisma Bribed the Bidens," *Washington Times*, February 15, 2024, https://www.washingtontimes.com/news/2024/feb/15/alexander-smirnov-ex-fbi-informant-arrested-accuse/.
10. Staff, Senator Chuck Grassley, "Grassley Grills FBI Director Wray at Senate Judiciary Committee Hearing," December 5, 2023, https://www.grassley.senate.gov/news/news-releases/grassley-grills-fbi-director-wray-at-senate-judiciary-committee-hearing.
11. Farnoush Amiri and Eric Tucker, "Why Republicans Are Clashing with the FBI over a Confidential Biden Document," *Washington Times*, June 7, 2023, https://www.washingtontimes.com/news/2023/jun/7/why-republicans-are-clashing-with-fbi-over-confide/.

12. Kimberley Strassel, "Sifting the FBI's Garbage," *Wall Street Journal*, February 22, 2024, https://www.wsj.com/articles/sifting-fbi-garbage-alexander-smirnov-indictment-says-nothing-good-about-bureau-b4302f22.
13. Amiri and Tucker. "Why Republicans Are Clashing with the FBI over a Confidential Biden Document."
14. Cf. Joy Pullmann, "6 Documented Instances of Systemic Pro-Democrat FBI Corruption," *Federalist*, May 18, 2023, https://thefederalist.com/2023/05/17/6-freshly-documented-instances-of-systemic-pro-democrat-fbi-corruption/.
15. Gabriel Hays, "White House Allegedly Blames Garland for Damning Special Counsel Claims about Biden," Fox News, February 10, 2024, https://www.foxnews.com/media/white-house-allegedly-blames-garland-damning-special-counsel-claims-biden-report.
16. Bradford Betz, "DOJ Indicts Missing Man Who Claims to Have Provided FBI with Info on Biden Family's China Business Dealings," Fox News, July 11, 2023, https://www.foxnews.com/politics/doj-indicts-missing-man-claims-have-provided-fbi-info-biden-familys-china-business-dealings.
17. Robert K. Hur, "Report of the Special Counsel on the Investigation into Unauthorized Removal, Retention, and Disclosure of Classified Documents Discovered at Locations Including the Penn Biden Center and the Delaware Private Residence of President Joseph R. Biden, Jr.," U.S. Department of Justice, February 5, 2024, https://www.justice.gov/storage/report-from-special-counsel-robert-k-hur-february-2024.pdf.
18. Tristan Justice, "Prosecutors Decline to Charge 'Elderly' Biden over 'Poor Memory,'" *Federalist*, February 9, 2024, https://thefederalist.com/2024/02/08/prosecutors-decline-to-charge-elderly-biden-over-poor-memory/.
19. Hur, "Report of the Special Counsel."
20. Congressional Staff, "Key Excerpts from Tony Bobulinski's Transcribed Interview," Committee on Oversight and Accountability, February 16, 2024, https://oversight.house.gov/wp-content/uploads/2024/02/Bobulinski-Transcript.pdf.
21. Justin Lahart and Nick Timiraos, "Hotter-Than-Expected Inflation Clouds Rate-Cut Outlook," *Wall Street Journal*, February 13, 2024, https://www.wsj.com/economy/consumers/what-to-watch-in-the-cpi-report-will-inflation-fall-below-3-ffc5859a.
22. Ramsey Touchberry, "Senate Border Bill Careens toward Defeat as McConnell Tries to Soothe GOP Outrage," *Washington Times*, February 6, 2024, https://www.washingtontimes.com/news/2024/feb/6/senate-border-bill-careens-toward-defeat-as-mitch-/.
23. Journalist Todd Bensman has hands down the best border coverage: Todd Bensman, "Front Line Field Reports from the Greatest Mass Migration Event in American History," February 15, 2024, https://www.toddbensman.com/reports-from-the-2021-border-crisis/.
24. "James Biden Transcript," transcript of speech delivered at Oversight Com-

mittee hearing, February 21, 2024, https://oversight.house.gov/wp-content/uploads/2024/03/James-Biden-Transcript.pdf.

25. "James Biden Transcript," 59.
26. Devine, *The Big Guy*, chap. 13, "The Coast Is Clear."
27. For a colorful account of the criminal downfall of legal mountebank Dickie Scruggs and accomplice Joey Langston, see Curtis Wilkie, *The Fall of the House of Zeus: The Rise and Ruin of America's Most Powerful Trial Lawyer*, AbeBooks, January 1, 1970, https://www.abebooks.com/9780307460707/Fall-House-Zeus-Rise-Ruin-0307460703/plp.
28. "Third Friday Management, LLC and Michael E. Lewitt," Litigation Releases, Securities and Exchange Commission, September 29, 2023, https://www.sec.gov/litigation/litreleases/lr-25869.
29. Ben Schreckinger, "Biden's Brother Used His Name to Promote a Hospital Chain. Then . . ." *Politico*, February 18, 2024, https://www.politico.com/news/2024/02/18/the-biden-name-how-the-presidents-brother-became-embroiled-in-a-hospital-fiasco-00141868.
30. Justin Kase, "City of Pineville Takes Control of Southeastern Kentucky Medical Center," WYMT, June 3, 2019, https://www.wymt.com/content/news/Mayor-Pineville-hospital-now-under-new-ownership-510781931.html.

**Chapter 18: Lean into the Harvest**

1. "Jason Galanis Transcript," interview delivered at Oversight Committee Hearing, February 23, 2024, https://oversight.house.gov/wp-content/uploads/2024/03/Jason-Galanis-Transcript.pdf.
2. Schweizer, *Secret Empires,* 34, Kindle.
3. Schweizer, 44.
4. "Jason Galanis Transcript," 8.
5. "Jason Galanis Transcript," 9–10.
6. "Jason Galanis Transcript," 10–11.
7. "Jason Galanis Transcript," 7–8.

**Chapter 19: The Beginning of the End**

1. Seamus Bruner and John Solomon, "Smoking Guns: Joe Biden Referred Business and Mingled Finances with Son Hunter, Messages Show," Just The News, April 14, 2022, https://justthenews.com/accountability/russia-and-ukraine-scandals/contrary-earlier-portrayals-joe-biden-referred-business.
2. "Jeff Cooper—Managing Partner," Flint Cooper, May 2, 2023, https://www.flintcooper.com/jeff-cooper-managing-partner/.
3. Oversight Staff, "Evidence of Joe Biden's Involvement in His Family's Influence Peddling Schemes," United States House Committee on Oversight and Accountability, September 13, 2023, https://oversight.house.gov/blog/evidence-of-joe-bidens-involvement-in-his-familys-influence-peddling-schemes/.
4. Miranda Devine, "Laptop Shows Joe Biden Attended Meetings between Hunter and His Mexican Business Partners," *New York Post*, July 1, 2021,

https://nypost.com/2021/06/30/laptop-shows-joe-biden-was-with-hunter-and-his-mexican-biz-meetings/.

5. Devine, "Laptop Shows Joe Biden Attended Meetings."
6. Schweizer, *Secret Empires*, 34.
7. Ben Feuerherd, "Rudy Giuliani Associate Lev Parnas Guilty on All Counts," *New York Post*, October 22, 2021, https://nypost.com/2021/10/22/rudy-giuliani-associate-lev-parnas-guilty-on-all-counts/.
8. The exchange can be found at "TC Shorts The Man in the Arena: Tony Bobulinski," Tucker Carlson Network, April 2, 2024, https://tuckercarlson.com/tc-shorts-tony-bobulinski/.
9. Ryan King, "Dem Rep. Jared Moskowitz Dons Putin Mask to Troll Republicans Ahead of Biden Impeachment Hearing," *New York Post*, March 20, 2024, https://nypost.com/2024/03/20/us-news/rep-jared-moskowitz-dons-putin-mask-to-troll-republicans-ahead-of-biden-impeachment-hearing/.

**Chapter 20: The Closer's Kid**

1. Margot Cleveland, "8 Unbelievable Claims from Hunter Biden's Deposition," *Federalist*, March 1, 2024, https://thefederalist.com/2024/03/01/8-unbelievable-claims-from-hunter-bidens-congressional-deposition/.
2. Oversight Staff, "Hunter Biden Transcript," redacted, House Oversight Committee, February 28, 2024, https://oversight.house.gov/wp-content/uploads/2024/02/Hunter-Biden-Transcript_Redacted.pdf.
3. Steven Nelson and Josh Christenson, "Hunter Biden Testified He Was 'High or Drunk' While Writing 'Sitting Here with My Father' $5m China Shakedown Text—but Still Got the Money," *New York Post*, March 25, 2024, https://nypost.com/2024/02/28/us-news/hunter-biden-arrives-for-impeachment-testimony-about-dads-role-in-foreign-biz/.
4. "What Hunter Biden's Testimony Showed," *Potomac Watch* podcast, *Wall Street Journal*, March 5, 2024, https://www.wsj.com/podcasts/opinion-potomac-watch/what-hunter-biden-testimony-showed/932a4e68-147c-448c-861e-9b636b96d9b3.
5. Bob Fredericks, "Jared Kushner Accused of Using WhatsApp and Personal Email for State Business," *New York Post*, March 21, 2019, https://nypost.com/2019/03/21/jared-kushner-accused-of-using-whatsapp-and-personal-email-for-state-business/.
6. "What Hunter Biden's Testimony Showed," *Wall Street Journal*.

**Chapter 21: The Hur Whitewash**

1. Hur, "Report of the Special Counsel," 345. The full quote: "We have also considered that, at trial, Mr. Biden would likely present himself to a jury, as he did during our interview of him, as a sympathetic, well-meaning, elderly man with a poor memory."
2. The very fact that Mark Zwonitzer, the ghostwriter, attempted to delete the interview points to the fact that Joe Biden knew full well this was classified information being shared with a person who had no security clearance. Hur, 12.
3. "Biden Books Go to Flatiron," *Publishers Weekly*, November 6, 2023,

https://www.publishersweekly.com/pw/by-topic/industry-news/book-deals/article/73268-biden-books-go-to-flatiron.html.

4. Joe Biden, *Promise Me, Dad: A Year of Hope, Hardship, and Purpose* (New York: Flatiron Books, 2017).
5. As Hur explained in our hearing, he did not exonerate Joe Biden. See Gabrielle Fonrouge and Steven Nelson, "Special Counsel Robert Hur Says He 'Did Not Exonerate' Biden, Claims President Lied about Sharing, Locking Classified Docs," *New York Post*, March 12, 2024, https://nypost.com/2024/03/12/us-news/special-counsel-robert-hur-says-he-did-not-exonerate-biden-claims-president-lied-about-sharing-locking-classified-docs/. The fact of the matter is, it is illegal to remove and store classified documents. See United States Code, 18 U.S.C. § 1924 (2018), https://www.law.cornell.edu/uscode/text/18/1924. Also recall that Joe Biden was not president or vice president at the time he was communicating with his ghostwriter, and therefore could not legally declassify anything. Note also that President Trump *did* have power to declassify any federal documents, and exercised it per Executive Order 13526, "Classified National Security Information," https://www.archives.gov/isoo/policy-documents/cnsi-eo.html. For an informative discussion on federal document classification see Harvey Rishikof and Josh Geltzer, "Dispelling Myths: How Classification and Declassification Actually Work," Just Security, February 19, 2024, https://www.justsecurity.org/86777/dispelling-myths-how-classification-and-declassification-actually-work/
6. Jordan Boyd, "Hur Highlights DOJ's Double Standards on Classified Documents," *Federalist*, March 12, 2024, https://thefederalist.com/2024/03/12/hur-highlights-dojs-totalitarian-double-standards-on-handling-classified-documents.
7. James Comer, "Chairman Comer's Statement on Transcribed Interview with Kathy Chung," press release, United States House Committee on Oversight and Accountability, April 4, 2023, https://oversight.house.gov/release/chairman-comers-statement-on-transcribed-interview-with-kathy-chung/. Kathy Chung has a colorful history with the Biden family. Hunter Biden got her the job with Joe Biden. See Gabrielle Fonrouge, "Hunter Biden Helped Hire Aides Who Mishandled Joe's Classified Documents," *New York Post*, March 4, 2024, https://nypost.com/2024/03/04/us-news/hunter-biden-helped-hire-aides-who-mishandled-joes-classified-documents/.
8. See James Comer, letter to Dana Remus, May 5, 2023, House Committee on Oversight and Accountability, https://oversight.house.gov/wp-content/uploads/2023/05/2023-05-05-Letter-Dana-Remus.pdf.
9. Marisa Schultz, "Comer Probing White House's 'Incomplete and Misleading' Biden Classified Docs Timeline," *New York Post*, October 11, 2023, https://nypost.com/2023/10/11/comer-probing-white-houses-incomplete-and-misleading-biden-classified-docs-timeline/; "Rep. James Comer Asks Why Discovery of Biden Classified Docs Wasn't Publicized in November," *Washington Times*, January 15, 2023, https://www.washingtontimes

.com/news/2023/jan/15/rep-james-comer-asks-why-discovery-biden -classifie/. And here is my own statement after the Hur Report was issued: James Comer, "Comer: Classified Documents Timeline Contradicts White House's and President Biden's Attorney's Public Statements," press release, United States House Committee on Oversight and Accountability, February 4, 2024, https://oversight.house.gov/release/comer-classified-documents-timeline-contradicts-white-houses-and-president-bidens-attorneys-public-statements%EF%BF%BC/.

10. Margot Cleveland, "Democrats Spun Biden's Classified Docs as 'Six Items,' but Special Counsel Report Reveals It Was 300-Plus," *Federalist*, February 9, 2024, https://thefederalist.com/2024/02/09/democrats-spun-bidens-classified-docs-as-six-items-but-special-counsel-report-reveals-it-was-300-plus/.
11. Kate Sheehy, "$54M in Chinese Gifts Donated to UPenn, Home of Biden Center," *New York Post*, April 9, 2022, https://nypost.com/2022/04/09/54m-in-chinese-gifts-donated-to-upenn-home-of-biden-center/.
12. Jordan Boyd, "9 Questions Biden Should Answer about His Documents Scandal," *Federalist*, January 18, 2023, https://thefederalist.com/2023/01/18/9-questions-the-white-house-should-answer-about-bidens-classified-document-scandal-but-wont/.
13. Margot Cleveland, "Biden Docs Confirm Hunter's Pay-to-Play Was a Family Affair," *Federalist*, February 12, 2024, https://thefederalist.com/2024/02/12/joe-bidens-classified-docs-provide-more-evidence-hunters-pay-to-play-was-a-family-affair/.
14. U.S. Department of Justice, Report from Special Counsel Robert K. Hur, February 2024, https://www.justice.gov/storage/report-from-special-counsel-robert-k-hur-february-2024.pdf.
15. Here's a report of my response to Tapper's blatant shilling: "Rep. James Comer Says CNN Is 'Playing to a Low IQ Audience,'" Analyzing America, December 27, 2023, https://www.analyzingamerica.org/2023/12/730282/.
16. Liam Donovan, "Opinion: Why Republicans Are Making a Big Mistake on Biden's Age," *Politico*, February 22, 2024, https://www.politico.com/news/magazine/2024/02/22/im-a-republican-strategist-bidens-age-wont-doom-him-00142492.
17. "Republican Rep. Ken Buck Leaving Office Next Week—Shrinking GOP House Majority to Just Two," *New York Post*, March 12, 2024, https://nypost.com/2024/03/12/us-news/republican-rep-ken-buck-leaving-office-early-shrinking-gop-house-majority-to-2/.
18. A comprehensive and damning account of the subversion of the DOJ, FBI, and CIA by left-wing and partisan ideology can be found in Waller, *Big Intel*.
19. To give one of several examples, we've been on the trail of private Joe Biden emails related to the various Biden family grift operations and NARA has tried to thwart us at every turn. See, for example, "Comer Demands Info on Biden's Business Pseudonyms," *Federalist*, August 18, 2023, https://thefederalist.com/2023/08/18/comer-demands-national-archives-fork-over-info

-on-bidens-business-pseudonyms/. For context, see Andrew Duehren and James V. Grimaldi, "Joe Biden Had Multiple Email Accounts as Vice President, Including Private Gmail," *Wall Street Journal*, February 2, 2024, https://www.wsj.com/articles/joe-biden-email-accounts-vice-president-hunter-biden-566bd720. Also Chad Pergram, "Eric Schwerin Confirms Joe Biden Used 'Robinware456' Email Alias while Serving as Vice President," Fox News, March 18, 2024, https://www.foxnews.com/politics/eric-schwerin-confirms-joe-biden-used-robinware456-email-alias-while-serving-as-vice-president. For more on the abundant leftist activism overtaking NARA, see Joanna Piacenza, "Labeling the Founding Documents 'Offensive' Is Just the Beginning of the National Archives' Spiteful Plans," *Federalist*, September 16, 2021, https://thefederalist.com/2021/09/16/labeling-the-founding-documents-offensive-is-just-the-beginning-of-the-national-archives-spiteful-plans/.

# ABOUT THE AUTHOR

**James Comer** represents Kentucky's 1st Congressional District and currently serves as the chairman of the House Committee on Oversight and Accountability, where he aggressively advocates for reducing waste, fraud, and abuse in government.